HISTORY OF THE
ONE TRUE GOD

VOLUME III: GOD-FEARING FAMILIES

GWEN SHAMBLIN LARA

Original Material Copyright © 1990
History of the One True God, Volume III: God-Fearing Families
Copyright © 2017 by Gwen Shamblin Lara
and Remnant Fellowship

The Remnant of the Kingdom of God (Remnant Fellowship) name and logo are trademarks.
History of the One True God, Volume III: God-Fearing Families
name and logo are trademarks.

All rights reserved. No part of this publication may be reproduced, distributed, or transmitted by any means, including photocopying, recording or other electronic methods, without the prior written permission of the publisher, except in the case of brief quotations where book and author are cited.

Printed in the United States of America
Remnant Publishing

Remnant Fellowship Publishing
Brentwood, Tennessee
1-800-844-5208
www.RemnantFellowship.org

ISBN # 1-892729-35-0

This Book Belongs To:

_____

But from everlasting to everlasting the Lord's love is with those who fear him, and his righteousness with their children's children. Psalm 103:17

Table of Contents

	Preface	8
1	Introduction to the God-Fearing Family	13
	The Family—A Startling Decline	17
	The Foundation of the Godly Family	20
2	Re-establishment of the God-Fearing Family	25
	A Loving Fear	28
	A Rich Inheritance	31
3	The Legacy	35
	The Remnant of the Kingdom of Love	38
	Spiritual Stewards	40
	Establishing a Legacy	41
	The Legacy for the Children	43
	Let Us Not Repeat History	43
4	The Royal Revival	47
	For God's Glory	49
	A Royal Righteous Society	52
5	A Man of Nobility	57
	Finding the Answers	59
	Offering Genuine Work	62
	Something Higher than Yourself	64
	A True Gentleman	66
	Making the Royal Choice	69
6	The Good Old Days	73
	The "Liberated" Wife	75
	An Age-Old Attack on Christianity	79
	Embracing Your God-Given Role	81
	A God-Fearing, Beautiful Woman	86
7	The Royal Wife	89
	Full Confidence	91
	Respect Your Husband	92
	Lay Down Your Selfish Ambition	94
	Work on Yourself First	98
	Appropriate Attire	99
	Turning the Other Cheek	101
	Building Up Your Husband	102
8	How to Raise Godly Children	107
	The Heart of a Child	108
	As You Walk Along the Road…	109
	Meet the Needs	110
	Essential Kindness	111
	Godly Direction and Redirection	111
	Praise and Encouragement	114
	Responsibilities of a Child	115
	Goals for School-Aged Children	115
	Intelligence and Academics	116
	Giving Back to God	117
	Bad Company	118
	Maintaining the Parent Relationship	119
	Take Time to Teach	120
9	Connected to the Heavens	123
	The True Emptiness	124
	A Sign of a Misplaced Heart	125
	Stand in Awe of God	126
	The Lord's Prayer	131
	A New Generation, a New Focus	132

10	**A LESSON FOR THE CHILDREN:**	**137**
	HONORING YOUR PARENTS	139
	NO ANGER	140
	NOT A HINT OF IMMORALITY	144
	LOVE YOUR NEIGHBOR AS YOURSELF	145
	IT IS ALL ABOUT GOD	146
	YOUR ONE GOAL	148
	TRUE CHRISTIANITY IS SUPERNATURAL	150
11	**GODLY ETIQUETTE AND COMPASSION**	**153**
	DO UNTO OTHERS	157
	RETURNING TO GOD'S FOUNDATION	159
12	**THE PERFECT DAY**	**163**
	HOW TO HAVE A GREAT MORNING	165
	A GRATEFUL HEART	167
	SPREADING HIS LIGHT TO OTHERS	169
13	**KINDNESS**	**173**
	TAKING CARE TO INCLUDE EVERYONE	175
	QUARRELING	179
14	**GODLY COMPETITION...THE PERFECT ATHLETE**	**185**
	AN OPPORTUNITY TO BE LIKE CHRIST	187
	A TEST SET UP JUST FOR YOU	190
	A CHANCE TO BRING JOY TO OTHERS	193
15	**A LESSON FOR THE YOUTH: SEEKING GOD**	**197**
	THE APPLE OF GOD'S EYE	198
	THE LIVING WATER	201
16	**THE AGE OF ACCOUNTABILITY**	**205**
	BABY DEDICATION	205
	BAPTISM	206
	CONFIRMATION	206
	CIRCUMCISION OF THE HEART	208
	IN MY FATHER'S HOUSE	212
	ONE FOCUS	214
17	**THE STORY OF JOSEPH**	**217**
	FAITHFULLY ENDURING PERSECUTION	219
	FROM A PRISONER TO A RULER	220
18	**SPIRITUAL GIFTS**	**225**
	GIFTS FOR THE CHURCH	227
	GIFTS FOR CAREERS	228
	A NARROW FOCUS	232
19	**MOTIVE OF THE HEART: A LESSON TO THE GRADUATES**	**235**
	THE DIFFERENCE	238
	A MOVING TARGET	240
	THE ONE CONSTANT GOAL	241
	MISPLACED DEVOTION	242
	ALL HONOR AND GLORY TO GOD	245
	JOIN IN THE RACE	247
20	**GODLY COURTSHIPS**	**251**
	APPROPRIATE TIMING	253
	LASTING RELATIONSHIPS	254
	RIGHTEOUSNESS IS ALLURING	256
	A BLESSED RESULT	259
21	**TWO BECOME ONE**	**261**
	OPPOSITES ATTRACT	262
	THE UNITY OF MARRIAGE	263
	A STRONG FOUNDATION	264
	LET NO MAN SEPARATE	265
	LOVING WITHOUT EXPECTATIONS	267
	TO ADD, YOU HAVE TO SUBTRACT	268
22	**HOW TO MAKE YOURSELF BEAUTIFUL**	**273**
	A GENTLE AND QUIET SPIRIT	275
	GOD LIFTS UP THE HUMBLE	278
	A PICTURE OF BEAUTY	280

    Being the Right Person....282
    Giving When Others Do Not Give....285

23 A Christian Husband....289
    Making Prayer a Priority....291
    Attention to the Needs of the Family....292
    The Godly Man....294
    The Driving Force for the Family....296
    Authority in the Workplace....298
    Providing for the Family....299

24 Divorce and Remarriage....303
    God's Example of a Faithful Marriage....304
    The Meaning of a "Faithful Spouse"....306
    The Unbound Unbeliever....309
    Legalism Versus God's Truth....312
    Liberty and Peace for the Oppressed....315
    Honoring the Covenant....319
    What God has Made Clean is Clean....322

25 The Meaning of Life....327
    This Too is Meaningless....330
    Satisfaction in Your Toil....334
    Enjoying Life....335
    Pleasing God....336
    Pursuit of the Eternal....341

26 How to Honor....345
    Outdo One Another in Showing Honor....347
    Honoring the Aged....349
    Honoring the Church Body....350

27 Showing Christlike Respect....355
    Genuine Respect....356
    The Purpose of Authority....360
    Advanced Spiritual Training....361
    A Spiritual Training Ground....362

28 Accepting Loving Redirection....367
    Clinging to Conviction....371
    Craving Direction....373

29 What does a Christian Household Look Like?....377
    The Care of the Home....383
    Personal Responsibility....385
    A New Job Description....386

30 A Picture of the Church....391
    Faith and Deeds....392
    A Unified and Humble Community....396
    Separating Good from Evil....399
    To Be Worthy of this Calling....400
    A Beautiful Vision....403

31 Taking Care of God's House....407
    Matthew 18...Love for God's House....409
    The Theft of God's Authority....412
    Pruning the Vine....417

32 The Super Community of Love....421
    The New Jerusalem....424
    A Transformed Family....429
    A Goal for Every Household....430
    Built on a Solid Foundation of Love....432
    A Dream of God's Kingdom....434

Appendix....438
    Note from the Author....455
    God-Fearing Family Resources....458

Preface

Greetings to all far and wide—to those who are seeking a deeper peace and purpose for life and for your children, and to those who are looking for solid ground for your family in this ever-capricious and unreliable world. We are all longing for a peaceful home, a loving family, and deep, genuine relationships founded on graciousness, nobility and kindness. It is a dream that is universal and is found in fairy tales, legends and fantasies in all cultures and all societies across the world.

However, this dream is far from reality as people are finding themselves increasingly isolated, overwhelmed and hurting. In a country where one in four adults lives alone, children leave home never to return, half of marriages end in divorce, and mental illness is ever-increasing, people are losing hope.[1] It is an utterly heartbreaking and unimaginable statistic, but it is true that the third leading cause of death in adolescents today is suicide.[2] We are living in a world that is far away from the picture of the royal, regal, *Holy Priesthood* called by God in Exodus 19:6a... *You will be for me a kingdom of priests and a holy nation.*

Early in life, I found a personal relationship with God and grew to love Him very much by trying to imitate King David of the Bible. And like King David, I wanted to be the apple of God's eye,[3] so I hung on to the Ten Commandments in Exodus 20 and to Mark 12,

---

1 USA Today, "Census: More Americans are living alone," 2013; Centers for Disease Control and Prevention (CDC), "Mental Illness Surveillance Among U.S. Adults," 2013
2 CDC, "Mortality Among Teenagers Aged 12-19 years: United States, 1999-2006"
3 *Keep me as the apple of your eye; hide me in the shadow of your wings. Psalm 17:8*

Preface

which tells us the greatest Commandment of all... *"Hear, O Israel, the Lord our God, the Lord is one. Love the Lord your God with all your heart and with all your soul and with all your mind and with all your strength." The second is this: "Love your neighbor as yourself." There is no commandment greater than these. Mark 12:29b-30*

As I shared this relationship with others, they also started finding this Kingdom of Love, which offers freedom from anger, disappointment, poor relationships, a lack of peace and emptiness. And now, as a part of this growing Body of Believers at Remnant Fellowship, God has led us to the meekness, humility and love that is found in the Sermon on the Mount recounted in Matthew 6, which in turn has led to answered prayers... answered all day long. There is no peace like moving mountains each day with prayer versus human effort, with prayer versus words or arguments, with prayer versus binge eating or drinking or other escapes.

The healing from these teachings was phenomenal. As a result of the right foundation of putting the words from the Bible into practice, people have laid down idols of food, drugs, depression and self-focus, money, anger, selfishness, envy and jealousy. Marriages have been healed, and children are being raised with kindness and respect. Personal responsibility and the spirit of self-control and peace permeate this Church, where there is no gossip or backbiting, but rather a support system for purity and humility, and abounding love for this compassionate God.

New Creations are seen here... ordinary people who have been transformed; they are laying down greedy and immoral behaviors such as overeating, over-drinking, anger, rage, depression, lust, overspending, drugs and all types of bad habits and attitudes. I have witnessed massive weight loss, recovered alcoholics, drug-free addicts, cured chronic fear-bound and anxiety-ridden worriers... all reformed from every stronghold or idol known to mankind! These transformations are permanent and profound because they have been approached correctly, in a humble and prideless way before the throne of the Almighty God. Countless men and women are turning away from the praise of man and man-made rules and are turning to the Great Physician—the Maker of our bodies, minds and souls—using His lead for hunger, for shopping, for making money, for speaking…and now these people walk by God's guidance and not by their own selfish desires.

At first it was noticeable, and then it became remarkable, and finally, over time it became increasingly amazing—defying statistics in every category. While the global economics and prospects for the future generations were diminishing, we were seeing the reverse. Our children are staying close to home, graduating earlier, excelling in the workplace, marrying earlier, buying homes earlier. They have less debt, more income, superior health, and a higher standard of living. This next generation's days look nothing like the days when I was their age, as they are making more friends at an early age and are keeping them for life—God-fearing friends around the globe.

We are watching trends being dramatically reversed with a depression-free, drug-free Church, with virtually no children with diagnoses such as Attention-Deficit Hyperactivity Disorder, anxiety or depression. Families are not having to spend money on counseling or therapy, but rather, they live joyful, hopeful and purposeful lives. Many of our youth are featured in concerts, plays and other community performances; they are employed quickly and promoted rapidly. They choose to stay close to family with a huge community-like support network. Rather than getting smaller, the families are becoming larger as they unite with others, and their children are not moving away. The unity, joy, peace, hope and love are priceless! These statistics are real, and it can happen to your family.

This is not a man-made doctrine or dogma about sacraments or rituals. It is not a mystery. This is an obtainable religion of putting the words of Christ into practice and experiencing a transformed life. Real religion, true religion, is a genuine love for God that will bring out a totally sacrificial, loving life all the way from the youngest to the oldest in the family.

It is all about who and what you love, and you fall in love with what you focus on. In a world of uncertainty, there is a message of certainty…there is nothing to lose and everything to gain. Beyond a doubt, this is an absolute possibility for your life and for the lives of those in your family—a deep healing is available for each and every person, as is liberation from unwanted habits, dependencies, lifestyle choices and behaviors that have been destroying our lives and relationships. You can experience the dependable power of the True Church, a Church built on the Rock of Jesus Christ who said, *But the world must learn that I love the Father and that I do exactly what my Father has commanded me. John 14:31a* It is an abundant life of hope, of beautiful relationships, of financial freedom, of health, and most important of all, of a relationship with God that is beyond anything we have ever experienced before. Read on to find out how this can be the reality for you and your family.

The foundation of a Godly family is having a loving fear of the Precious Creator and Heavenly Father above all. Saints—men and women and children— must adoringly fear the Lord to have this wonderful, peaceful, fun and blessed family life that you are longing for. You obey what you fear. Page 20.

Introduction to the God-Fearing Family

Chapter 1

You yourselves have seen what I did to Egypt, and how I carried you on eagles' wings and brought you to myself. Now if you obey me fully and keep my covenant, then out of all nations you will be my treasured possession. Although the whole earth is mine, you will be for me a kingdom of priests and a holy nation. Exodus 19:4-6a

It is time for a restoration of God's ancient calling of God-loving and God-fearing families… a Kingdom of Priests and a Holy Nation. There is a foundation that is essential for all families, and it is an **adoring** fear of God first and foremost. This is not merely an intellectual acknowledgment, but rather something felt deep inside—a feeling that a grave injustice on this Earth has been done to God, His Kingdom and the Heavens. It is an acknowledgment that it is time to right the wrong reputation of God—His will, His words, His undying love, His attention, His purpose—and then to right this grave injustice. The world has been blinded, and it has left the church and the family destroyed, for it is in the will of God that we live and thrive.

The family unit should mirror the Church structure, and each subunit builds the Church as they interconnect. The family unit is made of Christlike humans who represent the Kingdom of God and His Church. Each family member must accept their role and responsibility within their family and not put this off onto the Shepherds, Elders, Deacons, counselors and teachers of the Church. To have a family is a marvelous opportunity and responsibility to represent the most incredible God of the Universe. But without the right perspective, we cannot build the Kingdom of Love, for it will only turn into a selfish endeavor. Never did God plan for there to be anti-authority, rebellion, strife, rage, control, moodiness, greed, selfishness, financial stress and disrespect in any of these family units that He created.

Do we all not long for the examples of love, affection, respect, gentleness, companionship, humor and family unity with an atmosphere of building one another up? Can the miracle of this transformation happen within your family? The answer is yes—but it must start with the foundation of *you*. It only takes one family member committing to fearing God and being concerned for God's reputation. You must accept this responsibility and then change your behaviors, functions and roles into what God has chosen you to become. If He made you a man, then it is the loving husband and head of the household. If He made you a woman, then it is the gentle, submissive wife. Why does the husband shirk his responsibility in exchange for peace or approval of man? Why does the wife want to play ruler of the household, telling everyone what to do? Why do people resent how their Maker has made them and the role that comes with each fantastical position? If you think your God-given role is mundane, no doubt the cat or the dog would love to trade places with you. How could we ask for more if we have been created and made in God's image—made by choice to share eternity? What an honor!

If you are looking for a God-Fearing Family...if you are searching for beautiful peace between and among all family members, then start with yourself. How have you accepted your assigned height, body type, talents, roles, intelligence, circumstances and authority line? How have you shown full acknowledgement

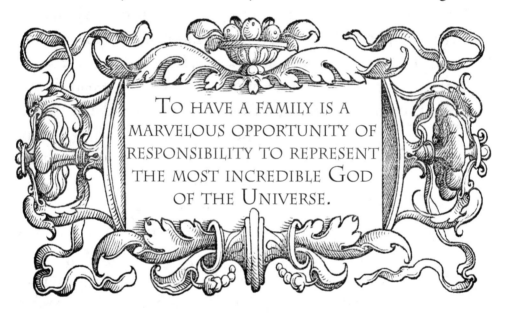

TO HAVE A FAMILY IS A MARVELOUS OPPORTUNITY OF RESPONSIBILITY TO REPRESENT THE MOST INCREDIBLE GOD OF THE UNIVERSE.

of such a high honor with taking care of your body and using the gifts God has given you? Have you tried in every way to tell God you adore Him and all His decisions by embracing your life as a wife or husband—are you the example that the world wants to follow? Or do you confuse the lines of authority and position?

King David was given everything, but he wanted more...so he took the wife of another man. Then, when David found out that Bathsheba was carrying his child, he essentially had Bathsheba's husband murdered on the front lines of war, then he married her, hoping that his sin would not be discovered. However, God sent the Prophet Nathan to King David and exposed his sin.

Then David said to Nathan, "I have sinned against the Lord." Nathan replied, "The Lord has taken away your sin. You are not going to die. But because by doing this you have made the enemies of the Lord show utter contempt, the son born to you will die." II Samuel 12:13-14

Notice that when the Lord spoils you with all you have and you still want the position or indulgence of more, the enemies rage at God as if He shows favoritism. In this case, King David—like lucifer or satan—was playing the role of immortal God and had thrown out his role of mortal man, who could not grab or make or remove human life from Earth. When you want the role or position of what has not been given you—and what is more, when you seem to get excused to just sin again and again—you are making God's court of decision very difficult, and you are making the growing of the Kingdom of God impossible. King David saved his own life but lost his child and then almost lost his kingdom because—for this moment in time—he despised the role he had been given and longed for something God had not given him.

> IF YOU ARE LOOKING FOR BEAUTIFUL PEACE BETWEEN AND AMONG ALL FAMILY MEMBERS, THEN START WITH YOURSELF.

What about you? Have you made it hard on God? Have you accepted your God-given role and looked at things from God's perspective? Have you lived to make God look good? And therefore, have you made God look good with your life, with your relationships, with how you have raised your children? Or have you made the enemies of the Lord show utter contempt? It is time to reverse this and accept what He has made and then glorify the CREATOR of the UNIVERSE with being the Royal Family, the Royal Priesthood, with men as Kings and women as royal Queens and the children as young Princes and young Princesses.

This Royal Family is the collection of the assigned Creation with all their individual roles that are beautiful in the sight of God and together is the glue that keeps the Royal Priesthood together. Let us take time to examine ourselves and all the roles of a God-Fearing Family so that we may glorify this marvelous God of the Universe, and may our families all be a beautiful offering before the Lord Almighty.

The Family—A Startling Decline

Sadly, God's beautiful vision of the family is becoming increasingly rare. We are living in a world where family, marriage and childbirth are facing a growing trend of reduction. According to the Centers for Disease Control and Prevention (CDC), 41 percent of all births in the United States are to unmarried mothers. It is the "new norm" among women under 30, since more than one-half of all the births in that age group happen outside of marriage.

The U.S. Census Bureau reports that in 2014, 48 percent of women between ages 15 and 44 had never had any children, which is up from 46 percent in 2012, so the trend of childlessness is increasing. This represents the highest percentage of childless women since the Bureau started tracking this data in 1976. The CDC also reported in 2013 that there were just 62 births for every 1,000 women between the ages of 15 and 44 in the United States—an all-time low.

The number of women ages 40 to 44 who only had one child roughly doubled between 1976 and 2014.[1]

Marriage numbers are declining. The percentage of married households in the United States has fallen to a historic low—down to just 50 percent in 2012 from a high of 72 percent in 1960. About one in five adults in the United States (about 42 million Americans) have never been married.[2] In addition, marriages are being dissolved at an alarming rate. In America, there is approximately one divorce every 37 seconds. That is nearly 2,300 divorces per day.[3]

Researchers say that America has been experiencing a "cultural retreat from marriage" that has several drivers: a growing number of men and women are living together instead of marrying; many couples have children outside of marriage; and fewer people are affiliated with religious institutions than in the past.[4] All of these facts have contributed to the current decline in marriages.

This decline in marriage is not just occurring in the United States. Marriage is decreasing worldwide. In the United Kingdom, the number of women in their early fifties who have never married increased by 150 percent over a period of 13 years, and the average marriage in England now lasts 11 years.[5][6] The Organization for Economic Cooperation and Development reports that across their 35 countries, marriage rates have fallen from 8.1 marriages per 1,000 people in 1970 to 5.0 marriages per 1,000 people in 2009.

---

1 *Pew Research Center, "The American family today," 2015*
2 *United States Census Bureau*
3 *National Center for Health Statistics, "National Marriage and Divorce Rate Trends"*
4 *Princeton University, Future of Children, "One Nation, Divided: Culture, Civic Institutions, and the Marriage Divide" 2015*
5 *The Telegraph, "Rise of 'Silver Singles' After Hike in Divorce Rates in 70s Put Them Off Marriage," 2017*
6 *The Telegraph, "Yes, Marriage is the 'Gold Standard,'" 2017*

Overall, they have found that there are "less people getting married, and those getting married are more likely to end up divorcing."[7]

So, there are more divorces worldwide and fewer people getting married … and among the smaller numbers of the married, fewer are having children. Greater numbers of women are waiting longer to have children or are not having children at all. Even in those households with children, they found predominantly only one or two children. This is a drastic reversal of historical replenishing of the Earth.

At the same time that this cultural retreat from marriage is growing and the number of women having children is decreasing, the culture of alternative, selfish lifestyles is at an all-time high. The younger population has rejected traditional religion and the family household as the center of life for the glorification of God. No doubt, this generation believes that marriage and family would inhibit their lifestyle—being married would limit what they can do and when they can do it. It is a culture of "live it up for self now." More than one in four adults in America live alone.[8] God does use singles, for they can give more of their time, more of their mind, and more of their strength to the Church, serving the body of Christ. But if one chooses to be single out of *selfishness*, this is not the all-important will of God. The person who has chosen the path of remaining single for the right motive would be married to the Church and its needs. You would know by their actions and their motives why they decided to remain single.

The increase in divorce and decline in families is also affecting the physical and mental health of the next generation. Overall, there has been an increase in psychotropic drug use and a corresponding

---

7   OECD, 2011, *"Doing Better for Families"*
8   *United States Census Bureau, 2014*

increase in mental illness. The CDC says that one out of two people will develop a mental illness in their lifetime.[9] And there has been a tragic rise in depression rates and suicides in youth and young adults. According to the World Health Organization, depression is the top cause of illness and disability among adolescents, and suicide is the third cause of death.[10] This demise of the family is frightening. What is the answer?

The Foundation of the Godly Family

Despite today's statistics, I have hope, for many have witnessed the reversal of these trends here at the Remnant. The foundation of all revivals for the Church and the family is based on a loving fear of God. It is based on the Will of the Heavenly Father. Deuteronomy 10:12 says to fear the Lord: *And now, O Israel, what does the Lord your God ask of you but to fear the Lord your God, to walk in all his ways, to love him, to serve the Lord your God with all your heart and with all your soul…*

The foundation of a Godly family is having this loving fear of the Precious Creator and Heavenly Father above all. Saints—men and women and children—must adoringly fear the Lord to have this wonderful, peaceful, fun and blessed family life that you are longing for. This fear is not about terror, but rather an adoring *respect*—to honor and uphold God, His genius, His decisions, His concepts of a glorious New Jerusalem, a City of Peace, which is the Kingdom of God. This God is to be praised for His flawless ideas of what should be in Heaven and what should be separated out from the infinite heavenly existence that is beyond this life. God knows exactly what

---

9 Centers for Disease Control and Prevention Report: *"Mental Illness Surveillance Among U.S. Adults,"* 2011

10 World Health Organization, *"WHO calls for stronger focus on adolescent health,"* 2014

evil is composed of and how this dark substance should be removed. With this loving fear comes a desire to do things the way that God would want things done. That is the basis of removing evil or separating good from evil.

God is building a Kingdom of Love. To do this, He is taking each glorious spirit or human that He creates and separating out the evil. The Kingdom of God is in the heart of man,[11] but it is made up of these interconnected wholesome hearts—all of the hearts that have gone thru a purification process of eradicating evil. They are tested, and then they are sent thru a refiner's fire, and miraculously the heat removes the tarnish and corruption.[12] What remains is uncorrupted purity, like pure gold.

> IN THIS KINGDOM OF LOVE, THE CHILDREN ARE EDUCATED IN THE FEAR OF GOD FIRST, AND THEN THE RESPECT FOR OTHERS NEXT.

But not only is God separating out and then gathering those who love with all of love's glorious components as described in I Corinthians 13, He is also separating out hate with all its miserable components of judgmentalness, pride, debauchery, lust and greed. God is taking this love that is left, and He is building a Super Community consisting of Pure Love that will be way beyond our imaginings and more formidable than any nation known to man. This love is found in God's subjects, in humans who have chosen His path of love. This Nation of love is divided into subunits called "family." The family unit is made up of the father, the mother, and the children, and in

---

11 Nor will people say, 'Here it is,' or 'There it is,' because the kingdom of God is within you. Luke 17:21 This is the covenant I will make with the house of Israel after that time, declares the Lord. I will put my laws in their minds and write them on their hearts. I will be their God, and they will be my people. Hebrews 8:10

12 He will sit as a refiner and purifier of silver; he will purify the Levites and refine them like gold and silver. Then the Lord will have men who will bring offerings in righteousness… Malachi 3:3

some cases, extended family members. It is a subgroup that reflects the Body of Christ. When the family gets large enough, it is almost like the tribes of Israel—interconnected families of love with all the units gathered together—and this is God's New Jerusalem, the City of Peace.

Think about this: God is building a Kingdom based on Pure Love, and the most powerful, influential substance in all the world is *love*. But this Kingdom can only be accomplished by separation—disconnecting the beautiful, the positive, the warm, the endearing, the delightful emotions and spirits, and completely severing them from the worst hateful emotions in the world. As a result, this society is beautiful at all times, kind at every moment, gentle all day long. This loving community is trained up in polished manners, showing respect for each creation of God, living purposely to help others with a clear understanding and motive that our reward is a relationship with God and building up God's Kingdom of Love. May our families also be known as God-fearing families made up of God-fearing men, women and children who treasure their assigned roles and live to promote this beautiful Kingdom.

In the Kingdom of Love, these children are educated in the fear of God first, and then the respect for others next. They are cultured, as a well-informed Royal Priesthood of Believers—living to adore and serve the only Being that matters, the Glorious GOD of the Universe. He is the Leader of this life-force that is free of any evil. He is the One and only Source; He is the only Intelligence and Brain behind this Super Community of Love. This Lord God Almighty is the true King, the true Czar, the true President, Emperor, Monarch, the only One who matters. He is the only Sovereign who was here from the beginning and the only Being that will live forever. He is the only Being that can create other life forms, the only Source that can extend life on Earth and then have life exist forever and ever and ever.

This Super Community was created and developed to belong to God, to this Great I Am who will exist after the great destruction here on Earth, and He will make a final and concise divide at that time, a division of all evil and all good. This is to be done at the end of time as we know it. If the Will of God was taught in this way, then God's Will *would* be done. If this Holy respect was understood—if every father, mother and child understood this—God's Will would automatically be done. Marriages would automatically become strong; children would be focused on their purpose and their goals. You would see plentiful marriages and families having many children and grandchildren. The Will of God would flourish, and peace and joy would abound. The Remnant of the Kingdom of Love was founded on that true loving, respectful, adoring fear and concern for God, His Will, and His Kingdom; therefore, we are witnessing the most beautiful and abundant marriages, a proliferation of beautiful, healthy births and strong, united families.

When we have a higher purpose—only pleasing God Almighty—and we are all united together in that one purpose, it does pull together an incredible organization called the Kingdom of God. It is time for this Holy Priesthood to flourish for the glory of God and His Son, Jesus Christ.

When you consider God and His Creation and that is what your mind is focused on, it becomes easy to build up His Kingdom. God is a genius, so it is easy—He is worthy of all our admiration! And from this fear and adoration comes this most esteemed wisdom for everyone in the family from the oldest to the youngest. Page 27.

Re-establishment of the God-Fearing Family

CHAPTER 2

Then God said, "Let us make man in our image, in our likeness, and let them rule over the fish of the sea and the birds of the air, over the livestock, over all the earth, and over all the creatures that move along the ground." So God created man in his own image, in the image of God he created him; male and female he created them. God blessed them and said to them, "Be fruitful and increase in number; fill the earth and subdue it." Genesis 1:26-28a

God created the Earth, and He created man and woman. God ordained marriage and the family. In the previous chapter, we read about the pain and disunity that can result from building a family without the foundation of a love for this Genius Creator first and the impact of not accepting your own God-given role.

The family is a unit that is like an individual cell in the body. Each family is very important, and we all take care to help each family become all that it should be. We care about the existence of each family, and like the cells in the body, we are all there for the good of the whole. God's brilliant and eternal work of the eradication of evil and the embellishment and the nourishment of everything that is good—from His Holy Personality, His Holy Spirit—should be paralleled in the home.

When Jesus came, his food was to finish the work of God.[1] Parents should take care of this responsibility first and foremost—to ensure that this priority is passed down to each child in each generation. Therefore, the purpose of the family unit is to do the Will of God… to be holy as He is Holy, and to be Christlike, *just* like our Christ. Upon laying down sin and living for God's Will as Jesus did, you automatically accomplish a unity that is impossible to destroy by the gates of Hades or the perpetual demonic attacks from the enemy. You see, the Church is built on the strength of each and every family unit, and therefore they are respected. Each family is valued equally as a part of this plan so that we work together, not in competition with each other as the world does. It is the opposite of the world because we help each other to be strong and upright.

> YOUR CHILDREN WILL RESPECT WHAT YOU RESPECT, AND THEY WILL WORSHIP WHAT YOU WORSHIP, AND THEY WILL ADORE WHAT YOU ADORE.

How do we pass this way of life down to our children? It starts in the heart. Each of us must lovingly fear God above all. This respect can be seen in your conversation—from the abundance of the heart, so the mouth will speak.[2] What is the conversation in your home? That conversation is a barometer of how much loving fear you have. When you have it, you will speak it to the family and then to the children and to the grandchildren. Children will respect

---

1 "My food," said Jesus, "is to do the will of him who sent me and to finish his work." John 4:34
2 The good man brings good things out of the good stored up in his heart, and the evil man brings evil things out of the evil stored up in his heart. For out of the overflow of his heart his mouth speaks. Luke 6:45

what you respect, and they will worship what you worship, and they will adore what you adore. If you are into self, they too will adore themselves in various ways. This worship of self, even in the smallest ways, breaks up, divides and destroys—first that person…and then their family.[3]

When you consider God and His Creation, and that is what your mind is focused on, it becomes easy to build up His Kingdom. God is a *genius*, so it is easy—He is worthy of all our admiration! And from this fear and adoration comes a most esteemed wisdom for everyone in the family from the oldest to the youngest… *The fear of the Lord is the beginning of wisdom, and knowledge of the Holy One is understanding. Proverbs 9:10*

By considering God with wonder-filled fear and awe, we will automatically find this wisdom and this knowledge of God, which is priceless! This fear of God is natural in the beginning of a child's life if the parent encourages it from birth and does not suffocate this fear of God with their own selfish ambitions on this Earth. God had the Israelites live very simply in life, living in tents where the doors opened facing the Presence of God Himself in the Most Holy of Holies at the center of the camp in the Tent of Tabernacle. Imagine growing up in that way…waking up and facing God every day, with a family that is getting up and sacrificing to God first thing in the morning, worshiping Him and praying to God throughout the day, living simply, waiting for the word from Moses, which would give the direction from God, watching the fire at night to go to sleep knowing that this warm, loving protection was over each family and each tribe in that cold night…then sleeping in peace and waking to

---

3   *The wise woman builds her house, but with her own hands the foolish one tears hers down. Proverbs 14:1*

the precious cloud by day that kept them cool and protected them from the heat of the sun. How wise will be the children raised up in this atmosphere! What is more, in God's genius, He rewards those who adoringly fear Him and give Him their love, time, respect and attention. Bottom line, those families who give their lives to this wondrous God will be rewarded.

A Loving Fear

Wisdom is a wonderful reward, but this essential loving fear gives back so much more than just wisdom. The family, in fact, will have no needs if this loving fear is the true pursuit of the father and the mother and the children. It is the fountain of life…

But the eyes of the Lord are on those who fear him, on those whose hope is in his unfailing love. Psalm 33:18

The angel of the Lord encamps around those who fear him, and he delivers them. Psalm 34:7

He will have no fear of bad news; his heart is steadfast, trusting in the Lord. Psalm 112:7

This is beautiful protection! But there is even more than protection. There is long life, the fountain of life. This loving fear prolongs your days…

The fear of the Lord adds length to life, but the years of the wicked are cut short. Proverbs 10:27

Through love and faithfulness sin is atoned for; through the fear of the Lord a man avoids evil. Proverbs 16:6

The fear of the Lord leads to life: then one rests content, untouched by trouble. Proverbs 19:23

Re-establishment of the God-Fearing Family

Humility and the fear of the Lord bring wealth and honor and life. Proverbs 22:4

This is insurance beyond insurance—no trouble, no fear, protection, a deliverance from evil, being given the fountain of life and the promise of a long life! What else could a mere mortal ask for? What more could a family need?

One important key in learning the fear of the Lord is gathering with like-minded Believers...*Assemble the people—men, women and children, and the aliens living in your towns—so they can listen and learn to fear the Lord your God and follow carefully all the words of this law. Deuteronomy 31:12* It is essential to take your children to the Great Assemblies in order to learn this fear and love and how to share it.

> WE LEARN BY PRACTICING SUBMISSION AT HOME, SHARING AT HOME, LOVING AT HOME, WITH THE GREATEST RESPECT FOR EACH INDIVIDUAL.

This does not refer to just "any" assemblies. As you grow closer to God in your life, there will come a time that you will have to make a choice of where you attend assemblies—where you go to church—for the sake of your children and children's children. This church must not just be there for your convenience, but it is there for the continuation of God's Kingdom and His Will.

Daily conversation about God is essential. Many verses point out that we need ears to hear... we need to listen, we need conversation, and we need to hear the Truth.[4] This matters. Truth makes all the difference. Truth sets you free; it completely changes your life. Truth is essential in this procedure to obtain this holy fear and this

---

4   Isaiah 32:3, Matthew 11:15, Matthew 13:15, Mark 4:9, Luke 8:8, Acts 28:27

loving adoration of God, and it is vital if we are to teach this relationship to our children.

This is about a relationship with God, but just the thought of a mortal being and an Immortal Being having the opportunity to build a relationship seems impossible. However, God in His Love allows each of us—a mere man, a mere woman or a mere child—permission to have a relationship with God Almighty. How could we neglect this great opportunity, this essential chance for life on Earth and life for eternity? This life of separating good and evil, starting with gaining a holy fear of God—which is the beginning of wisdom—is the most amazing life.

Better a little with the fear of the Lord than great wealth with turmoil. Proverbs 15:16

The fear of the Lord teaches a man wisdom, and humility comes before honor. Proverbs 15:33

He who fears the Lord has a secure fortress, and for his children it will be a refuge. Proverbs 14:26

For any of this to grow in our hearts, it is essential to adore Christ. Each family member practices all the characteristics of Christ as they learn about and apply God's authority lines—the correct roles for the father, for the mother, for the son, for the daughter, for the eldest child and for the line of authority all the way up. We learn by practicing submission at home, sharing at home, loving at home, with the greatest respect for each individual there, and demonstrating all the fruits of the Spirit at home…love, joy, peace, patience, kindness, goodness, faithfulness, gentleness and self-control.[5] If this is not done in the home, it will not be done outside the home. And if the family does not implement this, the whole Church suffers and will not be strong. It has to be taught and upheld in the home.

These family units were not a concept of man, and this is not made up of men's rules. This is the Will of the genius of God, the God who made all of Creation, and when all is done His way, you have the most glorious concept called the God-Fearing Family. This family will be the building block of the most glorious Kingdom of God, the Church…the Kingdom of Love. With each person fulfilling their God-given role—there to help each other with full respect, not just one day a week, but every day of the week from the morning to the night, treating your parents, your siblings, each other with the most regard and respect as each are Kings and Queens, Princes and Princesses, preparing each other for the next life to come—that is the sure way of passing the Truth of God and the Will of the Most High God down to each generation. May more attention be given to an entity that God has ordained on Earth from the beginning of time for the purpose of securing good and separating out the evil—so as to create the *beautiful*.

A Rich Inheritance

How do you create a God-Fearing Family? How do you expect your children to be what you are not? It seems impossible, and that is why it starts with the parents and the grandparents, because you cannot transfer to your children what you do not have yourself. Start *today* and make a connection with God in your life. You must have a genuine relationship with God to pass this rich inheritance to

---

5   *But the fruit of the Spirit is love, joy, peace, patience, kindness, goodness, faithfulness, gentleness and self-control. Against such things there is no law. Galatians 5:22-23*

your children. Your children do not need money or worldly education more than they need to see you with the fear and love of God.

> WHEN ALL IS DONE HIS WAY, YOU HAVE THE MOST GLORIOUS CONCEPT CALLED THE GOD-FEARING FAMILY. THIS FAMILY WILL BE THE BUILDING BLOCK OF THE MOST GLORIOUS KINGDOM OF GOD, THE CHURCH, THE KINGDOM OF LOVE.

The fathers and mothers who spend their efforts in acquiring money, thinking that possessions are the most important, will not have stable homes. Stable homes will belong to the parents who acquire a relationship with God and who spend their efforts, the rest of their living days, on being kind and uplifting, loving, respectful parents. This relationship builds stability, and these children will advance and will go far beyond all the children on the Earth. These children will have so much more than children who are given great material possessions, a large house, the biggest toys, exotic vacations and expensive cars. "Things" do not build the household that God desires. If the parents have this loving fear of God, if the father is strong enough to be loving and kind to the wife and if the parents reach out to the needy, then you will have a stable family and productive, stable children.

Since we have witnessed destruction of the family unit—and are now witnessing a revival—we all have a great responsibility to build up a true, God-fearing and God-focused family. You must read on. May we never forget this responsibility…may God's Will be done on Earth as it is in Heaven so that we can all point to this glorious Genius, our God, our King!

Re-establishment of the God-Fearing Family

David praised the Lord in the presence of the whole assembly, saying, "Praise be to you, O Lord, God of our father Israel, from everlasting to everlasting. Yours, O Lord, is the greatness and the power and the glory and the majesty and the splendor, for everything in heaven and earth is yours. Yours, O Lord, is the kingdom; you are exalted as head over all. Wealth and honor come from you; you are the ruler of all things. In your hands are strength and power to exalt and give strength to all. Now, our God, we give you thanks, and praise your glorious name. I Chronicles 29:10-13

The Legacy

CHAPTER 3

If you fully obey the Lord your God and carefully follow all his commands I give you today, the Lord your God will set you high above all the nations on earth. All these blessings will come upon you and accompany you if you obey the Lord your God: You will be blessed in the city and blessed in the country. The fruit of your womb will be blessed, and the crops of your land and the young of your livestock—the calves of your herds and the lambs of your flocks. Your basket and your kneading trough will be blessed. You will be blessed when you come in and blessed when you go out. The Lord will grant that the enemies who rise up against you will be defeated before you. They will come at you from one direction but flee from you in seven. The Lord will send a blessing on your barns and on everything you put your hand to. The Lord your God will bless you in the land he is giving you. The Lord will establish you as his holy people, as he promised you on oath, if you keep the commands of the Lord your God and walk in his ways. Then all the peoples on earth will see that you are called by the name of the Lord, and they will fear you. The Lord will grant you abundant prosperity—in the fruit of your womb, the young of your livestock and the crops of your ground—in the land he swore to your forefathers to give you… However, if you do not obey the Lord your God and do not carefully follow all his commands and decrees I am giving you today, all these curses will come upon you and overtake you: You will be cursed in the city and cursed in the country. Your basket and your kneading trough will be cursed. The fruit of your womb will be cursed, and the crops of your land, and the calves of your herds and the lambs of your flocks. You will be cursed when you come in and cursed when you go out. The Lord will send on you curses, confusion and rebuke in everything you put your hand to, until you are destroyed and come to sudden ruin because of the evil you have done in forsaking him. Deuteronomy 28:1-11, 15-20

Indeed, this passage holds true today; the world is witnessing a reversal of blessings for the next generation for the first time in our history. Incredibly, the children are seeing a shorter lifespan expectancy than their parents.[1] In a recent survey by the Pew Research Center, two out of three Americans believe that when this generation of children grows up, they will be worse off financially than their parents, and this belief was expressed by respondents regardless of their socioeconomic status, age or gender…rich or poor, young or old, men or women.[2] Similar, if not greater, pessimism was also apparent in 10 of 13 advanced nations polled by the Pew Research Center's Global Attitudes Project. Only when one refers to the lowest economic groups was there any optimism for improvement in the future of the next generation.

> LIFE IS NOT ABOUT THE ACCUMULATION OF WEALTH, BUT IT IS ABOUT SELFLESS PARENTS WHO LIVE SUCH RIGHTEOUS LIVES THAT THEY LEAVE A LEGACY OF BLESSINGS AND A CONNECTION WITH THE HEAVENS.

Other research showed that an employee "with the same degree, the same job and the same demographic profile is earning less today than they were in the 1980s," and that reality applies to both

---

1 New England Journal of Medicine, "A Potential Decline in Life Expectancy in the United States in the 21st Century," 2005
2 Pew Research Center, "What will become of America's kids?" 2014

white-collar office jobs and those in the service industry.[3] This means that if you recently graduated with a college degree, not only are you likely to be underemployed and working a job that does not require your degree, but you are likely under-earning when compared to your parents or grandparents years before the Great Recession leveled their opportunities. In fact, real earnings for recent college grads have declined by 10,000 dollars since 2000.[4] Experts say that what the younger generation has to realize, given the findings in the study, is that they are actually going to have a lower standard of living than their parents. Could this be related to the Deuteronomy 28 prophecy? I believe it can.

Life is not about the accumulation of wealth, but it is about selfless parents who live such righteous lives that they leave a legacy of blessings and such a connection with the Heavens that their children receive answered prayers—instead of leaving them in sin, with split families, debt and broken relationships, depression and bitterness. It is about being so God-like and Christlike that you leave the world behind a better place. By teaching this to our children and their children, our goal is not to just raise them and then leave them to fend for themselves, but to build a future for generations to come. There is a difference. Once we choose God and put His Commands and His House first, He gives back in increasing measure. I have lived long enough to believe in the impact of Exodus 20 (the Ten Commandments), and Christ's first sermon was about the Ten Commandments. The Ten Commandments have never been relaxed.

When I was a child, these Scriptures were just words. However, now that I have lived and experienced that Exodus 20 and

---

3   Forbes, "Millennials Earn Less Than Their Parents And The Recession Isn't To Blame, 2013"
4   The Atlantic, "The Graph That Should Accompany Every Article About Millennials and Economics," 2012

Deuteronomy 28 are living prophecies—as true today as they were 3,500 years ago—I know I never want to go back to the unpredictable outcomes that came from a peaceless, half-hearted relationship with God or half-hearted Christianity, a life where God is not totally at the forefront.

The Remnant of the Kingdom of Love

The history of this Remnant movement is that it has been led by God, based on the fact that Christ came to fulfill the Law (which is the first five books of the Bible) and the Prophets[5]—in other words, to fulfill the Old Testament—and that Deuteronomy 28 is still alive…with the blessings for obedience and the curses for disobedience.

The Remnant of the Kingdom of Love was founded on laying all idols down—having no hobbies or interests of the created over the Creator. Instead, we focus intently on the Word of God and His lead, applying that as a Church unit…and what has happened as a result? We became blessed. The early members would tell me how their lives were being drastically changed for the better. In the midst of testing, the blessings from God were impossible to mistake, for they came in increasing measure. Was this just random? That was my question. The choices were out there—testing and temptation were real, and therefore, there were standards that we had to selflessly choose between when we came to crossroads in our lives. Each time members made the choice to deny themselves, there was some suffering, yes, but when they chose the God-centered path, they felt God's good pleasure and experienced abundant blessings because of their choice.

---

5   *Do not think that I have come to abolish the Law or the Prophets; I have not come to abolish them but to fulfill them. Matthew 5:17*

We soon discovered this pattern of denying self and receiving blessings was not merely random chance—even though it was not always instant. In fact, in some cases, justice or reward took upward from three years to a decade, but the ever-increasing rewards were consistent and undeniable…in spite of the opposition. All the members of the Church were increasingly healed spiritually and relationally. We knew we were on to something and that we could not be silent or keep this Connection to ourselves. Indeed, I have been watching…taking note…how extraordinary and surreal the blessings were and still are. It is hard to keep up with them! Yes, upon examining the lives of the members, the correlating blessings were undeniable—lives increasingly fortunate, children progressively blessed, households rewarded with better jobs, finances, relationships and health. Members were experiencing blessings on their well-being, their physical health, their mental health, their joy…they had more friends, more help, more encouragement and love with no back-biting or gossip. The children developed life-long friendships, and as they grew into teens and young adults, they wanted to stay close to their family far more than ever. It is called the abundant life.

> LOOK AT ALL CREATION THAT GOD HAS MADE AND SEE HIS KINGDOM IN A BROAD STROKE OF ETERNITY. YOU ARE IN THE MIDDLE OF AN ENORMOUS PLAN…A PLAN WHERE EACH GENERATION BUILDS MORE STRENGTH FOR THE NEXT GENERATION, FOREVER.

For the families at Remnant, this did not happen overnight—but serious choices were made all along the way. This focus on God first and denial of self has brought blessings, and now offers even greater blessings to the children and grandchildren at earlier and earlier ages. However, our eyes have still not seen it all. I know beyond a doubt that each generation has more hope than the last. Here is the point: what God had orchestrated all along was not this tunnel vision where you are focused on yourself, your own life, your own accomplishments...but a much larger perspective to look at all Creation that God has made and to see His Kingdom in a broad stroke of eternity. You are in the middle of an enormous plan...a plan in which each generation builds more strength for the next generation, forever.

Spiritual Stewards

Look at the original example set by God thru the Israelites... think in terms of something longstanding—the tribes of Israel that span thousands of years. Instead of living only for ourselves and making the younger generation pay while we live it up today, God's plan is for us to sacrificially live to help the generations ahead of us with physical and spiritual inheritances. This goal is not about trying to get rich, but it does mean living out the Ten Commandments...and in that, each generation that loves God with all their heart has more opportunity than the previous generation did. This is about being good Spiritual Stewards for the generations to come. The world's history books document how the reverse is true—each generation that does not obey God is cursed, and their children often pay a price, too. Obedience means love...love for God first. Disobedience means love of self over others and over God. Disobedience is a form of hate toward God and His eternal plan. Those who love God will love the next generation more than their own selfish agenda.

Christianity was originally grounded in this...yet this has not been practiced as a whole in the past few decades, and more and more religious leaders have confessed to living lustful, greedy lifestyles with no shame. This has left many a follower with a disconnect from God. At the end of fiscal year 2016, the national debt of the United States was estimated to be 19.3 trillion dollars[6]—it is simply unthinkable to leave that amount of debt to our children, yet this debt continues to grow as our society shows no concern for future generations. Those who sincerely love are more concerned not for their own finances or their own retirement, but their concern is for the good of the whole—for the family, for the children, and for the great-great-grandchildren to come. Our concern is for the Church as it is connected to God and to His Business, His Kingdom. Having no laziness and seeking pure righteousness is sought after because getting rich without putting God first is like putting money in a pocket with holes in it.[7] It just disappears.

Establishing a Legacy

With the Jewish people, the twelve tribes, or families, started with the sons of Jacob. They were given territories around Jerusalem. These tribes lasted as one strong unit thru the times of King David and King Solomon, but after about 200 years, when Solomon's son, Rehoboam, came into office and then sinned, the tribes were divided by curses and strife. Ten of the tribes went to the north and had Samaria as the capital, but the tribes of Judah and Benjamin went to the south with Jerusalem as their capital. The tribes of the north continued to have unremittingly bad, selfish kings who permitted the worship of other gods and failed to enforce the worship of God

---

6   *Fiscal Year 2017 Federal Budget*
7   *You have planted much, but have harvested little. You eat, but never have enough. You drink, but never have your fill. You put on clothes, but are not warm. You earn wages, only to put them in a purse with holes in it. Haggai 1:6*

alone. Following the prophecy of Deuteronomy 28, God eventually allowed them to be conquered and dispersed among the peoples of the Earth, and strangers ruled over their remnant in the northern land. Following a conquest by Assyria, these ten tribes were allegedly dispersed and lost to history and were henceforth known as the Ten Lost Tribes.

But according to the New Testament, these tribes must have had a remnant remaining… *There was also a prophetess, Anna, the daughter of Phanuel, of the tribe of Asher… She never left the temple but worshiped night and day, fasting and praying. Luke 2:36a, 37b*

So these "lost" tribes were instilled with something… something that was still there, even after all that time, something noteworthy, something deep within the Jewish teaching. It was called a **legacy**. As time went by, the word "legacy" has evolved. It is now more likely to mean simply "fundraising" or charitable giving… something that collects money instead of the original sold-out life of right-living and love-living that connects you and your offspring to the Heavens.

I have witnessed the blessings and curses, and the prophecy is true: we reap what we sow.[8] Each generation that obeys God experiences fewer curses than the generation before. What we are experiencing now are children who are excelling in school and even completing college earlier, families who are now debt-free, peaceful households with loving spouses and families having blue-ribbon babies… the womb is so blessed. But now what is needed for this Remnant is not to think about just the next generation but to think in terms of a thousand generations out. We are just starting to experience God-sent blessings for His Glory alone. We take no merit for this ourselves, but it is only obtained by this Connection with God

---

8   *Do not be deceived: God cannot be mocked. A man reaps what he sows. Galatians 6:7*

and Christ. The blessings have come only by uplifting the Creator and totally following in the footsteps of Christ—not with any pride in ourselves, but with realizing that this is a gift. These blessings are treasures never to be accepted with haughtiness, but with humility. It is unbelievable!

THE LEGACY FOR THE CHILDREN

The children raised under this legacy are beautiful. There cannot be anything that God gives on Earth greater than the gift of a child, a human being. Children can feel their self-worth in the way that we dress them and in our actions and in our *deep* love for them. We are not there merely to clean up the outside and disguise the inside, as much of the world does. No, this starts on the inside first. It does not take money to do this...but it does take love. It is about honoring and being thankful for this gift that God has given us. **Life**...a human...a baby.

I have been there for the delivery of every one of my grandchildren. I just cry my eyes out, because I cannot believe God allows life to come from another life like that. Then I see all these other babies being born within our Church, and they are all so beautiful. It is unbelievable that God trusts us. Who are we that He would entrust us with a human being? We dress and care for these babies in a way that glorifies God because we value this life...we *value* the children. We *value* each and every human being. We value *life*. Tell me something that is worth more than that.

LET US NOT REPEAT HISTORY

Now, amidst all the blessings, there will be trials and tribulations for both the believer and unbeliever on this Earth—even more persecution and testing for the believer. However, those who are united in this true legacy will push to love God first and then live this life to leave a safe place for their offspring. The goal is to make specific efforts for God and His Kingdom. This is a superior goal with a superior outcome. Again…

If you fully obey the Lord your God and carefully follow all his commands I give you today, the Lord your God will set you high above all the nations on Earth. All these blessings will come upon you and accompany you if you obey the Lord your God. Deuteronomy 28:1-2

Live each day to make your offspring and future generations more stable and connected to the Heavens than the generations before, for the Glory of God alone. May we not repeat history and be the Ten Lost Tribes of Israel—rather, let us uphold this Biblical prophecy and live it out for a thousand generations strong until Christ comes back!

The Legacy

Greatness is not necessarily found in impressive armies of aggression, nor is it found simply in wealth, resources or public speaking skills. Nobility is not just made in castles. No, nobility is created altogether differently. Page 48.

The Royal Revival

Chapter 4

The word of the Lord came to me, "Son of man, if a country sins against me by being unfaithful and I stretch out my hand against it... even if these three men-Noah, Daniel, and Job-were in it, they could save only themselves by their righteousness," declares the Sovereign Lord. Ezekiel 14:12-13a, 14

We learned from Chapter 3 of the impact of the foundational promises and the warnings laid out in Deuteronomy 28. Think of the issues that face the world today: the threat of war, the strife in Israel, the refugees pouring into Europe, the bulging prisons, the great debt, and jobs being lost to countries overseas. What is the cause, and what is the answer? Does any wise man or any nation have the solution?

In every generation, the masses will search for great, noble and wise men to lead the way thru this challenging world. Noble, wise leaders are invaluable for guiding the way to shape a people and direct a society. People will rise only as far as the leader will take them. *Can* a people and a society be noble?

Royalty is dreamed about in the movies and in child's play. Vacations may center around this make-believe fantasy in Disney World—a pretend world of a different life. Yet notice that as much as a society guided by wise and noble men is fantasized about in reality, it is despised by some. The French Revolution led to turmoil and upheaval. The monarchy in England now has scarce influence and is little more than a figurehead. Times have changed, but should they have?

The more I read the words of the Prophets, the more I see that **royalty** is our calling. This kingly thread of fascination comes from the Heavens and not from Hollywood or a child's imagination. As we have read, Exodus 19:5-6a states: *Now if you obey me fully and keep my covenant, then out of all nations you will be my treasured possession. Although the whole earth is mine, you will be for me a kingdom of priests and a holy nation.*

Though we might be far from that image now, not only is it our calling, but it is God's delight. Psalm 16:3 confirms this: *As for the saints who are in the land, they are the glorious ones in whom is all my delight.* Not *just* God's delight—*all* His delight! We are here to please God, so this should be our priority. The Almighty wants to build His Kingdom of a Chosen People, a Royal Priesthood, a Holy Nation of God-Fearing men and women. God is calling mankind to transform into nobility, not to spurn it…yet how is this possible? How can our young boys go from the common to the extraordinarily uncommon noble man in this day and age?

Nations and kingdoms rise and fall throughout all of history. They have their moments tasting aristocracy, dignity and graciousness. They have even rarer moments with the wise and sage leaders who guide the citizens into greatness with a morally advanced civility, leading to advanced architectural engineering, progressive accomplishments and simply a superior society. Down deep, men search for justice and seek out great leaders for their countries; however, the secret to this progressive society is not created as you might think. Most societies promote their generals from war or the politicians of rhetoric. In America, one can run for office and use the forum of debate. Greatness is not necessarily found in impressive armies of aggression, nor is it found simply in wealth, resources or public speaking skills. Nobility is not just made in castles. No, nobility is created altogether differently.

For God's Glory

As you come to him, the living Stone—rejected by men but chosen by God and precious to him—you also, like living stones, are being built into a spiritual house to be a holy priesthood, offering spiritual sacrifices acceptable to God through Jesus Christ. For in Scripture it says: "See, I lay a stone in Zion, a chosen and precious cornerstone, and the one who trusts in him will never be put to shame." Now to you who believe, this stone is precious. But to those who do not believe, "The stone the builders rejected has become the capstone," and, "A stone that causes men to stumble and a rock that makes them fall." They stumble because they disobey the message—which is also what they were destined for. But you are a chosen people, a royal priesthood, a holy nation, a people belonging to God, that you may declare the praises of him who called you out of darkness into his wonderful light. Once you were not a people, but now you are the people of God; once you had not received mercy, but now you have received mercy. I Peter 2:4-10

Yes, God is calling for us to be the noble ones in whom is His delight; therefore, the world is in need of this God-fearing role model. According to Peter's passage above, this regal Priesthood can be built only if it knows and accepts its purpose: all is said and done for God's glory and not our own. Additionally, it is accomplished only when a man lines up with the capstone of Jesus Christ.

Why do so many reject nobility and stumble over The Stone? When a society loses sight that it is all about God's Glory, the world witnesses a moral reversal with a disgust toward authority and everything that portrays righteousness or nobility. People buy into a lie that all families are dysfunctional, so they give up. They give in to the crowd where the population is dressed with defiance, daring an authority to ask them to conform to polite society as they glory in shabby unisex outfits, multiple tattoos and piercings, with unkempt, frazzled looks. One of the most profound cultural changes of the twentieth century has been the rise of the casual, carefree look. Yet, I will still contend that down deep, people dream of better, and that is why the world pays to attend runway fashion shows—not vice versa.

The rebellion is real. Note that like the outside appearance, behavior is quickly growing more animalistic rather than refined or cultured. Where there was once a time when people would never display public anger or use the Lord's name in vain, now you see open and public displays of paramount projection and blame, often using the Lord's name freely. Having no respect and talking over others is at its zenith. Unfortunately, many of today's children have never seen a superior way. But there is hope.

In the midst of the strongest resistance to law and order and to "old fashioned" manners and etiquette…in the midst of the eradication of differences between men and women…in the midst of rejecting the role of ladies and gentlemen, rebuffing quietness in women and complete control of the tongue, applauding the smart mouth and what they would call the "freedom of spirit"…comes the Royal Remnant Revival, a calling to make the people of the world aware of their sin and deviation from God's Laws. The results of the revival of God's Laws have been thrilling—as man after man is reborn and family after family is transformed. We are now witnessing a *reversal* of this defiant, unruly, rebellious culture and a real rebirth of noble men and women of God.

How is this rare phenomenon taught? What can we do to ensure that God's Kingdom continues to come on Earth as Christ prayed?[1] Can something like this even take root today? My belief is that it can and it will, for all of God's Laws are programmed deep into the DNA of mankind and the world yearns for this revival, waiting for the sons of God to be born—though they may not know it.[2] Think

THIS REGAL PRIESTHOOD CAN ONLY BE BUILT IF IT KNOWS AND ACCEPTS ITS PURPOSE: ALL IS SAID AND DONE FOR GOD'S GLORY AND NOT OUR OWN.

about the growth of Disney's prince and princess movies over the past few decades.

An underground, grassroots resurgence is taking place. This is not about the spoiled rich, the snobbish, the upper crust blue-blooded. This is a calling of the humble, likable, engaging personalities who are full of the grace of God. This is a Nation that God is gathering, a Kingly Nation within a worldly nation, a Nation that has no race or color but is indeed a brotherhood of Christians. This is a nation

---

1 Matthew 6:9-13
2 *The creation waits in eager expectation for the sons of God to be revealed. Romans 8:19*

where the worldliness in the heart of man has been separated out like a sieve…separated out from the world while still in the world.

A ROYAL RIGHTEOUS SOCIETY

What does this Royal Righteous Society inside a worldly society look like, and how is it achieved? Well, it is all part of a spiritual war, and there are fundamentals of the authoritative men who are a part of this movement. Their training is somewhat like an obstacle course, and the exercises are tactical movements that are needed for combat. Peter made sure that those called out knew their purpose. As we read earlier, *That you may declare the praises of him who called you out of darkness into his wonderful light. I Peter 2:9b* Therefore, the life and death of each man is for the Glory of God. Without this foundational purpose, vanity will be exposed.

> THIS IS A NATION THAT GOD IS GATHERING, A KINGLY NATION WITHIN A WORLDLY NATION, A NATION THAT HAS NO RACE OR COLOR BUT IS INDEED A BROTHERHOOD OF CHRISTIANS.

Having a willingness to be different than the world is essential. This concept is something that weak men cannot stomach, so the faint of heart are left behind.

In the world, selfish promotion gives way to a rising self-conceit that is hungry for the praise of man, so this empty, ravenous man is willing to compromise his morals to get ahead, willing to use the excused little white lies in an effort to defend himself. With just this one wrong choice, when God's glory is pushed aside for one's own glory, the marriage suffers. When one elevates self over God, you see less peace and calm, a growing shame and embarrassment, while projecting harsh judgment on others. This one goal of glorifying self with money, jobs, cars and clothes only leads to fears and added anxiety and insecurity. It will exacerbate your neediness so that you become too loud, too intoxicated, driving too fast and often too angry. You will be a man who might try workaholism for financial gain, yet your pockets have holes in them, which then leads to cutting corners with taxes or tithing.[3] All of this develops phobias and suspicions. The worst characteristic is lying; if someone lies, it reveals something very deep-seated—corrupt morals, a twisted purpose in life. Lying reinforces that one is self-centric rather than God-centric. The solution is called "telling yourself the Truth." It cannot get better until men repent and develop a whole new goal, otherwise they will miss the high and gallant calling of this Majestic Knighthood—one for all and all for one—all for God Almighty.

Now you have a new "God first" goal, but how do you keep motivated? Time and energy are finite; therefore, look inward and never outward. You can begin this elite training once you readily ignore the faults of others, concerning yourself only with your own heart and your own shortcomings. You will have no projection toward others but rather will accept the task of overhauling your *own* bad attitudes. You get up and daily look into the spiritual mirror, concentrating on your own inadequacies. Ironically, you will evolve into the esteemed, valued man who radiates respected

> ALL OF GOD'S LAWS ARE PROGRAMMED DEEP INTO THE DNA OF MANKIND AND THE WORLD YEARNS FOR THIS REVIVAL, WAITING FOR THE SONS OF GOD TO BE BORN.

---

3 *You have planted much, but have harvested little. You eat, but never have enough. You drink, but never have your fill. You put on clothes, but are not warm. You earn wages, only to put them in a purse with holes in it. Haggai 1:6*

righteousness. Only the older and wiser soldiers can take the speck out of another's eye.[4]

Consider the workplace—people have a tendency to blame getting fired on the boss, or on downsizing, or on the supervisor's jealousy. Without a strong moral compass leading you inward, over time, employees who started with the same prospects will grow to be miles apart in character and opportunities.

> YOU CAN BEGIN THIS ELITE TRAINING ONCE YOU READILY IGNORE THE FAULTS OF OTHERS, BUT CONCERN YOURSELF WITH YOUR OWN HEART AND YOUR OWN SHORTCOMINGS.

Choosing the right road is challenging. We have to be different from the world but aim at imitating Christ so that we blend. Men seeking this path must beware… there is a strange wicked pride that is hard to detect with the common spiritual sieve. It is a pride of insisting on being unique and resisting imitation as if it were something brainless and foolish. It is a fear of "losing one's identity"…yet to insist on standing out speaks of a need for attention.

Copying, or imitating, Christ's characteristics is not a cop-out—it is genius. God gives uniqueness thru your spiritual gifts, and there is an etiquette in copying. True Nobility applauds duplicate noble characteristics, creating a God-fearing—and therefore holy—authoritative persona. We do not have to be identical, but take note of the Middle Eastern religious groups that hold close to ancient culture—they do not dress as the world, and yet inside their religious movement they are imitators. They lose their uniqueness in

---

4   *You hypocrite, first take the plank out of your own eye, and then you will see clearly to remove the speck from your brother's eye. Matthew 7:5*

order to give more attention to God. This says much to the world. This noble man brings glory to God thru all of his actions and builds the Kingdom of God thru daily and hourly putting his all into imitating Christ and living out those characteristics at work and at home. Read on, because there is more to learn about how a Godly man lives this out.

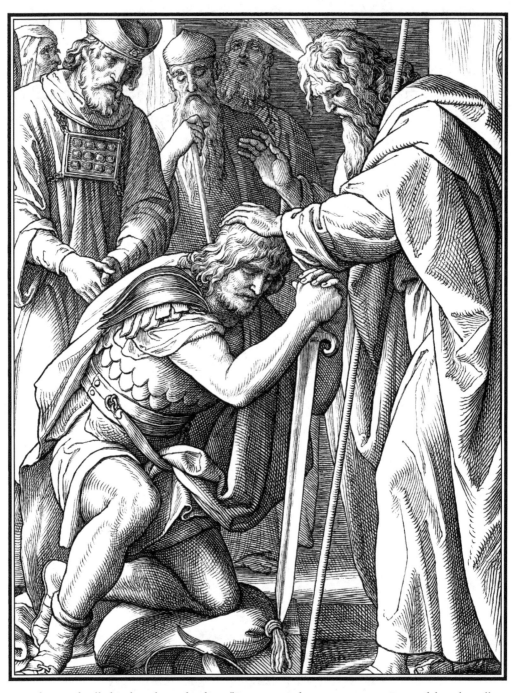

When God called Joshua, he said to him, "Be strong and very courageous. Be careful to obey all the law my servant Moses gave you; do not turn from it to the right or to the left, that you may be successful wherever you go. Do not let this Book of the Law depart from your mouth; meditate on it day and night, so that you may be careful to do everything written in it. Then you will be prosperous and successful. Have I not commanded you? Be strong and courageous. Do not be terrified; do not be discouraged, for the Lord your God will be with you wherever you go." Joshua 1:7-9

A Man of Nobility

Chapter 5

The God-fearing, noble man will stand out in this world just by taking personal responsibility at home and in the workplace. The moral-less world might steal, cheat and lie to justify their unsuccessful lives; however, fundamentally, God's men must not be lazy but must work. Second Thessalonians 3:10 says, *For even when we were with you, we gave you this rule: "If a man will not work, he shall not eat."* This is a rule with built-in behavior modification: no work, no food. Note that there is a difference between being lazy, or spending more than you are making, or being in debt… and being poor. Jesus said that there would always be the poor.[1] We have great empathy for those in needy situations, and the Church rejoices in helping. But the Scriptures are clear for the noble man about the importance of working:

He who has been stealing must steal no longer, but must work, doing something useful with his own hands, that he may have something to share with those in need. Ephesians 4:28

Make it your ambition to lead a quiet life, to mind your own business and to work with your hands, just as we told you… I Thessalonians 4:11

Hard work was not a new rule, but it is a lasting ordinance since the fall in the Garden of Eden.

---

1   *The poor you will always have with you, and you can help them any time you want. But you will not always have me. Mark 14:7*

To Adam he said, "Because you listened to your wife and ate from the tree about which I commanded you, 'You must not eat of it,' cursed is the ground because of you; through painful toil you will eat of it all the days of your life. It will produce thorns and thistles for you, and you will eat the plants of the field. By the sweat of your brow you will eat your food until you return to the ground, since from it you were taken; for dust you are and to dust you will return." Genesis 3:17-19

We are dust, and God is eternal. God has ordained hard work. God did not have the men work so that they could be rich but rather so they would keep the essential humility and dependence necessary for salvation. Extra money in the bank does not make you more moral, nor can money be blamed for the reckless behavior of some rich people. If you are unhappy *without* money, you will be unhappy *with* money. If you are unkind to your wife when you are poor, then money is not going to change your personality in your marriage. Having money does not instantly make you generous. If you were irresponsible in poverty, wealth may not guarantee that you will pay your bills on time. Money gives no power, nor does it give solutions to your own problems caused by your lack of personal responsibility.

Although the Bible seems to refer to some retirement, it does not say that a rich man does not have to work. This refinement eliminates laziness and stinginess. The love of money—and the pursuit of money—is not recommended by Christ, for he declared that it was harder for a rich man to go to Heaven because it competes with dependence.[2]

The curse given to Adam in the Garden was hard work, even, as we read above, "painful toil" at times working by the sweat of

---

2   *Then Jesus said to his disciples, "I tell you the truth, it is hard for a rich man to enter the kingdom of heaven. Again I tell you, it is easier for a camel to go through the eye of a needle than for a rich man to enter the kingdom of God." Matthew 19:23-24*

one's brow. If someone is a hard worker, they are rarely out of work. No work should be "beneath" you. We should be grateful for any employment, and many a man has had to temporarily work several jobs from time to time to get out of debt. Balance is key. Avoid a workaholic lifestyle but work to please God. A God-fearing man does not tolerate poor performance and is not in a habit of coming in late because "everyone else does." Instead of accepting a lower standard, he sets the example by giving more than asked, never

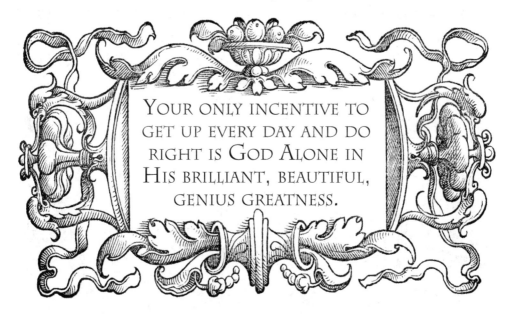

Your only incentive to get up every day and do right is God Alone in His brilliant, beautiful, genius greatness.

complaining, always keeping a task list and checking in with the supervisor, always having a "can do" attitude and becoming known as the "man who gets things done." Though you may not always be popular with the other employees, during economic downturns, your future will be more secure.

Finding the Answers

In today's society, you see the numbers of people who blame the government for the lack of jobs, the poverty, the debt of the country, the plight of the refugees and immigrants; however, this excuse is not that simple. Knowledge of history is essential to guide the future. Every time you think that your life is hard, someone else has it harder. Think back to the early days of America and the countless migrants and refugees who came on boats to America, at times fleeing for their very lives. Sometimes ships were even turned away at port as they came en masse. I remember the stories of the Germans, Irish, Polish, Jewish, Chinese and the boat people from Vietnam, all immigrants who crossed the ocean just to reach a country of freedom. They had nothing and knew no one when they arrived; they faced exclusion and discrimination, but they worked hard and

WITH THIS SOUND FOUNDATION, MEN FROM ANY CIRCUMSTANCES COULD BECOME A PRINCE OR A KING!

fed their families, and they kept their houses spotless. Even though wages were very low, they sacrificed to save, and they pooled their resources to help each other, so that by the early 1900s, most families were homeowners—without any government assistance.

Today, the government has spent billions on welfare and anti-poverty programs. After more than 50 years of the welfare state, many families are still struggling. Why? Which comes first: subsidies were offered, so everyone relaxed their morals because the government undermined incentives; or was it first a relaxing of morals, which then increased subsidies? Well, it is *neither*. Ongoing debates between more government spending versus limiting the government, increasing taxes versus decreasing taxes, and capitalism versus socialism continue to surface, but with no solutions. The secular world depends heavily on the government, and not just for food programs. Our banks and stock market are now dependent on the QE (quantitative easing) to stimulate the economy by the printing of money. However, the answer lies far beyond money and government policies.

Only God and His Kingdom hold the answers. Personal responsibility, when not emphasized by the Church, can give way to dependence and a loss of respect for persons and property. The Bible teaches that God cannot be mocked; a man reaps what he sows.[3] But this verse is not referring to money or worldly success. God is not promising that if a man works hard, he will get rich. This Scripture is in reference to pleasing the Spirit of God. God is not saving those who are rich in money, but those who are rich in Him. Repentance from greed improves your financial outcome. By the way, there are those who work hard every day and are proud of it, yet have never pleased God nor had a day of peace. The key is responsible, hard work to *please God*. The reward—your very great reward—is the favor of God, which brings everything!

The problems in this country will not be solved by government nor by politicians, for those entities are void of God. It is not about a wealth of incentives…nor a lack of them, for no one can force you to

---

3   *Do not be deceived: God cannot be mocked. A man reaps what he sows. Galatians 6:7*

take a lifetime of handouts, as tempting as it can be. You have to stand in long lines and fill out long forms for these various subsidies. No one can make you overeat or make you take unearned money. Some temporary welfare, in and of itself, is not right or wrong. Likewise, help from the Church is not right or wrong. However, one must not become dependent upon this help but instead accept God's Will and work hard so that we can help others less fortunate than ourselves.

OFFERING GENUINE WORK

But there is more! Look at the *quality* of work we are to perform:

Slaves, obey your earthly masters in everything; and do it, not only when their eye is on you and to win their favor, but with sincerity of heart and reverence for the Lord. Whatever you do, work at it with all your heart, as working for the Lord, not for men, since you know that you will receive an inheritance from the Lord as a reward. It is the Lord Christ you are serving. Colossians 3:22-24

God is asking for genuine work. Many men leave the house each day claiming they are "going to work," but are they? That may be true for some men, but between getting to work late, leaving early, taking longer breaks and lengthier lunches, socializing, spending time on personal emails, texting, web searching, Facebook, and drinking coffee, some are lucky to get in half a day of authentic work. The Gallup Polls found that almost 70 percent of workers in the United States are either not paying attention or not engaged to their assigned work.[4] In other words, only 30 percent of workers are driving their organizations forward. In companies with low engagement, this

---

4   Gallup, *"Majority of U.S. Employees Not Engaged Despite Gains in 2014,"* 2015

frustration often causes swift turnover of top talent since these hard workers quickly realize they are carrying the weight alone.

What about your attitude at work? God is asking for you to win the favor of your boss, yet it is not uncommon for employees to express a negative view of their employer. Nearly one in five employees would take company information such as customer data, price lists or product plans with them if they knew they were about to be terminated. Nearly one in six employees who have been let go have hacked a former employer's computing systems using their old identification cards. Employee theft is at an all-time high.[5] Light-fingered employees cost American stores (and consumers) more than shoplifters do; employee theft accounts for 43 percent of lost revenue.[6] True Christianity does not create a con artist who manipulates with flattering words, but it creates an employee who actually gives sincere service and respect as if working for God Himself.

> THE ROYAL REMNANT REVIVAL IS UNDERWAY…GOD IS REACHING OUT AND HIS VOICE OF ANCIENT PERFECT, FAULTLESS WISDOM THRU HIS BRILLIANT SPIRIT IS CALLING TO YOU.

The choice lies in the heart of a man whether to please God or self. You *can* choose to enter the Gates of the Kingdom with your own adoption of the Will of the Father—your food will be to do His Will.[7] What is essential is to be surrounded by men who have chosen this same path so you can focus on how rewarded and respected they are. It gives you the energy you need to survive in

---

5 *Harris Interactive*, 2013
6 *Fortune*, "U.S. Retail Workers are Number 1… In Employee Theft," 2015
7 "My food," said Jesus, "is to do the will of him who sent me and to finish his work." John 4:34

a world of negativity and apathy. Righteous men will escape the company of fools!

Stay away from a foolish man, for you will not find knowledge on his lips… A wise man fears the Lord and shuns evil, but a fool is hotheaded and reckless. Proverbs 14:7,16

Something Higher than Yourself

If you want to be a part of the noble, self-sacrificing Priesthood, the biggest hurdle to overcome is to admit that you are broke, overweight or sick from tobacco or that you have destroyed your marriage because of disrespect or greed…because you have *chosen* it. That is right—we all do what we want. When you are uncomfortable enough, you will choose to drink less, eat less, work more, spend less and love your family more because you *want* to.

The common denominator of God-fearing men is doing this for something higher than yourself, and then it becomes an adoration of the Creator. Your only incentive to get up every day and do right is God Alone in His brilliant, beautiful, genius greatness—words that are totally inadequate to describe a God so far superior than all that we can see or imagine with our finite minds. He is the only Immortal and the only Being that can give life—the eternal life that we all long for, a day that does not end, a life that gets to live forever and ever without aging. The answer has been here all along, right in the Ten Commandments that have been sitting by your bed all your life.[8]

When you live and work to please self, you will experience burnout; but when you live and work to please God, you experience

---

8   See Chapter 10 for more on the Ten Commandments.

the opposite. But these words must turn into *actions*…to love God above all, including the Commandment that a man shall not covet. Contemplate how different the environment of your family life would be if you lived out the Ten Commandments! No one would desire anything their sibling or neighbor has, for there would be no jealousy or strife. No one would dare look at what others have in a covetous way. Think of the peace of every man, woman and child if you were not comparing your life to your neighbor's life. Deliberate on the joy of households with no greed or lust if the Tenth Commandment was taken to heart. Just consider how your words

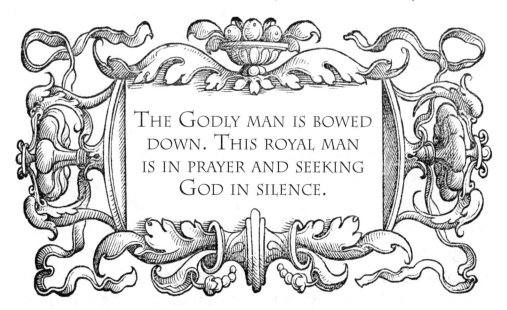

would always be gracious if the Lord's Name or any part of it was never used in vain. Consider the blessings of the households that put The Lord Almighty first in heart each day and night.

It is not just in the workplace that God wants us to be different, but in the home as well. Paul says in Colossians: *Husbands, love your wives and do not be harsh with them. Children, obey your parents in everything, for this pleases the Lord. Fathers, do not embitter your children, or they will become discouraged. Colossians 3:19-21*

Peter goes on to say: *Husbands, in the same way be considerate as you live with your wives, and treat them with respect as the weaker partner and as heirs with you of the gracious gift of life, so that nothing will hinder your prayers. I Peter 3:7*

How powerful it is to know that by doing this, nothing will hinder your prayers. Do not think that dying to self and instead working for the boss and for your wife and family is cramping your freedom and lifestyle. What is the use of going after hobbies and "self" time if you have no one to share it with in the end? When you give God your time and your hobbies and dreams, God gives it all back and much more. Faith is essential.

A True Gentleman

Yes, you can do this! Serving at work, home, and then serving others—once you have made these choices to please God and put others above yourself, something magical comes along. You transform and you no longer feel like you "deserve," but instead you owe to God and others honorable behavior as you consider others better than yourself.[9] The anger is gone, since anger is selfishness. Without knowing or expecting it, you win the respect of all around you because your choices have led you to a transformed graciousness, and you are esteemed as an educated gentleman, no matter if you had a formal education or not.

---

9   *Do nothing out of selfish ambition or vain conceit, but in humility consider others better than yourselves. Philippians 2:3*

All of this is lining up with the capstone, Jesus Christ.[10] This obstacle course and military-like training has been worth it, for it has value in every walk of life. It is wisdom, and it will walk before you, and the change in you cannot help but be noticed, for you will have peace from within. In its original meaning, the term "gentleman" denoted a man with an income derived from property in England. The word *gentleman* came in common use to signify not a distinction of mere wealth but a distinction of position, education and manners analogous to the Latin *generosus* or *nobilis*... one with virtues. History has rated the French as the most polite men in the world, and though these men were often associated with weakness, it pays to note that they were most often victorious in battle.

HE WHO FINDS GOD WITH HIS IMPECCABLE WISDOM FINDS LIFE.

It is all about how you treat other people that ironically brings honor and respect to you. Since the inception of Remnant Fellowship,

---

10 *Jesus said to them, "Have you never read in the Scriptures: 'The stone the builders rejected has become the capstone; the Lord has done this, and it is marvelous in our eyes'?" Matthew 21:42*

women have commented on how the men here are true gentlemen. In Zion, chivalry is not dead. This royal and noble behavior includes standing when a woman or someone of high honor comes to the table, opening doors, pulling out chairs and showing kindness and respect to everyone, especially the elderly. The etiquette rules of the 1800s that have an ancient moral base are still alive, such as a man may offer his arm but not take the arm of a woman. The husband, as a rule, never leaves his wife alone or unattended at a public function. The etiquette rules of eating and appearance are important because they are universally recognized as politeness and will make a lasting impression. Many manners progressed from those in an earlier century—such as the raising of the hat that evolved from knights raising their helmet visor when they met a friend rather than a foe.[11]

> YOUR INCENTIVE TO GET UP EVERY DAY AND DO RIGHT IS GOD ALONE IN HIS BRILLIANT, BEAUTIFUL, GENIUS GREATNESS—WORDS THAT ARE TOTALLY INADEQUATE TO DESCRIBE A GOD SO FAR SUPERIOR THAN ALL THAT WE CAN SEE OR IMAGINE WITH OUR FINITE MINDS.

Though some of these etiquette rules are outdated, the sincerity of the heart in making introductions is not. In fact, there are few mistakes a gentleman can make if you truthfully consider others better than yourself. You are honored, therefore, to meet or serve another human being who is made in the image of God. Sadly, so much damage is done with the loose tongue, no matter how many

---

11 *For more about manners and etiquette, see* Chapter 11 *on Godly Etiquette and Compassion.*

manners one might have been taught, for out of the abundance of the heart, so the mouth speaks.[12]

With this sound foundation, men from any circumstance could become a Prince or a King. When men fail to get the basics of a relationship with God, they remain insecure, so they will spend most of their day making moves to impress or show off, only to fail miserably. There is so much drama around the insecure, such as getting attention thru over-drinking and fits of rage. Those who are secure in the Lord will not boast, brag, show off, raise their voice or demand attention. People see thru false flattery and half-hearted efforts. It is about accepting who you are and your role as a man under God's Will—then you can forget yourself and focus on the needs of others.

Will there be suffering and opposition? Will you be tested with difficulties? Will the world try to drag you down amongst the common? Yes. However, you can now have empathy toward them for their behaviors were deeply instilled at a young age. *Father, forgive them, they do not know what they are doing. Luke 23:34.* How grand to behold, once again, a Camelot where men are gentlemen and never use disappointment or anger to manipulate or misuse their authority, and they are honored in their gentleness.

Making the Royal Choice

The Royal Remnant Revival is underway. God is reaching out, and His Voice of ancient, perfect, faultless wisdom thru His brilliant Spirit is calling to you. What God is speaking here is Truth, sound instruction, and a map for your day and for your life. But we must stop and listen… *listen*. If you fail to truly hear these words, you will

---

12 *You brood of vipers, how can you who are evil say anything good? For out of the overflow of the heart the mouth speaks. Matthew 12:34*

harm yourself and your family. The Godly man is bowed down; this man is in prayer; this royal man is seeking God in silence.

Listening is a choice. You must deny yourself one thing to get another. You cannot have the world **and** God. Choices…Choose God's approval over money or the praise of man. There is a world of doors out there, and we must teach our children to eliminate the unimportant, narrow the options, eliminate the superfluous, and open the door to God each day—watching for Him, waiting for Him—for this is your very life, and he who finds God with His impeccable wisdom finds life. These words that come from above were here before the Earth was made, when there were no oceans, before the mountains were set in their place. God's words were present before the deep waters were given their boundary and the clouds were spun into space. All of these words are true, just and prudent, and they give wisdom, knowledge, discretion and power. You will know that these are God's ancient and wise words because they protest wickedness, crookedness and perverse speech. Indeed, to fear God means to hate evil, to hate pride and arrogance. We are to see ourselves as apprentices, living by the side of Christ and of God day in and day out. Imagine yourself by God's side every hour of the day—living, learning, loving! Then you will rejoice in His Presence and be filled with delight forever. All effective, successful nobles who rule on Earth have this Truth, and by these words, you too can transform into Kings, Queens, Princes and Princesses.

Are you a part of this Kingly Priesthood movement? Then you will understand the "all" in loving God with **all** your heart, soul and mind.[13] Do you hunger and thirst for righteousness?[14] Do you eat

---

13 *Love the Lord your God with all your heart and with all your soul and with all your mind and with all your strength. Mark 12:30*
14 *Blessed are those who hunger and thirst for righteousness, for they will be filled. Matthew 5:6*

more spiritual food each day so as to fill up with the Spirit of self-control, kindness and gentleness? Do you follow the actions of Jesus Christ with all your passion—worrying less about your reputation than about God's? Do you labor for God's Kingdom, employing all your strength, giving to the needy to ease their burdens so that you can bring them to the love of Christ? Do you use every spiritual gift that God has lent to you for a time to its full extent for the assemblies of God?

Do you slow down to consider others better than yourself, seeking self-denial and humility? Do people see your seriousness and composure of spirit, patience, meekness, sobriety and temperance? For it is those who house the personality of God who are connected to God, and therefore who save themselves and others. Do you lay your life down for your wife and offspring with daily prayer and gentle instruction, pointing out answered prayers and a relationship with God? Do all those around you know that your one goal in life is to know, love and serve The One True God?

God's Holy Priesthood—His Royal Subjects—speak with authority because they are genuine, and they know how to lovingly lead their family with actions more than words. In the Kingdom of God, each family is strong, binding together to help each other so that the Church is powerful. Because their families are now strong and not needy, together they lead the way in this world into relieving the poor, helping the needy, subduing violence, deterring hatred, helping the prisoners, eradicating debt and advancing their employers. These are leaders with an answer to the global recessions, enormous debt, and the lack of jobs—answers that lead to a Holy City that thrives with protection and stability under any circumstance!

It is our life's journey to learn to love, serve, uphold and cherish those whom we have been given to love and honor—not to focus on others, but only focus on God—and then please your authority as unto God. Page 83.

Chapter 6

Wives, submit to your husbands as to the Lord. For the husband is the head of the wife as Christ is the head of the church, his body, of which he is the Savior. Now as the church submits to Christ, so also wives should submit to their husbands in everything. Ephesians 5:22-24

Chapters 4 and 5 addressed the role of Godly men in this transformation of the family and God's beautiful Royal Revival. All of the roles that God ordained bring peace to the home and our lives. It starts with an understanding of the essential line of authority; however, today there is a widespread resistance to this concept of "authority," a concept that is foundational for the existence of the Church, the family and eternal life. Indeed, I know of no other means to true freedom and the deliverance of being saved in this earthly life and in the life to come. Knowing and accepting God's authority line is essential in order to achieve the saving approval from the Heavens needed for eternity.

At a time when the world was experimenting with anti-authority and women's liberation, I experimented with getting under authority, and it became for me a miraculous salvation in every area of my life. God's beautiful, ingenious authority brought with it better relationships in all areas, as well as an increasing loyalty and love toward all authorities in my life. I have been uncovering and sharing this discovery for more than 30 years with astounding results for many…but unfortunately for most, this message seems to have fallen upon deaf ears.

This attitude of equality or even brazen superiority over our authorities is found even in the new Christian culture due to decades of false teachers who adopted this rebellion and have blurred the distinction between right and wrong. Religious studies departments in American universities have openly rejected the Apostle Paul's writings about women being submissive, and they have labeled him as a chauvinist, stating that he was prejudiced against women. But God's request of women

GOD IS NOT A RESPECTER OF PERSONS OR GENDER; HE LOOKS AT THE *HEART*.

to live in submission was made in Genesis after the temptation and the fall in the Garden.[1] It was a sacred, ordained precept that had nothing to do with the culture in Rome at the time of Paul. To bring back God's authority is a sleepy, resistant revival, waiting to be awakened. When it is awakened, it will conjure up the gates of Hades, inciting fear in some women who believe that this teaching of submission would take the women's liberation movement back 50 years.

---

1   *Genesis 3*

The "Liberated" Wife

How did this society go from a wife being under her Godly husband's authority to where we are today? In this generation, women shamelessly, openly, and publicly correct and rule over their husbands. Anti-authority is the signature of the "liberated" wife—she is a self-confident, independent individual, and this prideful anti-authority is actually supported and celebrated. It is applauded as freedom and advancement in civilization, but this blur of right from wrong has not made women happier.

According to a national survey by the Centers for Disease Control and Prevention and the Department of Justice, in 2010, more men than women were victims of physical violence, and more than 40 percent of severe physical violence was directed at men.[2] Men were also more often the victim of psychological aggression and control. Despite this, few services are available to male victims of partner violence. Recently, a YouTube video went viral of a woman attacking and cutting up a man while bystanders stood and watched. It was frightening and sickening. Who would have thought we would live to see such violence?

This is not just going on in the United States. Domestic violence against men is also rising in other parts of the world. A recent study in the United Kingdom found that more than 40 percent of victims of domestic violence are men, and the actual figures may be much higher since men were less likely to report the crime. Even with the lower reporting rate, the number of women who have been prosecuted for domestic violence almost tripled from 2004 to 2008.[3] What is going on? Why is this accelerating?

---

2   CDC, "National Intimate Partner and Sexual Violence Survey—2010 Summary Report," 2011
3   The Guardian, "More than 40% of domestic violence victims are male, report reveals," 2010

This exit from honor and respect toward the husband to an attitude of anti-authority has happened rapidly in my lifetime. It is not a new concept, however, as we see in the book of Esther. In Queen Vashti's day, under King Xerxes, there was a very real worry that if the King did not correct Vashti's anti-authority, it would cause a rapid and widespread discord in the kingdom. The exact words were, *"There will be no end of disrespect and discord."*[4] So the king acted quickly in punishing her disrespect by not allowing Queen Vashti to ever enter his presence again. This vice of anti-authority obviously spreads quickly.

Respect toward husbands was still strong in the first few decades of the twentieth century in America. Even in the 1950s, popular TV shows reflected strong family values. Husbands were greeted warmly at the door when they got home. The husband was the head of the household, and he was respected as he came in from a hard day's work. The wife sweetly served her husband and family at the dinner table. In Genesis, it says:

But for Adam no suitable helper was found. So the Lord God caused the man to fall into a deep sleep; and while he was sleeping, he took one of the man's ribs and closed up the place with flesh. Then the Lord God made a woman from the rib he had taken out of the man, and he brought her to the man. The man said "This is now bone of my bones and flesh of my flesh; she shall be called 'woman,' for she was taken out of man." For this reason a man will leave his father and mother and be united to his wife, and they will become one flesh. Genesis 2:20b-24

You see, the wife was a "helpmeet," a "suitable helper," in this Scripture, to support her husband as he laid down his life both day

---

4   Esther 1:15-20

and night for his wife and children. The parents were there to meet the needs of the children, and the children gave back much love and respect and pleasure. How beautiful was this original plan!

In the early days of America, women did not vote simply because it would be a waste to count it, for the husband and wife were in agreement—supportive and united. One man represented two people, like a delegate in Washington, D.C. By 1967, it was still shocking for most husbands and wives to see the women's liberation movement, and only a few women contributed to this group of aggressive women that was growing in anger with displays of overt noncompliance and public rage. The women's liberation movement has continued to grow since then and has all-time high support today. Surveys suggest that 82 percent of Americans believe that men and women should be equal socially, politically and economically. However, only 23 percent of women actually identify with the term "feminist."[5]

> TO ACTUALLY TAKE TIME TO CONSIDER OTHERS BETTER THAN YOURSELF AND PUT THEM ABOVE YOU BRINGS A MYSTERIOUS, MIRACULOUS HAPPINESS AND HOPE-FILLED JOY.

The anti-authority concept was a grassroots movement, and it did not just include women toward husbands, but employees with their bosses, students with teachers, unions with large corporations and citizens with government. All segments of the population together launched the anti-establishmentarianism movement. The idea began in a small way in the early 1900s, and its adherents were

---

5   Huffington Post, "Poll: Few Identify As Feminists, But Most Believe In Equality Of Sexes," 2013

very vocal by the 1960s. No doubt, with false grace comes sin, and with sin comes pain and hurt feelings as one moves further away from the fruits of the Spirit. More pain mixed with the lack of a relationship with the God of all comfort brings with it more self-protection, so that instead of the family units being strong, women started forming groups to fight for their rights as they unfortunately misdiagnosed the husbands and the men as the "enemy." Many men began opting for a single, unmarried life. There were more divorces, and some men even sought out the companionship of other men since they felt there would be less hassle. In fact, there are people

HEAVENLY AUTHORITY IS THE MOST BEAUTIFUL, LOVE-FILLED, PROTECTIVE ENVIRONMENT OF THE UNIVERSE.

now who would rather be with their pets than a spouse and who treat their animals nicer and as more of a companion than they do mankind.

People have increasingly become attached to pets over others because pets give you more attention. If you have been using attention here on Earth as a source of approval and comfort instead of God, then when the pet dies, you will tend to be unusually empty for an ungodly amount of time. Pets cannot replace God or His comfort, attention and love.

AN AGE-OLD ATTACK ON CHRISTIANITY

Those in subordinate roles felt a need to organize and fight for their rights since they did not know the righteousness that leads to answered prayers, and they did not have a relationship with God with all of His protection and salvation.[6] The nonconformist revolution became politically correct in the late 1960s and 1970s. It was given more justification as time went by, with exposed institutional and corporate scandals, such as Watergate and Enron. There was growing immorality in government, religious scandals and scurrilous law enforcement cover-ups; all of this left the undiscerning population in shock, while skeptics of any authority in any institution—even the home—felt justified. The anti-authority stance was satan's most prized attack on Christianity.

This concept has affected everything. So many women or wives seem to be frequently angry, and they are offended by anything and everything. A social psychologist was quoted as saying, "Women feel aggression is a form of empowerment. It has become so commonplace that it's not even shameful."[7] Women's crime rates are also increasing overall. According to the Bureau of Justice Statistics, the female local jail population increased 48 percent between 1999 and 2013.[8] But the sway of the public leans toward favoring the women—who would have thought that in our lifetime we would see a wife shoot her husband for calling her overweight and then get set free by an empathetic jury?

---

6   *The Lord is far from the wicked but he hears the prayer of the righteous. Proverbs 15:29*
7   The Daily Mail, "Why ARE modern women so aggressive?" 2016
8   Bureau of Justice Statistics, "Census of Jails: Population Changes, 1999-2013," 2015

This movement, however, did not start in the nineteenth and twentieth centuries, nor was it confined to western civilization. It did not just erupt with the Roman Empire, nor did Queen Vashti start it during the diaspora of the exiled Jews. It did not start in the wild days of Noah when God brought a flood to end the rebellion. It actually started as early as when lucifer was hurled to the Earth, and it was seen in mankind as early as the Garden of Eden.[9] Likewise, oppression and evil authorities did not start with the twentieth and twenty-first centuries—repressive subjugation has been here from the beginning of time. Lucifer himself actually started the first insurrection. Anti-authority is the ingredient of Hades and the opposite of Heaven. This anti-authority is a main warfare device of satan. The curse of the Garden was to help women get under authority—not to harm the female population whom God adores. Likewise, God-fearing authority is the basis of the Kingdom of God.

Heavenly authority is the most beautiful, love-filled, protective environment of the Universe. Without it, you cannot live. Without it, I would not *want* to live! Satan has tried to distort this saving authority from the beginning, and no doubt, we are witnessing a godless society and a "connectionless society."[10] However, here at the Remnant, we have witnessed that when men and women connect to God, the women become more submissive, the men regain their position as head of the household, and therefore the marriages come back together. We have seen it over and over with countless testimonies.

Being under authority, totally under authority, is elusive. Many assume that they are under authority automatically by designation;

---

9   *To read more about the Garden of Eden and the first attack on man, see History of the One True God, Volume I. Find out how to get your copy in the Appendix.*
10   II Timothy 3:1-5

you are an "employee," you are a "wife," a "child," "student," "military officer," "church member." However, merely having the designation and actually being respectfully under authority are two different things. It must be as unto Christ. We do not want to find out too late that we were really under the wrong authority or under our own authority.

Those who submit to their authorities and serve as unto Christ are known by Christ. Those who serve their masters as unto Christ will be known by their master, as Paul says in Ephesians 6:

Slaves, obey your earthly masters with respect and fear, and with sincerity of heart, just as you would obey Christ. Obey them not only to win their favor when their eye is on you, but like slaves of Christ, doing the will of God from your heart. Serve wholeheartedly, as if you were serving the Lord, not men, because you know that the Lord will reward everyone for whatever good he does, whether he is slave or free. Ephesians 6:5-8

Those who serve their authority as unto the Lord will know the Lord. It is ordained by God.

Embracing Your God-Given Role

The soul of a woman is equal spiritually to that of a man in the eyes of God. There is no male or female.[11] But their *roles* on Earth are different—it is a question of who is the authority to each. To the child, the authority is the parents, and they cannot pick and choose whether or not to obey their parents. To the wife, it is the husband; to the husband, it is the boss and the Church leaders…but the husband still has the responsibility to lay his life down for his wife.

---

11 *There is neither Jew nor Greek, slave nor free, male nor female, for you are all one in Christ Jesus. Galatians 3:28*

Just because there are evil authorities in this world, that has not changed God's mind and led Him to eradicate all authorities so that you can be your own boss. Though many wives, employees, or children could have a naturally higher IQ than their superior, this is not a sign that God is giving over the authority role to the subordinate. Just because your authority allows you to reason with him as God did with Abraham (where God agreed to let Abraham influence His actions), it did not make Abraham the god...with God becoming the subordinate![12] The Truth is that a good leader will always get the advice of many; Truth could even come thru the children—but just because the wife has a superior idea from God, this does not automatically promote the wife to the position of the head of the household. If the husband is forgetful or slower to make a decision, God still anoints His chosen, appointed authority over talent. The wife must accept her God-given role and God-given authority, because it has been hand-selected just for her. The man should accept his God-given role and his God-given boss or authority and show reverent respect as unto Christ with words and actions.

It is difficult to lead and to be the authority, so it is shameful and undermining for a wife to compete with her husband, even in trying to be taller or stronger. Even children by nature do not like this and from the earliest ages will say, "That does not look right." This is an innate law of God. The Godly wife does not compete with her husband. Children can sense this competition also, and they know right from wrong.

Again, it is so hard to lead that God gives empathy toward the leader. Either disrespect or heartfelt respect can be *felt*—you can feel it inside of you. Those who get out from underneath authority

---

12 Genesis 18

The Good Old Days

for selfish reasons, those who rebel, will sense God's disapproval and feel the Holy Spirit prompting them to radically change.

Now, there is always a case for standing up for the weak and for justifiable issues as with domestic violence, harassment, women with no property rights, equality in pay where it is deserved, and women's suffrage or the right to vote if it is needed. However, the anti-authority movement has moved far beyond just seeking justice for the oppressed, which is a Biblical thing to do. This concept has now permeated our culture so much that the youth believe that females do not need men, and likewise, men have lost sight that they need women. Why do men not want their role and women not want their role? It is because their world does not center around the Will of The Creator, and so it is impossible, because you cannot *make* a subordinate submit. It is our life's journey to learn to love, serve, uphold and cherish those whom *we* have been given to love and honor—not to focus on others, but only focus on God—and then please your authority as unto God.

Anti-authority is so accepted today that it is hard to detect. It is not always the blatant or "in your face" anti-authority—it is the mindless, habitual talking back, which tells its superior what it is going to do rather than asking for permission. It is the deceptive act of asking about some things and purposely not asking for permission about others because you are afraid that you are going to hear a "no"… sneaky anti-authority. It is the subtle, moody control—where you obey when you want to, and you disobey when you want to. The world will tell women to put their careers first, take care of themselves first. The husband has been trained not to upset or disappoint sensitive wives or children; the power is upside down, resulting in anger that is cruel and controlling. These spirits project; they cast blame. People are using anger more and more in this country to control others. Angry people are everywhere, people ready to pounce or project at a moment's notice. It is the pouting wife who controls the family.

This is hard to detect in yourself, for people think that they *are* under authority. They think they are under the calling of the Holy Spirit; however, they do not understand why they are not losing their weight or why they are on a roller coaster of going up and down on the scales or with other temptations. They do not understand why their husbands do not quite approve of them in public, and they do not understand why there is frustration from their spouse at home. Yet, Jesus did not consider equality with authority something to be grasped.[13] There was a big gap. Have you gone there? Do you consider yourself having equality with your authority?

It is no surprise that husbands are not confronting their wives and are slow to tell the Truth, scared to say anything to the children. No wonder the anti-authority wife feels lonely and in pain—it is impossible to have a relationship when you are trying to rule over the spouse who should be in authority. Respecting authority is the entire basis of a relationship. It is what is required for you to have a relationship. It must be practiced by the children at an early age so they can experience the blessings and peace that result from obeying authority.

The moral decline and the fractures in the stability of the family over the decades have resulted from the relaxing of the Laws of God in mainstream churches and that of submission to authority. In a country founded on "equality for all," those who have not accepted God's decision of inequality will continue to be unhappy as they

---

13 *Who, being in very nature God, did not consider equality with God something to be grasped.* Philippians 2:6

The Good Old Days

strive for and worry about how to be equal to or even superior to others. In addition, those who have not accepted their beloved, beautiful, God-given roles waste much valuable time boiling inside, thinking that life is unfair. This idea automatically leads to believing God is unfair.

God is not a respecter of persons or gender; He looks at the *heart*. There is equal footing when it comes to the souls of men and women. However, authority necessitates inequality in roles even in Heaven, so our role on Earth is our testing in preparation for salvation. If you cannot accept the idea of authority on Earth, you will, like lucifer, not accept this in Heaven. On the other hand, notice when you accept your role, and even *embrace* your role—being proud of the role that has been decided upon and designated by God—you become *thankful* for your role. You will feel peaceful, happier and more hopeful inside. Let these feelings guide you to Truth.

Note how merciful God has been to you! When you really evaluate the wrong choices you have made and the trouble you have caused God and others and you consider how little good you have done on Earth so far—you realize God is not only fair, He is *incredibly merciful* that you have been forgiven much…and those who have been forgiven much, love much.[14] God has given you more than you deserve. This is the breakthrough—God blesses those who adore Him and His beautiful and perfect Will, knowing His inequity is fair and beautiful because He will give more grace to the humble. To strive to be the most humble in your role, to actually take time to consider others better than yourself and put them above you brings a mysterious, miraculous happiness and hope-filled joy. Why? How

---

14 *Therefore, I tell you, her many sins have been forgiven—for she loved much. But he who has been forgiven little loves little. Luke 7:47*

does it work? It is because this is God's Will; it is achievable and will be immediately blessed and reinforced by God.

Ultimately, the choice to be under authority belongs to the subordinate, the one who must submit. I can testify that those who accept their roles are esteemed and respected. All roles are legitimate in God's eyes and in the world's eyes—for God is the one who brings honor to the humble, and He brings trouble and disgrace to the prideful.[15]

A God-Fearing, Beautiful Woman

In the beginning, no suitable helper for Adam was found. So the Lord God caused the man to fall into a deep sleep and He brought the woman out to the man.[16] Adam was pleased because he saw that this was finally someone like him—bone of his bones and flesh of his flesh. Husbands and wives are meant to be best friends and buddies and helpers, meant to have fun and not conflict. But it cannot be done when there are two heads, two authorities—it is impossible. There will be no peace in the woman ruling over the man, the employee ruling over the boss, the children ruling over the parents. For a woman to accept the beautiful, lovely, honorable feminine position is marvelous. This Genesis, beautiful woman has almost been lost in this society—may we all come out of this deep sleep and wake up to find the lovely, God-fearing, beautiful woman again. It is time to start over for the sake of the Kingdom of God. The next chapter has more...

---

15 *When pride comes, then comes disgrace, but with humility comes wisdom. Proverbs 11:2*
16 *Genesis 1:20b-24*

The Good Old Days

What is a Queen's duty? It is her subordination of self to the office, by her sheer will and love for God and for His Son, Jesus Christ. In the end, this amazing woman is strong and never idle, but take note: the quiet turns out to be the powerful because God works in and thru the submissive and humble. Page 104.

Chapter 7

A wife of noble character who can find? She is worth far more than rubies. Her husband has full confidence in her and lacks nothing of value. She brings him good, not harm, all the days of her life. She selects wool and flax and works with eager hands. She is like the merchant ships, bringing her food from afar. She gets up while it is still dark; she provides food for her family and portions for her servant girls. She considers a field and buys it; out of her earnings she plants a vineyard. She sets about her work vigorously; her arms are strong for her tasks. She sees that her trading is profitable, and her lamp does not go out at night. In her hand she holds the distaff and grasps the spindle with her fingers. She opens her arms to the poor and extends her hands to the needy. When it snows, she has no fear for her household; for all of them are clothed in scarlet. She makes coverings for her bed; she is clothed in fine linen and purple. Her husband is respected at the city gate, where he takes his seat among the elders of the land. She makes linen garments and sells them, and supplies the merchants with sashes. She is clothed with strength and dignity; she can laugh at the days to come. She speaks with wisdom, and faithful instruction is on her tongue. She watches over the affairs of her household and does not eat the bread of idleness. Her children arise and call her blessed; her husband also, and he praises her: "Many women do noble things, but you surpass them all." Charm is deceptive, and beauty is fleeting; but a woman who fears the Lord is to be praised. Give her the reward she has earned, and let her works bring her praise at the city gate. Proverbs 31:10-31

This passage paints the picture of a noble woman, with words describing subjects dressed in purple and scarlet—a queen of dignity worthy of a crown in this Royal Priesthood that God is calling. This passage is foundational for married and unmarried women alike. Think of the most celebrated queens and princesses on Earth. If any woman aspires to such a position—whether it is the empress of the household or if she is given the title of monarch by God as the highest position in the land—this breakdown of deeds and

EACH HOUSEHOLD IS A MICROCOSM OF GOD'S ROYAL KINGDOM.

characteristics found in Proverbs 31 is the place to go for all inspiration. The problem is that the world has forgotten the fact that each household is a microcosm of God's Royal Kingdom. God gathers these subgroups to make a Church, starting with the home and the husband as the King, the wife as the Queen, and the children as the Princes and Princesses. A true Christian household is connected to The Kingdom Of God. It is the ultimate Aristocracy with the most gracious of atmospheres as to reflect the Heavens and the glory of the King of Kings, the Lord of Lords. How quickly we forget, we are elected to be His Imperial Priesthood.

If you have a less than ideal marriage or a less than ideal household, you can, as the wife, begin to turn it around by taking the words of Proverbs 31 and following the example of a Godly, respectful woman. God distributes influence, and He has given great power to the wife. *The wise woman builds her house, but with her own hands the foolish one tears hers down. Proverbs 14:1* The wife has that sway—she can choose to build or tear apart. It is the power that God has given to the subjects under authority.[1]

Full Confidence

Note that the writer starts out with: *Her husband has full confidence in her... Proverbs 31:11a* Consider, her husband trusts her so much that he has **full confidence** in everything she decides to do. Just as men should ask themselves if they have their boss' full confidence, wives should ask themselves, do you have your husband's *full* confidence; and if not, how do you obtain such a trust in everything you put your hands to do?

First and foremost and without a doubt, the woman of noble character is dedicated to the Most High God and dwells in His Spirit. Without this, there is nothing successful, much less a successful marriage as described here, nor any relationship on Earth. True Nobility will depend on and pray to God constantly. Next, after committing to God, she is committed to her spouse as unto Christ. This is a commitment to building a Godly marriage relationship with no secret dream of another man, of unfaithfulness, or of another life. There is a knowledge that this is the husband (with the attached

---

1 For more about marriage and divorce, please see Chapters 21 thru 24.

circumstances that come with your spouse) given by God. Therefore, she is unswervingly dedicated to do all she can to help this one man and this one home.

When people think they can easily get another spouse, they are far too casual with this gift, and they are far too lax about building and protecting their relationships. They do not put their *all* into that one marriage. They do not throw everything into that investment because they always have another opportunity around the corner…or so they think. Over the years, I have seen people leave their spouse for selfish reasons, but they only find themselves in another difficult marriage later. God is setting up this test all over again for them to learn what is in Proverbs 31, but the number one lesson is to commit before it is too late.

> IF YOU SEE THIS LIFE AS GOD INTENDS IT—ONE SHORT OPPORTUNITY TO GUARD YOURSELF, TO PROVE YOUR LOYALTY—YOU WILL BE INSPIRED TO MAKE YOUR MARRIAGE AND YOUR HOME THE BEST POSSIBLE ON THIS EARTH.

If you see this life as God intends it—one short opportunity to guard yourself, to prove your loyalty—you will be inspired to make your marriage and your home the best possible on this Earth. You will have gratefulness and loyalty for the one and only life you have been given to live out. Commitment is another word for selflessness. Foolish people live frivolously with relationships and money and time, and then time runs out.

RESPECT YOUR HUSBAND

Once this foundation is in place, there are other essential characteristics to acquire in order to become this Noble Woman. Even after one chooses to commit, God allows couples to go thru many more trials, and unfortunately, the church has not stood her ground on the foundation of this important next element: respect. This is the sole request of Paul for wives: respect your husband.[2] A man can detect a lack of respect, and he can detect insincere devotion. Giving respect is a choice. You can change the world around you by choosing to give reverent respect.

Couples should hold a united front at all times, but especially during the hard times. Each young Christian man or woman should be brought up to expect the storms of life. Every one of our children should be taught, "Your time is coming. You are going to be tested. There is going to be a big storm that comes. It is going to shake and it is going to rattle your house. You have to get your spiritual house ready for a big storm because everyone will have one." If children are brought up that way, then they will not be so caught off guard when the testing comes. They will know to expect the storms, and they will be ready.

In both good and bad times, determine to build up your spouse. When the husband is down, how easy is it to add insult to injury—a sure sign of selfishness. When the husband goes thru testing, it is the wife's opportunity to encourage full acceptance of the Will of God, and the couple will grow closer as they are both on their knees crying out to God for salvation from financial, health or relational difficulties.

Why do people lose the spark in marriage? It is because instead of working for a common cause, they work against each other because of separate personal, selfish ambitions. Competition does not build; it tears down. The goal should not be divided, but there should be one leader in each home—the husband. The wife is never

---

2   *Wives, in the same way be submissive to your husbands so that, if any of them do not believe the word, they may be won over without words by the behavior of their wives… I Peter 3:1*

to compete, for there is no need. Have no fear, God gives the wife beauty and automatic favor, especially from the family members. From the smallest of the babies to the oldest, she is usually the most popular—notice how everyone wants her company at all events and to share with her all good things. Children cannot wait to show things to the mother. The foolish woman, however, will compete with her husband, and at that point, the hard times are seen as encroaching upon her own personal goals. I see women control with anger and disappointment, pouting, slamming doors and driving off. The greedy wife will focus on the husband's shortcomings. This is the faithless sin that believes that God is not intervening, failing to understand that God has set up this storm and that this testing, this circumstance, has been purposed since the beginning of time.

Criticism of others comes from having no belief in a God that transforms His subjects thru testing. In this scenario, the wife has to nag and coerce her husband to perform better financially, as if a human can make the testing of God disappear with money. This wife has godless, selfish ambition. How many households have been destroyed by wives who were controlling and correcting the husband for their own goals, wanting the husband to earn more money to secure their own personal life of indulging themselves?

Lay Down Your Selfish Ambition

Marriage means that you lay down your selfish ambition and uphold this newly combined union, seeking what is best for the whole. In Proverbs 31, the man worked at the city gate, which would be an official city or Church-paid position, and his wife worked as a retailer or wholesaler. She then bought land and set up a vineyard, which would also be for the market. She was very much a businessperson and manager of her own estate. Her husband had his work at the gates of the city, so she managed the home on her own, as well as being a businesswoman who was considering land and purchasing good property, selling her sewing, and of course, taking care of the children and providing clothes so that she and the children were dressed like royalty.

Too many women work at the home and then expect the husband to drop everything to support their endeavors—thinking that he is supposed to be centered on her, rather than the other way

YOU CAN CHANGE THE WORLD AROUND YOU BY CHOOSING TO GIVE REVERENT RESPECT.

around. Now, there are times that the husband calls the wife to be the breadwinner; but he has made that decision, and therefore, she is still in under his authority. Too many women are not helpmeets with finances and actually are just the spenders—creating constant conflict. Determine to make money and contribute to the bank account—not empty it.

Turn your selfish ambition into admiration. When facing financial trials or job changes, with wise contemplation, a wife should think of all the incredible qualities of her husband as unto Christ, knowing that this trial is only going to make him more Christlike. Help him, and thank God for how far he has come to be like Christ. Praise God for each of his righteous characteristics. Does your spouse get out of bed every day to work and provide money? Do you not understand that there are men who *never* work or bring in money? You should be grateful for the characteristics of Christ that

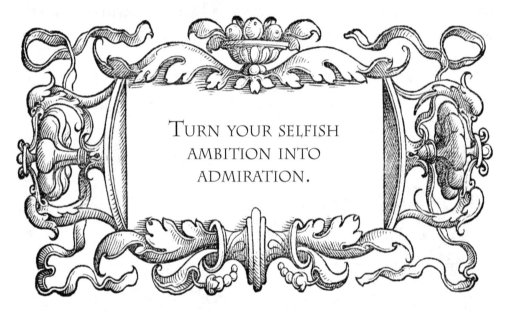

Turn your selfish ambition into admiration.

your husband has. There are a few men that God gifts with wealth as a steward for the Kingdom of God and not for selfish gain, but most of the world lives modestly. The husband who does not pursue or lust after wealth for selfish gain and who is not overspending to compete with his neighbor out of vanity is the man to be honored. This Christlike man has won already—he is far ahead in righteousness and peace, for he is one who acts correctly, pays back what he owes, pays his taxes and has good credit.

The love of money is the root of many evils.[3] Comparison with what other people or other households have brings on envy that leads to nagging your husband. Can you ever look at and notice other families and other homes? Yes, you can be happy for others because of what God has done for them, but you cannot be envious. "Thou shalt not covet" is one of the top Ten Commands of God; in other words, it is essential that we not covet.[4] There are times when it is good to observe other families in order to learn—taking note of the most efficient ways to clean house, raise children, please your husband, or make additional money for the household. God gives us good shepherding families to imitate for His Kingdom.[5]

The Good Wife is a helpmeet for life to build this Royal Home—to bring good into that house—and therefore this implies that there can be no moodiness. Self-focus and depression are prohibited. How is this done? Change your goals—your goal is not to please yourself but to please God and your spouse. That goal is time consuming, so there will be no time for depression. Think about the house and family you have been given. Make it the best and make the best of it—it is about this glorious Kingdom Home that is a subunit of the Church. Do not think of a church *building* as the Church, and then go home and think that your home is not the Church. Your home is a subunit of God's Church…a home to worship in and a home to live in so that it is glorifying God. Above all, in this home, give pleasure—be the

---

3   *For the love of money is a root of all kinds of evil. Some people, eager for money, have wandered from the faith and pierced themselves with many griefs. I Timothy 6:10*

4   *You shall not covet your neighbor's house. You shall not covet your neighbor's wife, or his manservant or maidservant, his ox or donkey, or anything that belongs to your neighbor. Exodus 20:17*

5   *For more about Shepherding Families, see http://www.remnantfellowship.org/Our-Leaders*

salt.[6] Salt makes everything better. Bring food to your spouse, give foot rubs or back rubs, bring laughter, bring good news, bring light. Bring Christ and God to each and every soul in your home and each and every room of your house, each and every hour. The wife is there for the good of the spouse, for the good of the children, for the good of the unit. She who helps the husband helps herself.

Work on Yourself First

We have discussed being committed to the husband, showing respect, and having *unified* ambition instead of selfish ambition, but now for something the woman has to know, or none of this will happen. The wife is not The Holy Spirit of the Alpha and the Omega, The Lord God Almighty, nor is she the conscience to correct a husband unless he asks for advice (and even then, he is usually not asking for advice but a sounding board). Be most slow to speak.[7] Many women have made it their career to find faults in the husband and nag until death does part the couple, but this is the opposite of dignity, the opposite of a Godly woman, the opposite of a Christ-fearing woman—and it is simply destructive. How many households have been destroyed because of the wife controlling and correcting the husband to get him to do more to secure their life of indulging themselves?

If you choose God's ways, then the wife of nobility will make sure that she works on *herself* and does not make the husband her project. Whereas before, you might have spent hours worried about and trying to fix your spouse, but now you are free! This focus on changing

---

6   *Salt is good, but if it loses its saltiness, how can you make it salty again? Have salt in yourselves, and be at peace with each other. Mark 9:50*
7   *My dear brothers, take note of this: Everyone should be quick to listen, slow to speak and slow to become angry... James 1:19*

yourself and not your spouse is mysteriously powerful because it gives the wife a whole new life. She has a completely new job description, and she no longer has "improving" her husband as a project on her checklist that day. A Godly helpmeet assists her husband but changes *herself*. She has all these hours now to check her heart, to get her extra weight off if needed, to get her life cleaned up, to get herself dressed and dignified and the children dignified and the household in order.[8]

THE GOOD WIFE IS A HELPMEET FOR LIFE TO BUILD THIS ROYAL HOME—TO BRING GOOD TO THAT HOUSE.

Appropriate Attire

This Royal Revival is made up of women who make their hearts beautiful and care about their appearance being glorifying to God; they do not sit around in a bathrobe all day. They get dressed and ready for the day. Wives and mothers taking care of themselves is a light to the world, and is not something that is frequently seen in modern society. Instead of dressing for others, most people are dressing for

---

8   For help on how to lose excess weight permanently or lay down other strongholds, see www.WeighDown.com

their own comfort…it is not uncommon to see people going thru the carpool line or out at the store looking like they just rolled out of bed.

There is also a modesty in dress—both a modesty in not looking like all you do is sit around and dote on yourself.[9] Neither are you to cut off all your hair so that you never have to take any time on yourself. Women are to look feminine, and we are to take care of ourselves and our appearance. This does not take much time or money; God can bless you with the best wardrobe from the local thrift store. I pray each morning for what God wants me to wear, and I pray when I get ready for the day, so that I can look the best for Him. Then I can forget myself and move on with the day, focused on Him!

We all come from different cultures and different parts of the world, but down deep inside of us, modesty is clear. There is a plumbline inside…we know when we are too exposed and when we are making others uncomfortable. Even pets know when they are too exposed—when you shave the cat or the dog, they will hide. It is wrong to dress in things that are too thin or too tight. The irony about immodest dressing is that it does not do what you hope it is doing…it is not flattering. There is something about a covering, and it is a beautiful thing. It is so honoring to your husband and pleasing to your family for the mother to take care of her appearance and make a good impression on others.

> IF YOU CHOOSE GOD'S WAYS, THEN THE WIFE OF NOBILITY WILL MAKE SURE THAT SHE WORKS ON HERSELF AND DOES NOT MAKE THE HUSBAND HER PROJECT.

---

9   *I also want women to dress modestly, with decency and propriety, not with braided hair or gold or pearls or expensive clothes, but with good deeds, appropriate for women who profess to worship God. I Timothy 2:9-10*

Turning the Other Cheek

A Queen of Nobility never takes things personally. It is wrong for a husband who has had a hard day at work to come home and take it out on the wife. But if there is a lack of peace in either spouse, look inward for just one more, better way to say something so that you are never sneaking in a correction, or you are never patronizing or defensive. Moodiness from either spouse will not be Heaven-bound. God is not temperamental. Christ is not sulky. Angels and Saints are not irritable, short-tempered, unstable or threatening. You should feel peace around God and around Christ. It is a sin of projection to blame the spouse for your pain and to be the eternal judge and jury of your spouse. The upright spouse has a calling; it is the higher law for the husband or wife to turn the other cheek and have compassion for the pain that is causing the eruption in the household…compassion for the hurting.[10] Your job is to turn the other cheek, be full of compassion and pray. For wives, trust God to correct the authority. The wife must remain the constant while reading the spouse's moods and being careful to honor this.

Be a quiet sounding board. As you are quiet, you will hear more words from your spouse; they will open up. They need the opportunity to think out loud without judgment. When he hears himself speaking, then the incredible Holy Spirit of God can come in and convict him without your help. You are not there to inflict even more pain. This is true also for husbands who do not know Christ.

Take all that energy you used to put into correcting and controlling and use it to make critical essential changes in yourself with no fear of when and how God will change what needs to be changed in your

---

10   But I tell you, do not resist an evil person. If someone strikes you on the right cheek, turn to him the other also. Matthew 5:39

spouse. Many times God will not allow the change in your spouse until you have fully changed into a wife who only focuses on her own faults and transformation first. Forgive your husband and hold no resentments, harbor no grudges. Rather, you become independently, fearlessly upright…how intriguing, how exhilarating! Change yourself again and again, then pray for your spouse, and watch God change and guide your husband when he needs guidance. How freeing! They will follow your changes. People look for the upright. They study it

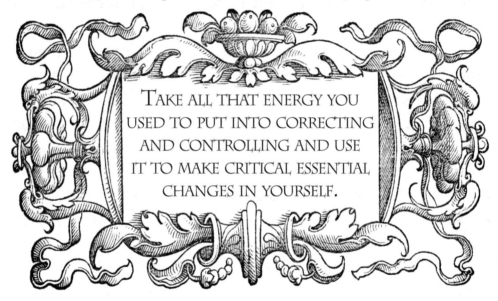

Take all that energy you used to put into correcting and controlling and use it to make critical, essential changes in yourself.

and want to be like you when you are upright, and then they are going to want your religion. How hopeful is that! The old saying is true—behind every great man *is* a great woman.

Building Up Your Husband

Do you want a great home and a great life? Slow down and rarely speak unless it is noble. So much is solved if we are quick to listen and slow to speak—if we are gentle and quiet, using the tongue only to encourage. Listening to your husband and teaching the children to honor and pay attention to what he says are ways to show honor to your husband. Offer a word of encouragement—never negative and patronizing—but rather uplifting. This takes faith and security in the Lord to point out something good in your husband every day. Look for it and then say something positive no matter what has been said to you. No matter what your day has been like, say something positive every day. In short, correct yourself—and build up your husband.

Using positive words requires thinking about the good. Some women have put others down so much that they have no idea that they are constantly judging, condemning and disapproving with their body language, all while defending themselves. If your conversations are always centered on what is broken around the house, what needs to be done or the family financial problems, you will be sure to have an unpleasant life. Learn to approach needed topics with prayer, like Queen Esther, without any patronization or reproach, being careful that this does not become simply your back-door approach for disapproval of something that he has done or one of his life choices.[11] It will be much better to focus on neutral topics until you can listen and not give opinions until asked.

Your husband is your lifelong companion. Appreciation for what the husband is and has done is the foundation of being as trusted as the Proverbs 31 woman. Show appreciation, which is respect—respond immediately when he calls, get the children to surround the father when he arrives home, point out the good of the day, point out

> NO MATTER WHAT YOUR DAY HAS BEEN LIKE, SAY SOMETHING POSITIVE EVERY DAY. IN SHORT, CORRECT YOURSELF—AND BUILD UP YOUR HUSBAND.

---

11 Esther 4

your husband's great traits, try to always make the atmosphere positive and fun, reassuring your husband of the commitment that nothing but God holds a higher place in your heart. You did not marry to use another for your own indulgence, you married to *build*. You are an architect…building, correcting and changing yourself and your actions, becoming the example as you build a mighty fortress of a home that all want to return to—not run away from.

> THE QUIET TURNS OUT TO BE THE POWERFUL BECAUSE IT PROVES YOU ARE FULLY DEPENDENT ON A LIVING GOD WHO IS WORTHY OF WORSHIP.

These are the things that build full confidence that you are neither jealous nor using your husband for your own selfishness. In the Book of Job, Job's wife was so upset about how his plight affected her when Job was tested that she only inflicted more pain, telling him to "curse God and die."[12] How selfish can you get? If you dwell on the negative and how a husband's testing affects your life, you will grow bitter like Job's wife. Speak and text words of respect each day, and this will nurture the relationship. This marriage is not about you but about building a union that will reflect the picture of Christ with his Bride—the Church. The power to either make or break a marriage is in your hands. It is God's day, and it is time to build! When you take that job description, there is never a boring day!

What is a Queen's duty? It is her subordination of self to the office, by her sheer will and love for God and for His Son, Jesus Christ. In the end, this amazing woman is strong and never idle, but take note: **the quiet** turns out to be the powerful because it proves you are fully dependent on a living God who is worthy of worship. And that is

---

12 His wife said to him, "Are you still holding on to your integrity? Curse God and die!" Job 2:9

when you win, and you and your spouse are both worshiping God together. This creates the royal, dignified woman and a noble family. Glorious extra time will be before you for profitable endeavors, receiving the praise deserved, dressing in purple linen, and laughing at the days to come.

The Remnant has employed so many of these ancient secrets in their homes. God has transformed many into Queens and Kings and into Princes and Princesses, all for His Royal Kingdom. Read on to learn more about raising up the next generation in this Royal Revival. May we continue with even more fervor to create and raise God-Fearing Families—for we have been called for this Imperial Priesthood, for the glory of our Most High God.

Now there was a man in Jerusalem called Simeon, who was righteous and devout. He was waiting for the consolation of Israel, and the Holy Spirit was upon him. It had been revealed to him by the Holy Spirit that he would not die before he had seen the Lord's Christ. Moved by the Spirit, he went into the temple courts. When the parents brought in the child Jesus to do for him what the custom of the Law required, Simeon took him in his arms and praised God, saying: "Sovereign Lord, as you have promised, you now dismiss your servant in peace. For my eyes have seen your salvation, which you have prepared in the sight of all people, a light for revelation to the Gentiles and for glory to your people Israel." Luke 2:25-32

How to Raise Godly Children

Chapter 8

Hear O Israel, the Lord our God, the Lord is one. Love the Lord your God with all your heart and with all your soul and with all your strength. These commandments that I give you today are to be upon your hearts. Impress them on your children, talk about them when you sit at home and when you walk along the road, when you lie down and when you get up. Tie them as symbols on your hands and bind them on your foreheads. Write them on the doorframes of your houses and on your gates. Deuteronomy 6:4-9

People often ask us what we teach to have such Godly children. Keep in mind, here at the Remnant of the Kingdom of Love, these children are not involved in any Sunday school programs that are divided by age. They are seated alongside their families, hearing the same words each week that the parents do, and they learn true passion from watching passionate people in this Church worship God. We are all united on the message of being born again with a heart to worship God alone. When the whole community lives to obey God and to be upright in all we do, it rubs off. People have moved here to help with changing their behavior and the behavior and hearts of their children. There is no greater influence than seeing people live out love and humility before God. Because of that, we trust each other to babysit, and we help each other in raising the children. The main responsibility, however, in raising these children is that of the father and the mother. The following are some of the basics that we teach each parent about raising Godly children.

The Heart of a Child

The heart of a newborn is a clean slate. The Bible tells us to raise up a child in the way that they should go and they will not depart from it.[1] A child's heart is made by the Lord, and God will program certain tendencies. However, it starts out fresh and clean and capable of accepting the influence of all types of impressions and inputs. Since the composition of a child's heart is such that it can accept the influences of both the good and the bad—the righteous and the evil—it is the responsibility of the father and the mother to incline the heart of the child either to good or to evil. This is an incredible responsibility.

> May you fulfill the will of the Father by talking about God when you are coming and going—in your home, car, at bedtime and mealtime.

Appropriately, God causes the child to only have eyes for the father and mother for quite some time. God programs the heart of a child to follow the parent. This gives the parent or grandparent all the advantage, power, tools, clout, authority and influence they need in the formative preschool years. The parent, first and foremost, must be devoted to God 100 percent themselves. Then they must be attentive to every word, action, interaction and deed of the child. This attentiveness is most important in the formative first three or four years of the child's life. A parent

---

1 *Train a child in the way he should go, and when he is old he will not turn from it. Proverbs 22:6*

should make this attentiveness their top priority and understand that this precious soul from the Heavens has been put into their hands to guide to eternal life. Forming their own genuine relationship with God that is humble, prideless, under authority and adoring, and then passing this down to their children is the beginning and the end of parenting, and especially concentrating on the oldest child. If you take the oldest one and help that child to do what is right, the rest will follow. Emphasizing family adoration and worship of God and praying to God is key. Indeed, having the child join in daily to worship and to pray and to converse about God is fundamental to raising a child.

As You Walk Along the Road…

May you fulfill the will of the Father as described in Deuteronomy 6 by talking about God when you are coming and going—in your home and in your car, at bedtime and at mealtime—and this does take time. If you have been blessed by having children, then you must understand that you have taken on a great responsibility, and you must let your old life go. The goal in God's True Church is to raise children to be like Christ, who loved The Father above all, as Jesus said in John 14:31, *But the world must learn that I love the Father and that I do exactly what my Father has commanded me.*

Children imitate what they see, and they can imitate Godliness as well as hypocrisy. Sometimes it can be an eye-opener, for parents pass down their sins to their children, so you must look inward and see if this is the sin that is in your own heart. Nothing is more important in child-rearing than to love God first with all of your heart and to crave more of His lead for your life daily. His Word or lead is not just found on the pages of the Bible, but it is alive, and it is in your heart and mind.[2] This is what we are to pass down.

MEET THE NEEDS

The parent should be very careful to meet the needs of the infant, and this is especially true in the first year of life. A baby's cries are only needs—the goal is to have a parent so attentive that the need is met even *before* the baby cries... not paying attention to a baby's

THE GOAL IN GOD'S TRUE CHURCH IS TO RAISE CHILDREN TO BE LIKE CHRIST WHO LOVED THE FATHER ABOVE ALL.

whimper is tuning out someone else's needs. Know your baby's whimpers! Try to anticipate needs of hunger, cold, sleepiness, the need for attention and love and the need to learn and be curious. The need to be taught is often overlooked. Babies love to learn, and they love it when the parent will tell them names of objects or show them their mouth and teach them words. They adore it! Learn to

---

2   *This is the covenant I will make with the house of Israel after that time, declares the Lord. I will put my laws in their minds and write them on their hearts. I will be their God, and they will be my people. Hebrews 8:10*

whisper in their ears to let them know what you are doing or what you expect. The attachment will be incredible. This precious time when they look to you for everything is so short and could pass you by. If you do not build this attachment now, thru love and attention, you may find that they will attach themselves to someone or something else as they grow up. Do not miss it! Know your baby's vocabulary and their body language. Babies are attached to those who know what they are trying to communicate. A calm, happy, secure child is the one whose needs are met.

Essential Kindness

Treat babies and children kindly. Kindness begets kindness. If we are kind to our children, they in turn will show kindness to others. Jesus was attentive and kind to children—even when he was carrying out his job responsibilities of preaching and evangelism.[3] He met their needs under all circumstances. He knew of the supreme importance of a child. Babies are very perceptive, and they respond to love and to those who are not selfish but attentive to their needs. Children will gravitate to those who are gentle and who whisper sweet, guiding words. They know who will pay attention and who will show them kindness.

Godly Direction and Redirection

When the parent feels that the child is able to discern between the good and the bad, then a more concentrated nurturing of the child should begin. The word "no" can be used to teach danger—such as

---

3 *Then little children were brought to Jesus for him to place his hands on them and pray for them. But the disciples rebuked those who brought them. Jesus said, "Let the little children come to me, and do not hinder them, for the kingdom of heaven belongs to such as these." When he had placed his hands on them, he went on from there."* Matthew 19:13-15

"No, hot," or "This will hurt the baby." You can whisper this in their ear. Do not be loud or harsh, and do not scare them.

By this point, you have spent so much time and attention on your baby in just meeting their needs that a deep bond has been created—they trust you and trust that you know what they want. So much of what is needed is just lovingly sweeping them up into your arms and sitting down on the floor with them, so they know you are not going anywhere—then putting your arms around them, telling them how much you love them, getting down on their level, playing with them and *really* listening.

These early years are strategic, and it is best to make it top priority before housework or socializing with friends. Fathers and mothers need to stay near their children and lovingly teach all they can. These little children are desperate for your approval. They adore you, and they want to be like you. If you put on a bracelet, they are going to put on a bracelet. If you put on a particular color, they want to wear that color. You need to watch everything you are doing and everything you are saying at this stage. They are going to be little clones of you because they adore you so much. This time is so important. Do not spend more attention on clothes or the outside appearance of a child than you do on the *inside* of a child. This is a soul that will live forever, a spirit that is preparing for eternal life, and nothing else matters.

As you spend time with your children, you learn all about them, and you see that every child is different. This is a golden opportunity to make sure your main goal is for your child to develop a relationship with God. There is no harshness in God nor Jesus Christ. There is only gentleness. Think about it: the discipline that God has given you has been extremely gentle. He has not disciplined you as your sins deserve. Have you not gotten away with a lot with God? I know we all have! He is so long-suffering and incredibly gentle, and you want your children to have those characteristics. To do that, they need to see these characteristics in *you* as you live that out. Then the children will be calm and long-suffering and gentle with each other as well.

When necessary, showing disappointment in your face is powerful. Children are tender and will naturally want to please. A parent should spend much time in gently making sure that the boundaries are clear. It is very unfair to correct a child about something they were not forewarned of. The parent should not dishonor or humiliate the child, nor should the parent highlight the child's fault publicly if possible.

Do not try to reason with the child and talk them into it. Leave your voice at a normal level because you want them to learn to be in tune to that frequency and tone. If they do not obey, do not raise your voice. Just take the action that needs to be made. If it is an electronic device, you step in and take it from them with no anger. Say, "No. We do not do that." You have been given the authority and you have the control of the billfold, the keys, the access to the Internet, etc. All you have to do is keep calm.

> TREAT BABIES AND CHILDREN KINDLY. KINDNESS BEGETS KINDNESS.

Trying to reason with a child is never going to work. God is quick in His redirection, and it gets your attention; you may trip or almost have a car wreck, and it fills you with adrenaline. God never raises His voice. He just takes things away one by one until we take the redirection, and then He gives it back one by one. It is simple, and it works.

How you handle issues must be for the child's good. This is not about the praise of man, but the praise of the Most High, glorious and brilliantly-loving God. Time, consistent training and gentleness are the keys.

Praise and Encouragement

Whenever the child displays a good quality or does a praiseworthy action, the parents should praise the child, and it is not wrong to occasionally give them a gift that will make the child happy. It is good to praise the child in front of others for Godly attributes.

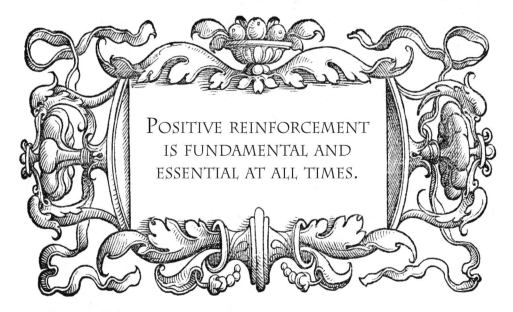

Praise Godly, Christlike morals. Make note of small progressions—celebrate, clap your hands, and reward and praise your child as appropriate. Positive reinforcement is fundamental and essential at *all times*. You cannot leave that out on any day. After all, God has used that so generously with you!

A key component of parenting, as has been stated earlier, is answered prayers. Again, this is huge. You must take time to sit down with your children, write down their prayers, and then follow up later so they will see that their prayer has been answered. This should be a constant part of your lives. Help them to see that the gadget that did not work was fixed, that the missing toy was found, or that they were able to get the answer to a tough homework assignment. If they stop and pray, then it gets done! Pray before you clean the house; pray before you eat; pray before they play with others. Sit down with them and pray, "Oh, God, make *me* the one who is loving today. Make *me* the one who gives up my toys, and God, help *me* to be that loving person." The answered prayers that these children in the Remnant of the Kingdom of Love are receiving are unbelievable. I am the most excited with my children and grandchildren when they have answered prayers and want to share that with me. We have this beautiful opportunity to get it right *ourselves* with God, and then teach our children the value of a relationship with God and receiving answered prayers.

Responsibilities of a Child

As the child begins to get older and can learn to do some small tasks, spend time teaching the child responsibility. Stay by their side in a helpful way as you teach them how to do things, but do not frustrate the child. They will gain faith in their abilities to perform tasks. Praise them for what they learn. It is beautiful to give them chores in line with their age. Let them know that they are performing an important function, and you will find them eager to help you out again!

Goals for School-Aged Children

During pre-teen years, children will go thru a needy time where they crave their parents' attention two or three times as much as they did before. Ask every day how their day was, and ask if there is anything they need. Pray on your knees with them daily, especially at that age. If you are not totally focused on them, they will have to do something to rattle you to get your attention. You cannot go wrong giving them more and more attention. They need you. They have so many questions. Use this phase as an opportunity to make up for any lost time. Keep a list of the positives about that child. Encourage them, and start all redirection with the positives.

Once you have set the stage for a beautiful relationship with the child and a relationship between the child and their Heavenly Father, they will have a solid foundation for school. School can be inside or outside the home. School-aged children should have a balance of play, exercise and studies. Too much of any one thing will dishearten the child. Teach the child to be active and not lazy—to work hard at their tasks. The relationship between you and the child will grow with each year. You are their counselor for friendships and answers to life. Every day be sure to spend time with your children and find out what is in their hearts. Pray with them…guide them…love them. Life is painful sometimes, but children who have secure relationships with their parents will be secure children.

> EVERY DAY, BE SURE TO SPEND TIME WITH YOUR CHILDREN AND FIND OUT WHAT IS IN THEIR HEARTS. PRAY WITH THEM; GUIDE THEM; LOVE THEM.

INTELLIGENCE AND ACADEMICS

At a certain age, schooling and academics start taking up a larger amount of a child's time. Therefore, academics should be in the context that an "intelligent person" is the one who seeks God with all of their heart and proves it by their good deeds. This true intelligence is rare and refreshing, and it is the stable person who knows the difference between this mortal world and the eternal life of the hereafter. You know that they are intelligent for they seek to attain a high rank of acceptance before God and Jesus Christ. The intelligentsia are those who look for God's approval and the limitless blessings of storing up their treasures in Heaven.[4]

If the child's initial upbringing is good, then the child will be more grounded and stable during adolescence. The world and its desires will pass away, but the child who does the Will of God will live forever.[5] Parents should clearly impress upon the mind of the child that the world is *temporary*—without permanence—and at some point will be nonexistent. Death puts an end to all the material possessions that you have acquired. The hereafter is the *permanent* home, and it is better…for everyone there is of one accord—they all love God for life, and they all worship God and obey Him. It is a place of peace and tranquility and a place of fulfillment, joy and satisfaction. Once this is understood, then the gifts of physical and mental skills should be recognized as coming from God, and therefore developed for the glory of God and the promotion of His Kingdom—not self. You cannot emphasize this concept enough.

Giving Back to God

"Will a man rob God? Yet you rob me. But you ask, 'How do we rob you?' In tithes and offerings. You are under a curse—the whole nation of you—because you are robbing me. Bring the whole tithe into the storehouse, that there may be food in my house. Test me in this," says the Lord Almighty, "and see if I will not throw open the floodgates of heaven and pour out so much blessing that you will not have room enough for it." Malachi 3:8-10

---

4   *Do not store up for yourselves treasures on earth, where moth and rust destroy, and where thieves break in and steal. But store up for yourselves treasures in heaven, where moth and rust do not destroy, and where thieves do not break in and steal. For where your treasure is, there your heart will be also. Matthew 6:19-21*

5   *The world and its desires pass away, but the man who does the will of God lives forever. I John 2:17*

It is so essential to help your children learn that everything belongs to God. It is all His. He is generously saying you can have 90 percent of what He is giving you … but none of it was yours to start with. This tithe is God's; it is earmarked for Him, and it belongs to His Church and the future of His Church. "Test me in this" does not mean wait until you save enough money to buy something you wanted or save up to buy a car. Teach your children that if you start off tithing, you will be blessed one-hundredfold from that. Otherwise, they will never get ahead. This needs to start at the earliest of ages with the youngest children. Whatever they are given in allowance, this percentage goes to God. Be sure they understand that it was never theirs to start with. Change the word "tithe" to "giving to the poor." We *get* to give a gift to the poor, and children need to grow up with charity and charitable giving. The fruit of this practice is truly immeasurable and exponential. In the end it will be the big untold secret.

BAD COMPANY

We are commanded by God as adults to stay out of the company of mockers, divisive people and those with rebellious spirits and bad morals—how much more so for impressionable little minds![6] This would also include being careful of what these impressionable minds watch—computer games, social media, television and movies. How easy it is to preoccupy the mind of a child with movies and computer games and let that be the babysitter so that you can be self-focused. However, it will eat up hours of your time later to undo the slang words and arrogant attitudes that the child has picked up.

Test and see if bad attitudes do not disappear upon replacing bad company with the company of the Saints who honor those who

---

6   *Do not be misled: 'Bad company corrupts good character.' I Corinthians 15:33*

respect their authorities and obey their parents. It is called peer pressure, in a good way! Teach your children examples of Godly heroes and heroines. Praise children who are righteous. Your children are gifted, full of the Spirit of God and therefore are a vital part of the family. Include them and let them see how needed and important they are. If they understand this, they might not look so hard for other companionship outside the family.

Maintaining the Parent Relationship

It is unfortunate that some parents use their children for friendship. It does not work that way. You are the parents, and this relationship is very rewarding, but respect for your authority must be maintained. It is irony... if you avoid correcting them for fear that you will lose them, then you *will* lose their respect and friendship. However, if you remain the parent in the relationship by directing, encouraging and guiding them, you will gain their respect, and they will desire your company. As the years go by, the relationship will grow more and more. God has called you to train your children in the way that they should go so that they will not depart from it.[7] He expects you to be loving but direct. Again, ironically, you will lose the relationship between you and your child if you have not raised them to love God more than you. Expect

> What could be a better hobby, preoccupation, or legacy than training children up from young to old to help them find this relationship with God and the peace that results from it?

---

7   *Train a child in the way he should go, and when he is old he will not turn from it.* Proverbs 22:6

no relationship with them later in life if you do not raise them to love God more than anything else on Earth.

TAKE TIME TO TEACH

Spend time with your children and love them. Teach them to get out of "self." Teach them to be grateful. Teach them to be thankful for having eyes that see, ears that hear, arms and legs that work. Have them focus on Jesus Christ who loved the Father above all and did not consider equality with God a thing to be grasped.[8] Jesus Christ was humble. Teach loyalty, faithfulness, truthfulness, honor, courage and devotion. Teach them to be unified with others who are here for God's Kingdom and who have the Kingdom of God in their hearts. There is no greater joy than seeing your children walking in the Truth.[9] Raising a child is a big responsibility given to us from God, but it is also a golden opportunity. If you are selfless, you see it as an enjoyable opportunity, second to none. A selfless parent jumps to take care of the child—and only selflessness will see the face of God.

Be involved with your children. Are you worried about the amount of time they spend with God? Don't you ask your children if they ate lunch? Would you not be very worried if they had not eaten all day? Consider, are you as concerned with their spiritual meals as you are with their physical food? Be aware of their heart and focus…be sure that their evenings are ending with Truth. Are there devotionals at home? Time for confessing and sharing? What could be a better hobby, preoccupation, or legacy than training children up from young to old to help them find this relationship with God and the peace that results from it.

---

8   *Who, being in very nature God, did not consider equality with God something to be grasped.* Philippians 2:6
9   *I have no greater joy than to hear that my children are walking in the truth.* III John 1:4

How to Raise Godly Children

When getting to know the Creator as a family, you cannot do it if you leave out His Creation, so take time to share in what God is doing with the seasons and to learn about His animals and the world He made.[10] You can make everything a lesson to learn about what God has designed and to point out His love and His incredible details.[11] God's Creation tells you everything about Him—His kindness to His creatures and how He feeds them, as it says in the Psalms, *These all look to you to give them their food at the proper time. When you give it to them, they gather it up; when you open your hand, they are satisfied with good things. Psalm 104:27-28.* God provides food for each one of them! The beauty of the world says so much about God. It all reflects who He is. You are accomplishing the number one goal in life, and that is knowing God and helping your children to know God as well.

Ultimately, God will be the One who gets the credit for the beautiful behavior of a child because you cannot raise a child without Him. He is the best Father of all. And in the next chapter, you will learn more about the vital importance of building on this foundation for your children. May you be challenged to use your time to raise these children who will be leading the next generation in protecting this Truth—even if you have no children of your own right now. May this be our goal, and may God bless our efforts so that the Princes and Princesses of the Royal Remnant Revival may be the most powerful defenders of God, His Church and His Truth on the face of the Earth.

---

10 *For since the creation of the world God's invisible qualities—his eternal power and divine nature—have been clearly seen, being understood from what has been made, so that men are without excuse. Romans 1:20*
11 *A beautiful book to read with your children about God's Creation is The Garden of Eden Children's Book (see www.WeighDown.com to get your copy)*

*Teach your children to pray every day. The prayer Jesus taught us is a **daily prayer**. "Give us this day our daily bread." Help your children to connect to the Heavens before it is too late and their hearts grow cold. Page 133.*

Connected to the Heavens

Chapter 9

God has given us all so much—we have life, and life with blessings! We woke up today with a beating heart and maybe even eyes that can see and ears that can hear! We have clothing, we have food, and we have shelter. On top of all of this, we have the Truth, and we have happiness—the two most valuable things in the world! What a day and what a life and what a God to provide all these things. But there are people in the world who are not happy with life. They do not see the many blessings, and they may not even want to live.

For those who have known me for years, you know I have warned that when times get hard, you see the real heart of man. There will be chaos in the streets—each man for himself. Well, chaos has dominated the news in recent times, and it has not just stemmed from adults but from the youth as well—there has been a wave of criminal "flash mobs" in the United States and in Europe. Teens can communicate and congregate at a moment's notice to overwhelm the police force and terrorize bystanders. Whereas at one time these groups formed for concerts and dancing and entertainment in the streets, some now throw rocks to break out windows, loot, rob and destroy. They have burned businesses and have even murdered business owners.

Besides violent mobs, there have been reports of youth committing murder of their peers or parents or teachers. One 15-year-old killed his parents and then texted out to everyone to come over to the house that night for a party. These are children who are cold, calculated and unconcerned. Jesus predicted this exactly in Mark 13 when he said that children would cold-heartedly murder or put their parents in jail.[1]

THE TRUE EMPTINESS

It is important to note that the youth involved in the rioting and violence came from all income levels. After they removed the masks of the young adults involved, they found that some of these teens came from the homes of millionaires. Money, or the lack of it, is not the key. These youth tend to be from troubled homes in general, which would include many of the problems straight out of Deuteronomy 28 referenced in Chapter 3. These are unblessed homes where the children have many needs and many problems. They have needs for love, attention, approval and sometimes physical needs. But even more, they do not know how to fill this emptiness that is deep in their souls. They do not know **God** and how to get connected to God. Instead they have been raised to project— their problems are everyone else's fault, and the world owes them something, so they grab for what they want. Others are the source of their own pain and poverty thru their poor choices that have been based on bad role models.

The world does not understand the connection contained in Deuteronomy 28, so these angry youth congregate and feed off one another. They are hurting, and they feel a little better seeing others

---

[1] *Brother will betray brother to death, and a father his child. Children will rebel against their parents and have them put to death. Mark 13:12*

in pain as well. It is like a modern-day version of the ancient coliseum where people would entertain themselves by seeing others fighting for their lives, in pain and hurting. Their parents are empty, and mainstream religion has offered them nothing. They have no answers. According to Romans 1, there is no excuse—God and His Eternal Deity and power are evident.[2] These teens have chosen evil and wickedness. Generations have rejected the Word of God, neglected a relationship with God, and we all are reaping the results. The contrast of life choices is becoming more black and white these days. Again, what is in the heart comes out during hard times, not during the good times. A life full of love or a life full of hate will illuminate what people have been sowing. You *will* reap what you sow.[3] Today's prisons are full of anger and full of youth, and this trend continues to grow. We are witnessing children who are out of control. They say they are "bored," but that is just another word for *purposeless*. They have only selfish standards to live by, and therefore they are miserable, lonely and full of hate.

A Sign of a Misplaced Heart

Everyone is looking for answers on how to respond to this increasing youth crime rate and rising hate. While the world is pondering this, we know that here at the Remnant, we are witnessing something that is amazing… something right out of the Prophecies from ancient times that God *is* instructing and teaching each one of these children, and they are on the right path. God has given us the direction and the answers. What is this answer?

---

2 *For since the creation of the world God's invisible qualities—his eternal power and divine nature—have been clearly seen, being understood from what has been made, so that men are without excuse. Romans 1:20*
3 *Do not be deceived: God cannot be mocked. A man reaps what he sows. Galatians 6:7*

As parents, we must be careful not to allow the child's world to center around themselves. Rather, teach true morals—to focus on God and Christ—and at the same time, *love* your children. Passing down an empty way of life with no morals, creating selfishness in the children, breeds hate and anger in the child, and the child winds up hating *you*. However, when you gently guide them, they will love you.

The first sign of misdirection is when children are outwardly respectful and nice to other people, but at home they are disrespectful to the parents. They may seem quiet or sweet, but you cannot really count on them to do what you ask them to do. By the teen years or early 20s, they have no respect for anyone. Often, they are poor students because they do not respect the teacher. They may also be poor employees because they do not respect the boss. If they get married, they make poor spouses because they cannot keep relationships or jobs. The bottom line is that they wind up destroying their own life along with the lives of others.

How a child treats the parent is so reflective of how the child really feels and what is *really* deep in their heart. It is a reflection of their relationship with God, an essential barometer. You cannot bypass this. Children being lovingly respectful and listening to the voice of the parent is everything. We must stay on top of the hearts and minds of our children, teaching each child the love of God and the love for man. Teaching them *all* the precious Commandments and how to obey them and living it out thru our own actions every day; this is a wonderful, selfless, full-time job. What better preoccupation could one have?

STAND IN AWE OF GOD

We have found our Connection to God, and thus the answer to how to raise our youth thru respectful obedience to God. Then they get the blessings! And what makes an even greater contrast is **answered prayers.** When you go in prayer to God (see the Triangle below) in the name of Jesus Christ, without fretting or manipulating anything to make it happen, God will answer your prayer.[4] Do not think this pathway is necessarily slower than doing things your own way—in fact, it could be faster. This builds your faith! When you go to God and refuse to grab for yourself, you develop a relationship with and a dependence on God. You stop being the forceful and controlling person, and you start seeing what a great God He is. God can give you the desires of your heart. You can go to bed at night with no guilt for over-eating, overspending, over-talking, over-drinking, or grabbing. You have no worries, and it is beautiful!

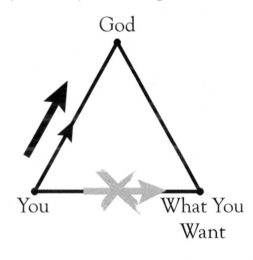

The greatest of all things that has ended the anger in these children is the ability to *communicate with God* and then feel His approval, which is what we are all looking for. If you have been around the Remnant you have heard the expression, "Who are we that we have been given so much?" This was first voiced, of course, by one of the ancient Prophets who said in Psalm 8:4: *What is man that you are mindful of him, the son of man that you care for him?* What does this really mean? Well, this Universe is vast. The stars and the planets are unfathomable. Our sky and the birds and creatures that inhabit

---

4   *For more about the Triangle and how to get answered prayers, see Weigh Down Works! Chapter 16, "How to Get the Spirit of God." See the Appendix for how to get your copy.*

it are beyond counting. The sea and all the water and all its creatures are immeasurable. Yet God cares for each creation. He knows all of them. It says in Matthew 10:29, *Are not two sparrows sold for a penny? Yet not one of them will fall to the ground apart from the will of your Father.* God is aware of all the animals and birds, but how many billions are out there… all the creatures on the Earth, all the trees, all the plants? Then add mankind on top of all of these creatures and all that is happening with them every second of the day. The Earth is *huge*! There are over seven billion people as of 2017—an incomprehensible number to keep up with, even if they were all obedient and predictable. Now add to this concept the "free-will factor," the "rebellious factor," in mankind, which you do not have to deal with in animals. Then you have a chaotic exponential factor that challenges the highest number ever thought of by mankind to process all of this constantly changing information. If you do not keep the vast nature of the Universe in mind, you might expect something from God, but if you wake up every day with the correct perspective, then you would understand what Solomon wrote in Ecclesiastes:

Guard your steps when you go to the house of God. Go near to listen rather than to offer the sacrifice of fools, who do not know that they do wrong. Do not be quick with your mouth, do not be hasty in your heart to utter anything before God. God is in heaven and you are on earth, so let your words be few… Much dreaming and many words are meaningless. Therefore stand in awe of God. Ecclesiastes 5:1-2, 7

Stand in *awe* of God. We need to watch our words. On the other hand, the Psalmist was right—who are we that God is mindful of man? Out of all the objects to capture His attention, how is it that we get to have even have one second of God's time? And not only that, we have personal answered prayers! Who are we? Even though we cannot comprehend it, we have to come to the conclusion that we *must* be important to God. If you love God, He will love you back and respond to you with answered prayers. Love is that valuable! I can tell you that an answered prayer is unfathomable to me...this concept of being able to communicate with and reach God! We know that it is true from our own multiple answered prayers each day. We need to combine the two thoughts. Yes, let us never forget that God is *incredible*. He is the Almighty God, and we are one of billions here on Earth. Yet this super-busy, massively genius God *hears and answers us.* A personal Connection thru the sea of creatures and people—

> WHO ARE WE THAT GOD IS MINDFUL OF MAN? OUT OF ALL THE OBJECTS TO CAPTURE HIS ATTENTION, HOW IS IT THAT WE GET TO HAVE EVEN HAVE ONE SECOND OF GOD'S TIME?

a personal Connection from an awesome God—that is what calms people down. It will calm you down and calm your children down. God cares deeply for all of the obedient animals and His children who seek Him.

In the Gospel of John, there is a story of the man who had been born blind and was healed by Jesus. The pharisees called the healed man in to question him, but they did not believe his report:

A second time they summoned the man who had been blind. "Give glory to God," they said. "We know this man is a sinner." He replied, "Whether he is a sinner or not, I don't know. One thing I do know. I was blind but now I see!" Then they asked him, "What did he do to you? How did he open your eyes?" He answered, "I have told you already and you did not listen. Why do you want to hear it again? Do you want to become his disciples, too?" Then they hurled insults at him and said, "You are this fellow's disciple! We are disciples of Moses! We know that God spoke to Moses, but as for this fellow, we don't even know where he comes from." The man answered, "Now that is remarkable! You don't know where he comes from, yet he opened my eyes. We know that God does not listen to sinners. He listens to the godly man who does his will. Nobody has ever heard of opening the eyes of a man born blind. If this man were not from God, he could do nothing." John 9:24-33

WHEN YOU GET YOUR FIRST ANSWERED PRAYER, IT IS A PROFOUND MOMENT, ONE YOU ARE LIKELY NEVER TO FORGET.

Remarkable indeed! God does not listen to the unrighteous but the *righteous*. How did the pharisees get this wrong? Everyone else knew it. Those who are right before God can get their prayers answered. James pointed out, as we read earlier, that when you are greedy you do not get your prayers answered. You are asking for the wrong reason.[5] You have to have the right motive in your heart.

---

5   When you ask, you do not receive, because you ask with wrong motives, that you may spend what you get on your pleasures. James 4:3

Jesus said that when you are right and you love God, you can move mountains.[6] Unbelievable answered prayers!

THE LORD'S PRAYER

If you have been brought up in the midst of mainstream religion, you may forget to pray because your old prayers were rote, stale, and unanswered. It was just a ritual or something the preacher did on Sundays. When you get your first answered prayer, it is a profound moment, one you are likely never to forget. When you find the true Jesus Christ, and you find how to pray and get answered prayers, it is amazing! So how do you do it? Prayers need a foundation, and Jesus taught us how to pray:

Our Father in heaven, hallowed be your name, your kingdom come, your will be done on earth as it is in heaven. Give us today our daily bread. Forgive us our debts, as we also have forgiven our debtors. And lead us not into temptation, but deliver us from the evil one. Matthew 6:9b-13

Jesus starts the prayer off with a focus on God, His Kingdom and His work. *"Our Father in Heaven."* You are awesome…You are everything! Then he gets our focus off of ourselves by asking for our basic needs for that day, *"Give us today our daily bread."* That allows us to move on and not worry about our basic needs. *"Forgive us our debts…"* Oh God, get *my* heart clean. *"…as we also have forgiven our debtors."* You are freed from anger toward others by forgiving them, and you can start with a clean slate with no focus on self or man. This gets everything out of the way that could hinder you, and finally, you

---

6   He replied, "Because you have so little faith. I tell you the truth, if you have faith as small as a mustard seed, you can say to this mountain, 'Move from here to there' and it will move. Nothing will be impossible for you." Matthew 17:20

come back to a focus on God and the Kingdom, "*And lead us not into temptation, but deliver us from the evil one.*"

A good way to teach your children this prayer is to put it all together by adding at the bottom, "Again, God, You are everything. Therefore may Your Kingdom come and Your Will be done on Earth as it is in Heaven." Your prayer is focused on God and focused off man, off yourself, off your worries, and focused back on God. Plus, now you have everything out of the way and are ready for the new day. "May we start this day off right, God. Now, this day I am getting everything focused on getting Your Kingdom work done." That is the genius of Jesus.

The prayer must be prayed in Jesus' name, because God gave Jesus the power. It is such an awesome idea! What a prayer! Is life not about just focusing on God and His Kingdom? The biggest roadblock is the focus on man or yourself...the worry of man, how you were wronged, your anger or the praise of man. When you pray correctly, then you will find that you do not focus on man at all, but only on the Will of the Father. When you do, then you are free from needs and worry or anger, and it makes for a wonderful day. This is everything!

A New Generation, a New Focus

As part of this Royal Revival of a Holy Priesthood, we are called by God to raise our children differently. You can see that in the Remnant, it is not just the Church that makes the difference. It is the *parents* who make the greatest impact; the parents are responsible. You cannot take that away, because God *wants* you to have that responsibility. It is a part of your training so that you can understand Him and your relationship to Him. You *must* teach the children to find God, and reinforce the greatest lesson with that relationship is that of answered prayer, turning off the television, having devotionals, praying, and the next day pointing back to the answered prayers. Teach your children that God listens to the Godly man who does His Will and that the prayer of a righteous man is powerful and effective.[7] Ask other families to come over and share stories about their children's answered prayers or their own answered prayers. Teach your children to pray *every* day and throughout the day. Help your children to connect to the Heavens before it is too late and their hearts grow cold.

Anger, hate and violence are signs of being *disconnected from THE VINE*. Thru social media, there is a new vine of communication that teens are plugging into, and it is made up of angry mobs who are all connected to the pit of Hades. Why? They do not know, they have not been taught, they have not experienced that they can get anything they need from God, so they grab and take, they steal and harm. When you see the transformed lives at the Remnant, you are seeing miracles like the one of Jesus healing the man born blind. These people are *healed*. Many of them were near death because of being obese, and they were brought back to life. Relationships were broken, and then they were repaired. The answered prayers are quite remarkable, and here everyone understands that God listens to the Godly parents and the

> I PRAISE GOD FOR JESUS CHRIST AND HIS LIFE AND HIS DIRECTION. THIS DIRECTION CAN SOLVE ALL SOCIAL ISSUES. JESUS CHRIST COULD ERADICATE ALL THE ANGER IN THE WORLD.

---

7   *Therefore confess your sins to each other and pray for each other so that you may be healed. The prayer of a righteous man is powerful and effective. James 5:16*

Godly youth who do His will.[8] That is why we *want* to be obedient. We do not want to ever lose the answered prayers and the blessings.

Many Remnant parents testify that the attributes of Christ came out in their children after joining this Royal Revival: their child became joyful, kind, calm, respectful, patient, charitable and very loving; it was a parent's dream. With good parental guidance they became under authority, steady, loving, patient. We have all seen these miracles in our children since we have been here. It has been amazing—a city of respectful and happy children. It is the miracle of Christ in us that we are witnessing hundreds of children with the same Christlike behavior!

> PARENTS, LET US MAKE A DIFFERENCE IN OUR OWN HOMES BY FOLLOWING JESUS CHRIST, WHO WAS SELFLESS AND BRILLIANT IN MAKING THE WILL OF THE FATHER CLEAR AND PRACTICAL.

I praise God for Jesus Christ and his life and his direction. This direction can solve all social issues. Jesus Christ could eradicate *all the anger in the world*. Jesus spent his life seeking and saving those who were blind, the ones who did not know—not those who were prideful and arrogant. He taught us how to connect to the Heavens thru obedience to our awesome God. Then he taught us to pray with not too many words but straight to the point. It is a prayer that is God-focused and gets us off ourselves so that there is no need for greed or worry or selfishness or anger toward others. It is a prayer that in itself is *brilliant,* and it is amazingly effective in keeping our focus off of ourselves and onto building the Kingdom of our Almighty God.

---

8   *The Lord is far from the wicked but he hears the prayer of the righteous. Proverbs 15:29*

Jesus was also assigned and accepted the position of mediator of these prayers, so that he is selflessly busy, like his Father.[9] Jesus was given this power, and in light of these troubled times, let us thank God that we have a Sanctuary, a place with answers that will give us hope for our children in these troubled times. Parents, let us make a difference in our own homes by following Jesus Christ, who was selfless and brilliant in making the Will of the Father clear and practical and in helping us to be personally connected, so that we could all find our way back home to the heart and love of the Father and therefore be saved from the life of hate. Let us teach our children how to connect to the True Vine:

I am the true vine, and my Father is the gardener. He cuts off every branch in me that bears no fruit, while every branch that does bear fruit he prunes so that it will be even more fruitful. You are already clean because of the word I have spoken to you. Remain in me, and I will remain in you. No branch can bear fruit by itself; it must remain in the vine. Neither can you bear fruit unless you remain in me. I am the vine; you are the branches. If a man remains in me and I in him, he will bear much fruit; apart from me you can do nothing. If anyone does not remain in me, he is like a branch that is thrown away and withers; such branches are picked up, thrown into the fire and burned. If you remain in me and my words remain in you, ask whatever you wish, and it will be given you. This is to my Father's glory, that you bear much fruit, showing yourselves to be my disciples. As the Father has loved me, so have I loved you. Now remain in my love. If you obey my commands, you will remain in my love, just as I have obeyed my Father's commands and remain in his love. John 15:1-10

---

9   For there is one God and one mediator between God and men, the man Christ Jesus. I Timothy 2:5

"'Hear, O Israel, the Lord our God, the Lord is one. Love the Lord your God with all your heart and with all your soul and with all your mind and with all your strength.' The second is this: 'Love your neighbor as yourself.' There is no commandment greater than these." Mark 12:29b-31 Page 148.

Chapter 10

And God spoke all these words: "I am the Lord your God, who brought you out of Egypt, out of the land of slavery. You shall have no other gods before me. You shall not make for yourself an idol in the form of anything in heaven above or on the earth beneath or in the waters below. You shall not bow down to them or worship them; for I, the Lord your God, am a jealous God, punishing the children for the sin of the fathers to the third and fourth generation of those who hate me, but showing love to a thousand generations of those who love me and keep my commandments. You shall not misuse the name of the Lord your God, for the Lord will not hold anyone guiltless who misuses his name. Remember the Sabbath day by keeping it holy. Six days you shall labor and do all your work, but the seventh day is a Sabbath to the Lord your God. On it you shall not do any work, neither you, nor your son or daughter, nor your manservant or maidservant, nor your animals, nor the alien within your gates. For in six days the Lord made the heavens and the earth, the sea, and all that is in them, but he rested on the seventh day. Therefore the Lord blessed the

Sabbath day and made it holy. Honor your father and your mother, so that you may live long in the land the Lord your God is giving you. You shall not murder. You shall not commit adultery. You shall not steal. You shall not give false testimony against your neighbor. You shall not covet your neighbor's house. You shall not covet your neighbor's wife, or his manservant or maidservant, his ox or donkey, or anything that belongs to your neighbor." Exodus 20:1-17

These Commandments are God's treasures that He gave to us on stone tablets for us to know how to have a relationship with Him. We are to have no other gods before Him—no other loves, no other passions, no other interests other than God and His love and what He wants. Love for God must come before anything else on this Earth, and then everything else will be added unto you.[1] The first four Commandments are about your relationship with God, and the last six are about a relationship with God's children. If you love God, how could you not be extremely outgoing, kind, loving, generous and patient to the object of His affection—mankind? If He loves mankind, then you will love them also. God has chosen mankind to love and to do special things for, so how could you be ugly toward something that He has approved of and He loves, and whom He has made in His image? You cannot. It is His hobby—loving man and being kind—so it should be your hobby as well.

---

1 But seek first his kingdom and his righteousness, and all these things will be given to you as well. Matthew 6:33

A Lesson for the Children

HONORING YOUR PARENTS

Loving your father and mother and honoring them are paramount. It is so important that you need to hear it every day. You should honor your parents by obeying what they have asked you to do. *Children, obey your parents in everything, for this pleases the Lord. Colossians 3:20* You honor them with your good behavior, with your dress, with not arguing and with being grateful.[2] You honor them by greeting others with respect and good manners, by being kind and offering to help others. Your parents will be delighted, and God loves it!

If your parents tell you to turn the TV off, you cannot be angry at their decision. If they tell you to do your homework or ask you to try a certain food, respect their requests, even if you would rather play, or what they are offering is not your favorite food. When you do what your parents tell you to do, you will be healthier and happier. You will sleep better, and you will perform better at school. Listen to your parents. Dress how they want you to dress, and do not waste their time when getting ready; you might make them late for work if you argue or talk back. Honor your parents' requests. Now, you may offer your opinion if they allow it. If you say, "May I give my opinion, please?" and they respond, "No, not this time," then you politely agree. Then maybe you can ask another time. If you wear the outfit they have helped you select, just see if you are not complimented on your clothes that day! If you stay inside God's boundaries and pray to Him, then you can accept whatever God allows for you, because it will be perfect. Be careful to never respond to your parents disrespectfully by saying "whatever" or rolling your eyes. You should live

---

2   Philippians 2:14

out the acceptance of "not my will, but yours be done," just as Jesus prayed in Luke 22:42.

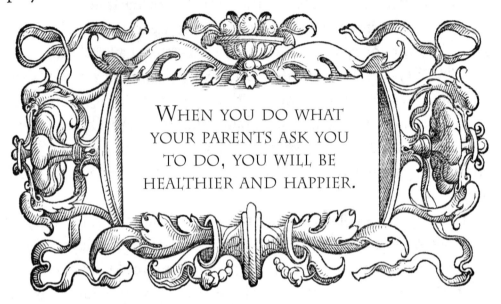

WHEN YOU DO WHAT YOUR PARENTS ASK YOU TO DO, YOU WILL BE HEALTHIER AND HAPPIER.

NO ANGER

In Matthew 5, Jesus says… *You have heard that it was said to the people long ago, 'Do not murder, and anyone who murders will be subject to judgment.' But I tell you that anyone who is angry with his brother will be subject to judgment. Again, anyone who says to his brother, 'Raca,' is answerable to the Sanhedrin. But anyone who says, 'You fool!' will be in danger of the fire of hell. Therefore, if you are offering your gift at the altar and there remember that your brother has something against you, leave your gift there in front of the altar. First go and be reconciled to your brother; then come and offer your gift. Matthew 5:21-24*

You do not want to be angry. Make sure that you love everyone sitting next to you. Do you go to school and get mad at other children? You cannot do that. If you feel anger inside, you need to talk to your parents or a Godly authority and let them know. They will help you learn to change your focus so you see things from God's perspective, and they will help you find the positives in every situation. Feeling anger toward those around you goes against the Ten Commandments.

When you look at the causes of anger, having jealousy or envy in your heart is a telltale sign that you have lost your focus and dependence on God. You should never want what someone else has, so stop staring at how others look or at what others have. If you depend on God and you are so appreciative of what God has given you, starting with life and the breath that you have, even to just live one day on this Earth, then you will not be given to jealousy.

Make sure you know that jealous feelings cannot be anywhere near the heart of a Christian. There are many scriptures that back this up:

A heart at peace gives life to the body, but envy rots the bones. Proverbs 14:30

And I saw that all labor and all achievement spring from man's envy of his neighbor. This too is meaningless, a chasing after the wind. Ecclesiastes 4:4

But if you harbor bitter envy and selfish ambition in your hearts, do not boast about it or deny the truth. Such "wisdom" does not come down from heaven but is earthly, unspiritual, of the devil. For where you have envy and selfish ambition, there you find disorder and every evil practice. James 3:14-16

If you keep on biting and devouring each other, watch out or you will be destroyed by each other. Galatians 5:15

It is obvious from these Scriptures that jealousy and envy are cruel and destructive to both the beholder and to others. If you master jealousy, then you are ready to help others who have not mastered it. How do you master it? By finding something to compliment them on and reaching out to them no matter how they treat you. You can fulfill the law of love by overcoming their evil toward you with good.[3] With trust and focus on God, His throne in Heaven, and Christ sitting beside Him, you can bless those who are being unkind to you, just as Stephen did when he was being stoned.

When they heard this, they were furious and gnashed their teeth at him. But Stephen, full of the Holy Spirit, looked up to heaven and saw the glory of God, and Jesus standing at the right hand of God. "Look," he said, "I see heaven open and the Son of Man standing at the right hand of God." At this they covered their ears and, yelling at the top of their voices, they all rushed at him, dragged him out of the city and began to stone him. Meanwhile, the witnesses laid their clothes at the feet of a young man named Saul. While they were stoning him, Stephen prayed, "Lord Jesus, receive my spirit." Then he fell on his knees and cried out, "Lord, do not hold this sin against them." When he had said this, he fell asleep. Acts 7:54-60

Jesus loved on his mother and took care of her and forgave others while he was on the most painful cross for hours. He had absolutely no envy of what others had, what others were doing, or the life that they were going to continue to live, and he had no jealousy about the life that he was giving up. He was completely tuned into God and God's plan for him that hour and every hour. The main sign that someone still has jealousy is what comes out of their mouth; they are envious of something someone else has or for another person's appearance or how other people are treated, so they hate it, and it results in gossip and slander. This would all end with putting envy

---

3   *Do not be overcome by evil, but overcome evil with good. Romans 12:21*

and jealousy to death by focusing on God every hour for whatever He wants to give us and being satisfied with that.

If you have felt envy or jealousy before, make sure to confess that to God and then to your parents and those close to you, and then pray. We must end envy, covetousness and jealousy because if you

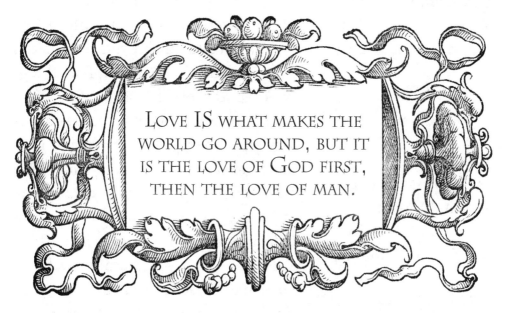

LOVE IS WHAT MAKES THE WORLD GO AROUND, BUT IT IS THE LOVE OF GOD FIRST, THEN THE LOVE OF MAN.

have that, then you will have the rest of the evil that was addressed in the Ten Commandments. This is backed up in Romans…

They have become filled with every kind of wickedness, evil, greed and depravity. They are full of envy, murder, strife, deceit and malice. They are gossips, slanderers, God-haters, insolent, arrogant and boastful; they invent ways of doing evil; they disobey their parents; they are senseless, faithless, heartless, ruthless. Although they know God's righteous decree that those who do such things deserve death, they not only continue to do these very things but also approve of those who practice them. Romans 1:29-32

Not a Hint of Immorality

There are so many distractions in today's world. Social media, TV shows, movies, music—the world is bustling all around us. It is important to take care to never *ever* let your eyes wander—never get caught up in what the world is chasing after. This is called lust. Never, ever touch it, because it will bring you down. Lust will destroy your mind and make you sick. You need to quickly run away, flee, if you see pictures of inappropriate things on computers or television shows. Turn the TV off, leave the movie, and shut the computer down. Run from ugly things. Get away, because lust is a sticky trap that wants to grab you and take you under and drown you in a sea of obscenity from which you cannot escape. There is no way out if you are not careful to flee that temptation. You cannot let your mind go there, and God hates it. So get far away from anything that tempts you like that—far away from inappropriate music, foolish talk, coarse jesting (which is making jokes that are inappropriate or that make reference to rude things) or anything that is out of place in God's Holy Priesthood.

> WHAT IS INCREDIBLE IS THAT WHEN YOU OBEY AND FOLLOW GOD'S PRECIOUS COMMANDMENTS, YOU ARE TRULY TRANSFORMED INTO A NEW PERSON, A NEW CREATION.

But among you there must not be even a hint of sexual immorality, or of any kind of impurity, or of greed, because these are improper for God's holy people. Nor should there be obscenity, foolish talk or coarse joking, which are out of place, but rather thanksgiving. For of this you can be sure: No immoral, impure or greedy person—such a man is an idolater—has any inheritance in the kingdom of Christ and of God. Let no one deceive you with empty words, for because of such things God's wrath comes on those who are disobedient. Therefore do not be partners with them. For you were once darkness, but now you are light in the Lord. Live as children of light (for the fruit of the light consists in all goodness, righteousness and truth) and find out what pleases the Lord. Ephesians 5:3-10

LOVE YOUR NEIGHBOR AS YOURSELF

You must make sure you continue to love those around you. The word "neighbors" can refer to those who live in your community, but it also refers to the people who are right next to you throughout the day. If you love your neighbors—because God loves them so much and all of His children are so special—how could you even take something as small as one of their pencils when they are not looking? We do not steal. We do not take anything that belongs to someone else, not even a pencil. God gave *them* that pencil; it is not yours. We also do not steal ideas or answers to questions on a test by cheating. That is not your answer, and you cannot take it. We do not even look longingly at what others have and make them feel bad about having it. Pray to God for what you want. Then if you let God take care of you, you will never have to panic—you realize you will get your prayers answered, because He will feed you, He will clothe you, and He will give you what you need.

You shall not give false testimony against your neighbor. Giving false testimony means lying. We are to never lie. God hates it when you lie about someone. Lying and Hades are associated.[4] Telling the Truth and salvation go together, because God loves the Truth. If you are

---

4 *But the cowardly, the unbelieving, the vile, the murderers, the sexually immoral, those who practice magic arts, the idolaters and all liars—their place will be in the fiery lake of burning sulfur. This is the second death. Revelation 21:8*

in trouble, never lie about it. Parents need to be so careful to uphold this. It should be the biggest rule that the child should not lie—you have to tell the Truth so that you can go to Heaven! The Truth and Heaven are connected. If you have done something wrong, that is when it is most important that you tell the Truth. If you were at fault, admit it. Let your parents and those you have wronged know that you are sorry, and you will make it right. You will feel so much better about the situation if you do whatever you can to make it right—an honest apology makes things so much better.

Do not ever covet what someone else has. Do not long for their clothing, their situation or their house. If you are coveting, then you are telling God you are not happy with what He has given you, and you are hurting His feelings. Stay focused on what *you* have, and thank God every day—just the fact that you are breathing is a miracle! Being able to see is another miracle. Can you use your hands and your legs? Do you have working kidneys and a functioning heart? You can run, you can jump, you can act, and you can play. These are all unimaginable riches and you should want nothing more beyond that. Life is priceless, and it is unbelievable all that we are given! We are beyond blessed.

It Is All About God

The last six Commandments are also all about a relationship with God, because why would you steal if you knew about the Triangle (asking God for what you want rather than grabbing for yourself) and knew that you can pray about what you want?[5] Why would you covet if you were thankful for what you already have? Are you even taking care of what you have been given already?

---

5   See Chapter 9, "Connected to the Heavens" for more about the Triangle.

If you are not following these Ten Commandments, you are hurting God's feelings. *Everything* on this list is about a relationship with God and about never, ever hurting His feelings. You can put these Commands in your heart by understanding what God wants, and what He wants is for you to trust in Him. He wants you to love Him. If you love Him, and you trust Him, then you will not take more food than you should. You will not steal someone's pencil. You will not talk about someone else and gossip to make yourself feel better.

All of these precious Commands are so that you can have a relationship with God. If you do that, you will stay connected to your parents as you honor them, and you will have good relationships with everyone around you. People who follow the Ten Commandments are happily married; they have children who honor them, and they have gathered little by little.[6] They have never stolen anything. They have enough to pay their bills, and they are truly happy. They have many friends—Godly friends. They sleep well at night, because they are not longing for more food or lust or something else that is not theirs. They have sweet sleep, and when they wake up, they enjoy another full day with a relationship with God and a good marriage and children who love them inside an orderly home. They are happy with what they have. They have good health and they live a long life, because they have honored their mother and father, and they have faith that God will provide everything they need. Then they go to bed

> TRUE CHRISTIANITY TRANSCENDS ALL RACE, ALL COLORS OF SKIN, ALL EDUCATIONAL BACKGROUNDS, ALL LANGUAGES AND ALL GOVERNMENTS.

---

6 *Dishonest money dwindles away, but he who gathers money little by little makes it grow. Proverbs 13:11*

again for another night of sweet sleep, and they wake up prepared to start another day of pleasing God.

In contrast, people who do not follow the Ten Commandments may end up in jail, divorced, or with terrible finances. They constantly want more, but they will never get it…and they do not know why. They are empty, unhappy, angry and have no friends. They use people and want things, instead of using things and loving people. They need drugs or alcohol to numb their pain, and they go to bed filled with anger and hate. They lose their sleep, they lose their health, and they get back up the next day, and they are worse.

Which do you want? Do you want the Ten Commandments in your heart? I know I do! I love God, and I honor my parents. I do not want something that is not mine—I would rather give and would never want to take from others. I want to love people. I am genuinely happy when others are blessed with something, and I would never want to bow down to something else and mislead people or hurt God's feelings. I want to remember His Sabbath. I want to do what He wants me to do. So I praise God, because I love Him, and I love His people, and I love you!

Your One Goal

Of all of these, what is the most important Commandment? What is the foundation of true religion? What is the most important thing in the world that you should pursue? What is the summum bonum, the supreme good? Jesus was asked that very same question. His answer in Mark 12 was, *"The most important one,"* answered Jesus, *"is this: 'Hear, O Israel, the Lord our God, the Lord is one. Love the Lord your God with all your heart and with all your soul and with all your mind and with all your strength.' The second is this: 'Love your*

A Lesson for the Children

neighbor as yourself.' There is no commandment greater than these."
Mark 12:29-31

As you grow up, many people will ask you what you plan to do with your life. What are your goals? What career will you choose? What will you study? What should it be? Well, it is **love**! Love God first! Then love your neighbor as yourself! If you reverse the order, it stops the world from spinning on its axis. Love IS what makes the world go around, but it is the love of God *first*, then the love of man.

If you have humanism—this means that you consider human interests above everything else in the world—and you love man first over God, you completely stop the world from spinning. It stops everything because it stops the Holy Spirit, which is love, from coming into your heart. It blocks your Connection to God. Pride also blocks the Connection because pride believes that it does not need to repent. It thinks it does not need to get anything out of its heart so that God's Holy Personality can come in. There is no more room in your heart.

True religion is truly delightful because it is very simple. What are the rules that give you the crown? Love God with all your heart and soul and mind and strength, and love your neighbor as yourself.

Again, your home should be a microcosm of the Church. A microcosm means a community or place that represents on a smaller scale the qualities of something much larger, so if your home is representing the Church, then it should be the most loving place there is. Start with the people right next to you and love them, respect them and care for them. Wake up every day to love and honor your parents and your brothers and your sisters. Ask yourself what you would want them to do for you, and then you do it for them! First you love at home, and then take this love to school and share it with the others you encounter.

When you get up in the morning and you go to God before you start your day, He will fill your heart up. Call on Him in the middle of the day, reach out hour by hour. Learn about God by listening to All Access and reading His Word. Recharge your batteries by coming to Church and worshiping your Creator.

TRUE CHRISTIANITY IS SUPERNATURAL

What is incredible is that when you obey and follow God's precious Commandments, you are truly transformed into a new person, a new creation. As you put these Commandments in your heart, you will feel His Spirit grow inside of you, and there will be joy, elation and even more happiness as you live out your faith. You will truly be living in a supernatural state.

Superman, the Avengers, Iron Man, Spider-Man—these superheroes are fascinating to all, but why? Because they are supernatural. People cannot fly, but Superman can fly. People cannot climb a wall, but Spider-Man can scale the highest wall and leap from building to building and use his supernatural power to fight evil. Well, if you obey God's Commandments, *you* are Superman. *You* are Spider-Man and Iron Man when you obey. **True Christianity is supernatural**.

The creation waits in eager expectation for the sons of God to be revealed. Romans 8:19 People around the world are searching for and seeking these gallant examples of royalty. They are looking for those who have self-control, who respond beautifully, who lose graciously, and who have a higher cause than just themselves, especially in children and young adults.

The world wants to see children who can obey, Princes and Princesses with graciousness and kindness who can sit still, respect their parents, focus, serve and love. They are in awe of people who are getting answered prayers. That *is* supernatural! It is supernatural to directly communicate with the Heavens. It is supernatural to be able to deny yourself and put others first. Where are you getting this supernatural power? It is from the Heavens…it is called the Holy Spirit, the Spirit of God. And the Spirit of God has love, joy and peace. The whole world is looking for peace, and now you have been shown the answer.

True Christianity transcends all race, all colors of skin, all educational backgrounds, all languages and all governments. It is THE government of governments. The Apostle Peter said, *How true it is that God does not show favoritism but accepts men from every nation who fear him and do what is right. Acts 10:34b-35* You have the chance to be a part of something that is unbelievable and unified. Everything God created is beautiful: every race, every language, every look. It is all for His glory and exceeds the greatest superhero or fairy tale story that has ever been told.

If we all would do unto others as we would have others do to us, then from the youngest to the oldest, we would be trained automatically in the world's etiquette and in true etiquette. Stop expecting others to serve you, and instead serve others. You go first. Then a miracle occurs, and your eyes are opened to how much is being done for you. Page 158.

Godly Etiquette and Compassion

CHAPTER 11

This is what the Lord Almighty says: "Administer true justice; show mercy and compassion to one another." Zechariah 7:9

The word "etiquette" comes from the French word "estique," which means to attach or to stick. The dictionary describes "etiquette" today as the requirements of behaviors according to society for various occasions, including ceremonies, courting, formal events and everyday life. I feel like the definition used by Merriam-Webster is closer to my belief of "the rules indicating the proper and polite way to behave." However, a changed behavior was initiated or started by God Almighty, The Source of everything, and Christ showed us the path to a superior way of life. God is the one who made manners and expects us to have His heavenly manners for eternal life.

Almost every religion in the world teaches their followers the required morals, behavior, etiquette and rules they believe their god expects. In the Middle East, the Muslim religions teach the children their customs, traditions, and their expected behavior; the Jews impart morals to their children; the Hindu religions educate their children, and in the Far East, Buddhists' morals influence the Chinese children. In the beginning, Christian laws, rules and moral behaviors for each member were taught. However, at some point in time, the Western religious culture divided, starting with the Catholics and Protestants, and continued with ever-growing divisions... there was disunity about what was right and wrong. In the Western Christian religions, they abandoned the role of teaching rules of behavior, since there was so much division on which rules to follow, and it was finally given over to the schools and universities, the society and the government to teach. Because no two denominations could agree, the Bible became less of a source, which in turn removed the solid-rock, immovable standard of the ancient Words of the Bible and gave way to an ever-changing and evolving sets of rules—for example, whereas at one time there was a high standard

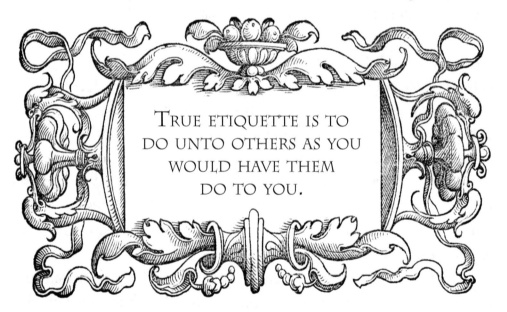

True etiquette is to do unto others as you would have them do to you.

of behaviors regarding authority, dating, and respect for parents and employers, these have all digressed to a low standard or to no standard at all.

Why did this happen? Besides the unprecedented divisions in Christianity that resulted in no standard of behavior, it was also due to elevating one law over the foundational teaching of God. It is true that Christ taught us not to judge others before first judging oneself correctly and that Christ and the Prophets taught never to correct mockers or share pearls before swine lest they turn and attack you and trample the pearls of Truth. But when this law became elevated above the foundational teachings that we are to speak to our neighbors with Truth, never uphold man's rules above God's rules, and must respect and fear God above man—that is the time in which it became socially unacceptable to talk about God, Christ or your religion. This persuasion became so strong that Europeans or Americans would blush if you brought up your religion or the subject of Christ or your relationship with God.

American and European church teachings on behavior went from being the responsibility of the church to what they called "finishing schools," which emphasized the social graces. These expensive schools and seminars replaced the church rules and became the place where young men and women could possibly meet suitable spouses. Time passed and society changed so that now these finishing schools have had to adapt and learn to downplay submissive behavior and change to emphasize the new culture of self-assurance and pride. Since the 1960s, many of these schools have even closed as a result of financial difficulties caused by changing societal norms. Now, no matter what culture, the term "etiquette" has almost been reduced to how to eat properly—and is now taught thru department stores and hotels to promote their fancy dinners. For most of American society, anything goes, and rules are random or completely abandoned.

Meanwhile, religions that never divided became bolder and open with proclaiming their allegiance to God…something that would be terribly uncomfortable for an American. For example, in the Middle East, you see the entire population of Muslims bowing down to pray to God five times a day with a public call to prayer, and the name and praise of Allah, which is Arabic for God, is spoken frequently in conversation. Note they typically have no "etiquette classes" in these cultures.

These measures in the United States that were originally intended to avoid offense have become an effort to promote an agenda. This strong, godless persuasion in America was eventually called "politically correct" language and policies. In other words, etiquette started with Christian customs, but the changing standards opposed God's Laws and evolved into rules that God never intended for mankind—and indeed, God would have us live quite the opposite way. God wants us to share the Truth about what He wants, about Him and His Christ and the Bible.

God has spoken His mind on many subjects and is clear about what He calls a sin, but this has been ignored. The Lord God Almighty calls us to tell the Truth about sin. You need the foundation of God's morals, not modern American etiquette, which has evolved into merely which fork or utensil is used first at the table. Although these facts can be helpful, true and proper etiquette begins in the heart with the Ten Commandments and their summary given by Jesus Christ in Mark 12. We are to love God first and then love others as ourselves. Both passages express showing love and obedience with all you have—all your heart, soul, mind and strength. It is an overwhelmingly encompassing attitude and a search to put God first and foremost by making Jesus the Lord of your behavior. That is true etiquette. Without that foundation, you are disingenuous. You could know how to properly cut your food with a knife, but at the same time, your words could be sharper than a knife, cutting another human down and discouraging their spirit. Here at Remnant Fellowship, we have tried to restore the original etiquette taught by

God thru Moses, and genuine love and manners are making a comeback.

Do Unto Others

So in everything, do to others what you would have them do to you, for this sums up the Law and the Prophets. Matthew 7:12

The Golden Rule was written by God, and almost all etiquette rules have been stolen words from the Bible... for true etiquette is to do to others as you would have them do to you. This is one of those subjects that is so deep and so vast. It is so time-consumingly intricate trying to think about all your emotions, wants and dislikes... and then thinking about someone else's emotions, wants and dislikes, yet it is so ignored or just considered passé or unnecessary and tossed out like an old rag.   Oh, to explore exactly what another human would want and need. We instinctively know what we would want. We all want and need thoughtfulness, caring, empathy, concern, love and affection, but the process of automatically employing that principle onto the person standing right beside you takes a surrendered and charitable mind. It takes a tremendously disciplined, thoughtful adult or child who can put down their phone, put down their electronics or their computer games, and instead give thought to the needs of others. They are considerate, so they can be confident about knowing what others would want, and they are able to extrapolate their own feelings onto another. They are confident enough that they have read the needs and emotions of the human being beside them, so now they can act and express and provide and extend, touch and love, and give the support that person needs. These people who are always salt

> STOP EXPECTING OTHERS TO SERVE YOU, AND INSTEAD SERVE OTHERS. YOU GO FIRST.

and never pepper...they always make things better, and they never offend.[1] They always think the best of others. At the same time, they always tell the Truth about what the Heavens want, holding that line to be able to give graciously without offending the other person. Those people are so valuable, and they are rare.

To employ the Golden Rule is the most important lesson in your life. You cannot toss it aside as just one more little fact. If you learn nothing else in your home, in school, in Church, thru all the sermons and all the reading of the Bible, except learning to love God and to do unto others as you would want them to do unto you...then you have an essential, profound foundation and purpose.

> IMAGINE A HEAVENLY COMMUNITY...A PLACE OF GENTLENESS, KINDNESS AND GRACIOUSNESS... TRUE ETIQUETTE AND MANNERS, A POSITIVE ATTITUDE AND LOOKING FOR THE GOOD IN EVERYONE.

If we all would do to others as we would have others do to us, then from the youngest to the oldest, we would be trained automatically in the world's etiquette and in God's true etiquette. Stop expecting others to serve you, and instead serve others. You take this step first. Then a miracle occurs, and your eyes are opened to how much is being done for you by others and by God.

While the world teaches secular etiquette and rules that are politically correct, it is time for a comeback to true etiquette as laid out by God. Doing what the Heavens expect was given to Moses and the Prophets and Christ and his Apostles. It was based on the Ten Commandments and Mark 12, which all boiled down to love—love

---

1   Salt is good, but if it loses its saltiness, how can you make it salty again? Have salt in yourselves, and be at peace with each other. Mark 9:50

that is shown thru genuine compassion for God and for humans, devoid of harsh judgment, for after all, even after we all have sinned, God has given us forgiveness and compassion.[2] *I will betroth you to me forever; I will betroth you in righteousness and justice, in love and compassion. Hosea 2:19*

The world will talk about having respect for others, being honest and trustworthy, putting others at ease and showing kindness to everyone—that is all a part of universal success classes of Western culture—but when you leave out God and His never-changing Word, these are shallow, manipulative manners, and their standards are ever-changing because they are based on what the fickle man wants. This will only prove to bring destruction on the community. The irony is that when you care to make God and His Business look good thru your words and behavior, you will attract a like-minded spouse and obtain a good job. You will win over both Saints and the world with your good behavior. Love, indeed, is the summary of the Law.

Returning to God's Foundation

The Western culture is proud but confused—just turn on the television to hear of governments quarreling and see news of discord, interruptions and arguments...with blatant disrespect for leaders. You feel your blood pressure rise as no Truth can be proclaimed. When our society stopped talking about our love for God and upholding His Commandments and it became politically incorrect and embarrassing to share openly about our faith, then society became just a free-for-all for whatever anyone wanted to say. The loudest child in the classroom, the squeaky wheel, got the grease. And if one of the children started talking back to the teacher

---

2 *For more about compassion, see Chapter 21, "True Compassion" in* <u>The History of the Love of God, Volume II</u>.

or punching the other classmates and it was not corrected, then that became the new standard. Everything has turned upside down—with children controlling parents and teachers, students destroying campuses, wives ruling over husbands. The Western culture has lost the foundation that God set forth. You will not see finishing schools in the Far and Middle East...but what the world needs came from the Judeo-Christian background.

> THE ETIQUETTE THAT WILL BE TAUGHT IN THIS ROYAL REVIVAL IS FOR THE GOOD OF GOD AND HIS KINGDOM FIRST, FOR HIS GLORY—TO MAKE HIM AND HIS BUSINESS BE THE BEST BUSINESS IN THE WORLD.

But there is hope. As we have returned to this foundation of God's etiquette and His Commands, we have seen a transformation in our own lives and in those around us. Imagine a Heavenly Community...a place of gentleness, kindness and graciousness...filled with true etiquette and manners, a positive attitude and looking for the good in everyone. We experience this daily, and our children are grounded on this foundation, but I know that there is even more to go—this is exciting. The Bible teaches that good behavior is not an option, and God's rules are standard and timeless.

The etiquette that is taught in this Royal Revival is for the good of God and His Kingdom first, for His glory, to make His Business—His Church and His Kingdom of Love—the best Business in the world. This true etiquette exists to honor His Son Jesus Christ who came down here to show us this behavior, and for everyone to honor their parents. If you behave correctly, you will win over both Saints and the world with your good behavior. Learn the true etiquette taught by the Heavens, for it is our behavior that will be evaluated in Heaven. My prayer is that the word etiquette, meaning "to stick," will stick to us and be a part of our moral fabric. May God and His etiquette rule the world. May His Will and His beautiful etiquette and manners be done on Earth as they are in Heaven.

PRAYER

Dearest Father, we are so in awe of you. You wrote all the etiquette rules. You are the one who came up with and studied behavior so much that you could program these things into our hearts and then prick our consciences. You have put a conscience inside of each man, each woman and each child. You have been the one to guide us, teach us and then somehow keep it all alive thru years and years of people going the wrong direction. You have shown us how to right that wrong and set us in the right direction. And if it is given a foundation, it will last. Father, we want to put all this into action. May it go from our head to our heart and into our muscles, with all of our effort given to make this happen. May we be totally living out Christ's behavior, who was imitating your behavior, so that the world is full of you and Christ and your beautiful etiquette and manners. I pray that every family, every husband, every wife, every child puts so much more into it than they have in the past, and may it all be blessed. In the name of Jesus Christ, Amen.

Each of you should look not only to your own interests, but also to the interests of others. Philippians 2:4 Constantly and consistently looking for the needs of others and putting the characteristics of Christ into practice all day long will lead you to the perfect day! Page 170.

The Perfect Day

Chapter 12

As we learned in the previous chapter, etiquette is only possible when you genuinely love GOD and His Ten Commandments from deep inside your heart. However, etiquette courses and multiple finishing schools all claim to teach proper etiquette. People pay for and take courses to polish the outside, but they never achieve appropriate social interaction, so they never seem to have true friends or maintain relationships of any depth. They are instructed on how to greet others, on the polite way to eat, the proper use of cell phones, and they are given general business etiquette tips. However, these learned skills are never natural, and true etiquette never becomes a part of their heart or their defining characteristics—and you will see the difference in their behavior, especially at home. They may smile, but underneath they are full of hate toward you, the world and their life situation. In fact, Psalm 55 points this out: *His speech is smooth as butter, yet war is in his heart; his words are more soothing than oil, yet they are drawn swords. Psalm 55:21*

Notice that in the world's etiquette classes, there is no credit given to the Bible…no credit given to God, the Creator of all social graces—The Lord God Almighty and His Son, Jesus Christ, the true Sources of this beautiful behavior. In addition, beautiful behavior is taught and lived out by His Prophets and Angels. There is a proper way to behave, and our bodies are here to house the sacred Spirit of God, the characteristics of the Heavenly Father. There is only one way to lay a foundation for proper behavior and God's course of etiquette, and that is with God's Holy, perfect Spirit that gives you His behavior, which is from the Ancient of Times—behaviors that He has selected to be the very ones that are the perfect way to live and respond so that there is a world of peace about us.

How do you get this beautiful Spirit and gracious etiquette from above? You cannot buy it, nor can you obtain it from simply begging for it from the Heavens. The Bible teaches us that the only way to obtain this priceless Spirit is to empty out and cease your old behavior, and then to act in a new way of life following Christ. You have to stop loving idols—end what you have been doing, and then start a new way of life of loving God more. Another way to express this is to surrender or give up your old wants and ambitions and now become a servant of the Most High God. Jesus Christ would call this "repentance," and we must have genuine, true and sure repentance and then be baptized into the love and the life of Jesus Christ. Then you will receive the Holy Spirit of God, and it will continue to grow as long as you live in obedience to the Will of God in your life. Jesus described it like a spring of everlasting water where you will never be thirsty.[1]

Note that obtaining this Spirit is dependent on our actions. These actions must come first, and then God will come and make His home inside your heart. This is worded so beautifully by Jesus

---

1   But whoever drinks the water I give him will never thirst. Indeed, the water I give him will become in him a spring of water welling up to eternal life. John 4:14

in the Gospel of John, where it says, *Jesus replied, "If anyone loves me, he will obey my teaching. My Father will love him, and we will come to him and make our home with him. He who does not love me will not obey my teaching." John 14:23-24* God's Spirit of love resides in those who obey. Then and only then will you have etiquette of the heart. If you work on the inside of your heart first, then you can clean up the outside and polish gracious behavior. This behavior will be sincere, not striving to flatter or impress mankind, because those who are trying to do that could still have bad thoughts inside, but you are doing it solely for the glory of God. We must have the right purpose every day! Get your heart right so you can glorify the Father who made you, and then extend the credit back to Him.

How to Have a Great Morning

Etiquette starts in the early morning when you awaken and give glory to God by praising Him for another day and His beautiful sunrise. He has been merciful to allow the world that is so full of evil desires to continue to spin another day. He is doing that in hopes that the lost will find His goodness. We must praise God for His patience and pray to imitate this patience with every human or situation that we come in contact with each day, even to our animals. We awaken with joy, and then we extend joy. If we find it hard to awaken early, then go to bed early, for the evening is less productive and the morning is extremely productive with a lot more time for the Spirit of God to guide you into good for the day.

We must not get out of bed until we pray to live a life that will salt the Earth all day. This prayer is with praise, and then directed love— to bring joy to our fellow man, which is the Kingdom work of God. This joy will come from the heart and give a morning smile to the face and a gentle, quiet, cheerful disposition to all around. For many there will be a need for mercy, patience and service for those around you—knowing that the world is only still in existence because of the extraordinarily deep patience of God.

Once you get out of bed after praying, you must know that healthy hygiene is essential to glorify God, so you must shower or wash your face, brush your teeth and comb your hair to ensure that you are fresh and clean, wearing clean clothes. Once you are ready for the day, before you leave the bedroom, you must pray the Lord's Prayer to be led not into temptation for idols and to be sure you have nothing but forgiveness and mercy and patience for others. In this way, you fulfill the Law and the Prophets and all that God has asked of you.

> ETIQUETTE STARTS IN THE EARLY MORNING WHEN YOU AWAKEN AND GIVE GLORY TO GOD BY PRAISING HIM FOR ANOTHER DAY AND HIS BEAUTIFUL SUNRISE.

How is this accomplished? I will give you the Truth from the Word. When you surrender your old life of anger and pick up the new life of love along with a control of the tongue, then you will be able to do what is right that day. So much of it is learning to depend on God rather than man for your bread for the day. Notice the Lord's Prayer, *"Give us this day our daily bread."*[2] It does not tell you to look to others—such as looking to your employer to give you a satisfying and well-paying job or looking to your siblings to do all the chores or looking to your parents to give you inheritance…but rather, "Dear *God*, give us this day our daily bread." We are not to be independent and lean on ourselves and our own smarts, but rather, we are to lean on the Father. That means our real job description is to be childlike. In Proverbs it says, *Trust in the*

---

2   *For more about the Lord's Prayer, see Chapter 9, "Connected to the Heavens."*

The Perfect Day

Lord with all your heart and lean not on your own understanding; in all your ways acknowledge him, and he will make your paths straight. Proverbs 3:5-6

When you lean not to your own understanding but rather to God all day, expectations and anger go away. When anger is gone and love is present, you are a light to the world, and you do not bring negativity or pessimism to those around you. It is wrong to complain and be negative. That will eat up your life and ruin your day. Being complaining, grouchy and irritable means that you are not focused on God and are not depending on Him. Complaining is the clear sign you have lost your focus. Start the day with a dependency and focus only on God. This focus will become stronger and stronger, and your words will become more positive every day.

A Grateful Heart

There must be NO whining or complaining. Why? Because the Bible tells us very clearly:

1. Complaining makes God very angry.

Now the people complained about their hardships in the hearing of the Lord, and when he heard them his anger was aroused. Then fire from the Lord burned among them and consumed some of the outskirts of the camp. Numbers 11:1

Don't grumble against each other, brothers, or you will be judged. The Judge is standing at the door! James 5:9

2. His Will for us is to not complain but only be thankful.

Give thanks in all circumstances, for this is God's will for you in Christ Jesus. I Thessalonians 5:18

Do everything without complaining or arguing. Philippians 2:14

Offer hospitality to one another without grumbling. I Peter 4:9

3. To be a child of God, to be a Godly young man or young woman for God, anger must leave. This is very clear:

But now you must rid yourselves of all such things as these: anger, rage, malice, slander, and filthy language from your lips. Colossians 3:8

Bear with each other and forgive whatever grievances you may have against one another. Forgive as the Lord forgave you. And over all these virtues put on love, which binds them all together in perfect unity. Colossians 3:13-14

Refrain from anger and turn from wrath; do not fret—it leads only to evil. Psalm 37:8

When we depend on God and Christ for all things every minute of the day—with any obstacles, with any oppositions, with any hardships—then we will not project and cause a problem by blaming others. We will be at peace. And when you learn to do these things, you will have graduated from the hardest and most difficult subject in the school of life. There is no university that could assist your life or eternal life more than this training. This topic must be the reminder on every cell phone or device or on every sheet of paper. To have proper behavior and etiquette, you must pray without ceasing… all day long. And when you do this, you give your first frustrations of the day and your last frustrations of the day to God in the name of Jesus Christ. In doing this, you will watch all anxiousness and frustration and fears leave because God is working and answering your prayers thru Jesus Christ. He is taking care of everything. This turns your worry into ecstatic joy because you have the Most

𝕻𝖔𝖜𝖊𝖗𝖋𝖚𝖑 𝕮𝖗𝖊𝖆𝖙𝖔𝖗 out there working for you and taking care of everything.

To get God's Spirit and then depend on Him hour by hour will clean you up on the inside. It will end complaining and anger. Look to Him, and all concerns will be resolved, and then all of these behaviors you have been trying to stop will disappear.

Spreading His Light to Others

This new life—this dependence, this love, this turning to God and obeying Him—covers the first four of the Ten Commandments.

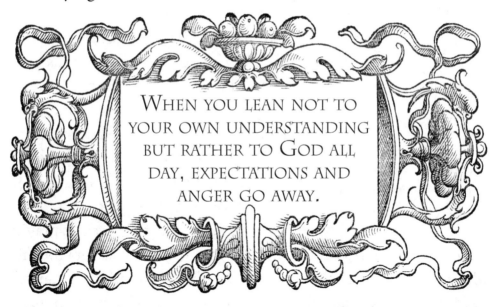

WHEN YOU LEAN NOT TO YOUR OWN UNDERSTANDING BUT RATHER TO GOD ALL DAY, EXPECTATIONS AND ANGER GO AWAY.

With these foundational characteristics in place, you may leave your bedroom. You are now ready to open up the door and face the world, ready to put into practice the last six of the Ten Commandments and be a glorious, successful light to all men on Earth. If your brothers and sisters who are right outside your bedroom door need help, the most commended goal for you is to consider the needs of your siblings. This is putting the highest Law first in the earliest part of your day, and your Heavenly Father sees this and will reward you because you are spending this beautiful day to glorify Him and spread His light to the world. *Each of you should look not only to your own interests, but also to the interests of others. Philippians 2:4* Looking for how you can help others get ready for their day's work sets a beautiful example, and you are living out the Law. You can help make lunches or help a younger sibling get dressed; you can encourage them and help them find needed articles of clothing or school books or whatever they may need for the day. This makes everyone's day better!

> IF YOUR BROTHERS AND SISTERS NEED HELP, THE MOST COMMENDED GOAL FOR YOU IS TO CONSIDER THE NEEDS OF YOUR SIBLINGS. THIS IS PUTTING THE HIGHEST LAW FIRST IN THE EARLIEST PART OF YOUR DAY.

The morning is the time for thoughtful quietness. After a night that has been dark and quiet, it takes time to gear up for light and sound and noise. And family members are waking up and spending time in prayer, so you have to be respectful. Remember to do to others as you would have them do to you.

As you continue to get ready, pray to God for what to wear and how to do your hair; do it all for God and with God and for His glory. Then get dressed and forget yourself and how you look, and then you can look past what someone else has on and into their heart, praying that God will show you their needs.

So you now have a routine for getting up and getting your heart ready, to the point that you are opening that door truly ready to leave the house. The major point is not to lose your focus or your dependence on God. James is very clear: *My dear brothers, take note of this: Everyone should be quick to listen, slow to speak and slow to become angry, for man's anger does not bring about the righteous life that God desires. James 1:19-20* Keep this focus and this dependence on God, and then when anything goes wrong, you cry out to God. When He answers your prayers and fixes everything, then you praise Him and continue to be in this beautiful, wonderful good mood.

Even at the end of the day, continue in this same pattern: *In your anger do not sin: Do not let the sun go down while you are still angry... Ephesians 4:26* Now you have gone thru the entire day and your heart feels pure and at peace with all men and with God. That is the picture of a perfect gentleman and a perfect lady. Praise God for His etiquette and a perfect day!

Luke 5:17-20 tells the story of the deep compassion of four friends of a paralyzed man. They were so concerned about their friend that they opened a hole in the roof so they could get him into the presence of Jesus Christ.

Kindness

Chapter 13

Make sure that nobody pays back wrong for wrong, but always try to be kind to each other and to everyone else. I Thessalonians 5:15

A very high standard of God's etiquette necessitates being kind. Yes, kindness is essential for a person who calls themselves a Christ follower, and it is a foundational concept for parents to teach to their children. You cannot just expect your child to instantly be kind. How sad to see parents get angry and upset at their own children missing the mark of kindness, and yet they have no kindness in their hearts toward their children. This anger comes from embarrassment… and embarrassment comes from wanting the praise of man. We must start over as parents and only desire God's approval, and then the anger will subside. Be patient, parents, and live out and show kindness with your actions while gently correcting with soft words, or, if you are in public, gently whispering in the ear to redirect the child.

What if your child is learning one of the most supreme and most challenging lessons from the Heavens, and that is to be kind to *everyone*, especially when it entails returning evil with good, and yet they miss the mark? Expressing disappointment is appropriate, followed with encouragement that they can do better because they are called out by God to be a part of this Royal Priesthood.[1] Yes, again, I consider kindness toward others the most paramount and most important objective for each Christian on Earth, and it is a most

---

1   I Thessalonians 5:15; II Timothy 2:24; I Peter 3:9

exquisite subject. To focus on the life of Christ who reflected God is the answer. Only God is the resource of kindness, and our Christ lived it out perfectly with perfect motives. It will take much patience and effort on the parents' part and concentration on the child's part, but when you see how important this is to the Heavenly Father and how essential it is to be able to blend in with the Angelic Staff in Heaven forever and ever, you will want to make every effort to take your child thru the steps toward celestial kindness.

> GOD'S GOOD ETIQUETTE IS TO BE COMPASSIONATE TO ALL.

His divine power has given us everything we need for life and godliness through our knowledge of him who called us by his own glory and goodness. Through these he has given us his very great and precious promises, so that through them you may participate in the divine nature and escape the corruption in the world caused by evil desires. For this very reason, make every effort to add to your faith goodness; and to goodness, knowledge; and to knowledge, self-control; and to self-control, perseverance; and to perseverance, godliness; and to godliness, brotherly kindness; and to brotherly kindness, love. For if you possess these qualities in increasing measure, they will keep you from being ineffective and unproductive in your knowledge of our Lord Jesus Christ. But if anyone does not have them, he is nearsighted and blind, and has forgotten that he has been cleansed from his past sins. Therefore, my brothers, be all the more eager to make your calling and election sure. For if you do these things, you will never fall, and you will receive a rich welcome into the eternal kingdom of our Lord and Savior Jesus Christ. II Peter 1:3-11

Note that Peter makes a list in ascending order of noble characteristics that starts with faith and ends in love. It starts with a mental acknowledgement of faith and ends in the ultimate action of love. Each progression is a higher level of godliness than the next, and that leads all the way to love, which he then says is necessary for our entrance into salvation. But note that the level that is second only to love is the gift of kindness. Do you see how pleasing kindness is to your God? Kindness is necessary and is also a sign to the world that God is with you—that God and Christ have made their home in your heart and that you indeed have the Spirit of God in you.

But the fruit of the Spirit is love, joy, peace, patience, kindness, goodness, faithfulness, gentleness and self-control. Against such things there is no law. Galatians 5:22-23 Again, kindness is a fruit of having God's Spirit in you. Jesus, who was full of the Spirit, was kind to all people. In fact, it says in Matthew, *When he saw the crowds, he had compassion on them, because they were harassed and helpless, like sheep without a shepherd. Matthew 9:36* The Scriptures go on to say that Jesus had compassion so he healed them, gave them sight and insight into Truth, and he fed them.

Kindness is not just shown thru deeds, but it includes kind words as well. *An anxious heart weighs a man down, but a kind word cheers him up. Proverbs 12:25* A kind word is something everyone can give.

Taking Care to Include Everyone

One of the kindest things you can do for your brothers and sisters in Christ is to include them. You might think that you do include others, but do you really? Have you ever been out with a couple of friends on the playground swinging and the two of them just leave and do not tell you where they are going? In other words… have *you* ever been left out? It hurts! On the other hand… have you ever left anyone out? Have you ever been with your friends and told one of them, "Let's go back inside and play" and then just left the other children outside? Then you are guilty. Have you ever heard others call out to you, "Wait up! Where are you going? May I go with you?" That is sad, because it is cruel and impolite that others are having to run after you to find out where you are going. You did not have the kindness to tell them where you were going or what you were doing.

God's good etiquette is to be compassionate to all. Slow down… inform your friends of your exit. Whether you are at a table having a meal or outside playing with a crowd of friends, ask to be excused, and let others know what you are doing. Ask forgiveness for leaving and let them know that you are reluctant to leave their presence because they mean so much to you.

Kindness means including and informing. Kindness is communicating generously to everyone, making it easy to include everyone. What if you want to stop swinging and go inside and get a drink or snack? If the group is divided on what to do, then say, "Why not those who feel led to stay outside, please do. It is a beautiful day in God's Creation. However, if you feel a need for a break from the sun or are thirsty or hungry, please join me." You have been polite with proper etiquette to let everyone know that you are excusing yourself—but not because you do not love them or have not enjoyed their company.

> ONE OF THE KINDEST THINGS YOU CAN DO FOR YOUR BROTHERS AND SISTERS IN CHRIST IS TO INCLUDE THEM.

People, especially children, are very sensitive, and God wants unity, but satan wants to divide. When people have the wrong spirit, they might try to divide or separate friends or show off that they have the most friends. There are those who are proud and feel powerful that they can control others, but this is not from God at all. Indeed, this spirit is from lucifer and is evil. Could you see me rudely leaving a dinner party with all my dear friends with no explanation? How discourteous. What is everyone to think, "She has abruptly left; maybe she does not like us, or she is upset." That is not being the salt of the Earth but rather a damaging hot pepper that destroys friends and hurts people. How much better to ask to be excused because you unfortunately have prior engagements, for it says clearly that you have truly loved the company and the fellowship of all your sisters and brothers, and you regret having to leave their wonderful company.

Kindness is communicating generously to everyone.

What if there is an activity, such as a slumber party or a movie, that you are not invited to? Well, you know that it is impossible to have everyone at every event all the time, and you should feel happy for those who are getting to go. Pray with a sincere heart that they have a good time, and know that God will let you have your day and your fun and your activity at some point. God is never going to leave you out, especially when you obey.

What about sports? How rude to leave out others in games when you think that they may not be the best athlete or they are not your best friend or they are new in town and you do not know them very well. How well-trained, educated, mature and kind you appear if you look around and meet the needs of others, making sure to include new people. As we have learned, we are never to say an unkind word or make fun of others, but rather, God wants us to build each other up. You must be the salt of the game or activity or fellowship, making every situation better. Always involve everyone around you, and never leave anyone out. If one of the children does not want to play a contact sport, ask that person to keep score or be a referee or help out in another way. Do you understand how painful being left out is? Have you ever had a burn, a bad cut or broken a bone? It is painful physically, but I can tell you that the pain of being hurt in the heart from being left out is even greater because that type of pain is not alleviated with medicine—no pills can help the deep ache of being left out nor the agony of the parents for their child. Oh, the heartache that could be stopped by merely showing an act of kindness to those left out.

Kindness is your calling…a part of the new clothing when you take off the old and put on the new. *Therefore, as God's chosen people, holy and dearly loved, clothe yourselves with compassion, kindness, humility, gentleness and patience. Colossians 3:12.* What a beautiful picture of how we are to look!

To be kind, you must slow down. Slow down and look around you. How ill-mannered it is not to be kind and include everyone. This does not mean just being kind to your best friend or to those who can give something back to you, but it means being kind to those who cannot give anything back, to the hurting or the needy, not expecting anything back in return...

He who despises his neighbor sins, but blessed is he who is kind to the needy. Proverbs 14:21

He who oppresses the poor shows contempt for their Maker, but whoever is kind to the needy honors God. Proverbs 14:31

He who is kind to the poor lends to the Lord, and he will reward him for what he has done. Proverbs 19:17

QUARRELING

What causes fights and quarrels among you? Don't they come from your desires that battle within you? You want something but don't get it. You kill and covet, but you cannot have what you want. You quarrel and fight. You do not have, because you do not ask God. James 4:1-2

How do you end anger and quarreling? The opposite of being kind is being selfish, and when you have selfish desires, you only want to play the game *you* want... and you do not want to play the game someone else has suggested. Think about this: you passionately want what you want to do, and you are equally passionate that you do not want to play what someone else wants to do. You want to play basketball, but the other children want to play soccer. Or one child wants to go swimming, and the other children want to play games inside. If you did not have any selfish desire, then you would not quarrel or be angry, and you would enjoy going along with what someone else really wanted to do. It is possible to suppress your desires, to give up your will, to make peace, to make others happy and to please your parents and God. Yes, you *can* give up your desires and be kind. It is possible to give up your selfish desires, and it is possible to learn to find joy in making others happy. Both of these actions make God happy and bring peace to the Earth. We may have desires, but we need to go to God for our desires… we should not try to make it happen on our own.

Praying is the key to kindness. Kindness starts with the oldest sibling in the family, and it can start as easily as this: a gentle word turns away wrath.[2] Show kindness when your sibling gets hurt; be empathetic to your brothers and sisters instead of ignoring their pain and tears. Try this at home the next time your siblings want to watch a certain TV show but you want to watch a different show: first, make sure your heart is right. Then ask God to lead everyone to a show that is good or helpful or something you can learn from. Call out to God and pray to change the TV channel, letting God know you want to watch only what He wants you to watch. You do not have to use pouting, crying, getting angry or quarreling to get your

---

2   *A gentle answer turns away wrath, but a harsh word stirs up anger. Proverbs 15:1*

way. **Just pray**. And watch God change the channel without a word. It works for everything. Obey God and be kind... and with prayer, you are taken care of. You will see that God can give back even better games to play, with more love and peace with your siblings and your friends! Amazing! It is a beautiful way to live.

There are no exceptions when it comes to being kind. Be kind to everyone, and especially parents—look them in the eyes and offer only kind words. This also includes other adults, too. If you are at a friend's house, make sure that you are respectful if their parents ask you what you would like and never be flippant or short. For example, if they ask if you would like a snack, do not just say "no." How polite it would be for everyone to learn that when people offer you food, you can say, "How kind of you to offer, thank you! But no thank you for right now." That is the appropriate way for you to excuse yourself from eating something you may not want or for which you are not hungry.

It is all about the motive of the heart. For years, parents have tried to teach children to say, "May I be excused?" before leaving the dining table. But parents, if you do not teach the children about the love behind it and the reason why a person should ask to be excused, children will not truly feel it nor remember it. They will wind up rolling their eyes and sighing sarcastically, "May I be excused?" because it has just turned into a rule. If this action comes from love, it is genuine and it is felt, because they will want those at the table to know how much you care about each person and how much they mean to you. Then from the child will come the beautiful words, "Oh, I love everyone here, but could you please forgive me and excuse me?" It will be heartfelt and real. The *motive* behind kindness is essential.

Children, be kind to the adults, to other children, to your friends, to your siblings, to everyone. Be patient, and pray for what you would like, expecting nothing from man but only from God alone. When you learn all this, you will be known as a kind person, and you will gain much respect. Your kindness will be contagious. In the end, you are not only helping others, but you are benefiting yourself. *A kindhearted woman gains respect, but ruthless men gain only wealth. A kind man benefits himself, but a cruel man brings trouble on himself. Proverbs 11:16-17*

God wrote the book on the good etiquette of kindness: *Finally, all of you, live in harmony with one another; be sympathetic, love as*

brothers, be compassionate and humble. I Peter 3:8

The Bible tells us that the righteous man is even kind to his animals.[3] How could anyone not be kind to the helpless? There is judgment for those who are cruel and for those who find secret

---

3 *A righteous man cares for the needs of his animal, but the kindest acts of the wicked are cruel. Proverbs 12:10*

pleasure in leaving others out, being divisive or inflicting pain on others. They will see God's justice one day.

In summary, you might think that people are impressed if you are intelligent, but I know now that the whole world is more impressed with kindness. It is time to work at slowing down, not being overly self-confident. Show kindness and be selfless…it is all about loving the children that God made. God loves His creations, and you must love and take the best of care of His offspring. Look back at the scripture from Peter earlier in this chapter. Be kind…for it is second only to brotherly love in its progression to the ultimate goal of love and godliness. It takes energy and determination to work from faith all the way up to kindness, but it is worth it. The acts of kindness feel so much better than cruelty, rudeness, jealousy, anger, and quarreling.

> IT TAKES ENERGY AND DETERMINATION TO WORK FROM FAITH ALL THE WAY UP TO KINDNESS, BUT IT IS WORTH IT.

Kindness keeps you from falling and ensures a warm welcome into eternal life! Jesus did kind deeds. To be kind, he had to have noticed what others needed. This is a whole new mindset to consider others better than yourself and notice what they need over your own needs.[4] Trust me, God will come back in and take care of you thru others when you take care of them first, and it will be better than just grabbing for yourself. Do you see what God has created with everyone taking care of others before themselves? He has created a community of the Kingdom of Love. This kind love is the ultimate goal and makes the world go around.

---

4   *Do nothing out of selfish ambition or vain conceit, but in humility consider others better than yourselves. Philippians 2:3*

There are physical athletics and spiritual athletics. Jesus Christ exercised the highest standard of spiritual athleticism.

Godly Competition... The Perfect Athlete

Chapter 14

We are learning to be more like Christ in all areas, but to be like Christ when it comes to a game can be challenging. Sports can be a lot of fun, but they can also conjure up characteristics that are totally unlike Christ and unlike God. We need God to learn how to play games and participate in sports in the way that Jesus Christ would have done.

We all have different personalities, and there is always someone who wants to lead the game and someone who wants to make up more rules for it. When it comes to sports, so much of it is based on opinion; that is why they have replays in football, so they can go back and look at the replay to see if the referee actually called a play correctly. And even with replays, you still see players getting into arguments with the referees and the other team.

In America, arguments around games, referees and rules are abundant, and it is even worse in other countries; sometimes you will hear of knockdown, drag-out fights. At one soccer game in Egypt, more than 70 spectators were killed when a riot erupted between rival fans.[1] Sometimes a whole country is fighting against another country. People are mad at the referee, they are mad at the

---

1 New York Times, "Egyptian Soccer Riot Kills More than 70," 2012

coach, they are mad at the players, and the players are mad at each other.

On top of that, sports often involve gambling. Gambling is when spectators bet money on the outcome of a sporting event—who will win and who will lose. When people gamble, it can make them even angrier at the game and the players. This all leads to "Monday Morning Quarterbacks" where people watch the games over the weekend, and then come into work Monday morning arguing with one another about the various calls and actions in the game.

Competitiveness is an emotion that gets the adrenaline up and causes people to take sides. Many times it can make you feel like you need to defend yourself. Sadly, there can be situations that are very unjust in sports because people do cheat, and they do get angry and act out. This even happens on the playground—you may have seen someone get mad, take the ball, slam it down and storm off when they are called "out" in a game. That is a sad thing to witness. You are taking something that was a game and turning it into something unpleasant. Everyone is in shock, and it takes the fun and enjoyment out of the game. This person has also taken time away from others because when they slammed the ball down, it did not go to the next person in line, and someone had to run to retrieve the ball. This bad attitude robs both fun and time from your friends and playmates.

> EVERY TIME YOU PLAY A GAME, YOU NEED TO KNOW THAT HOW YOU HANDLE THIS COMPETITION WILL BE A TEST OF YOUR CHARACTER.

You will stop that kind of behavior when you understand that no one is impressed with whether or not you did well in the game. They will not remember how you played, but they are going to remember if you were angry. People will remember your anger because it made everyone very uncomfortable, especially when you were mad about something like being called "out" in a game. The next time they play, they are not going to want to include you. What is even worse is that if you keep doing it, they are not going to want to hang out with you at all.

Your goal is to show the characteristics of Christ no matter how you are playing that day.

Children in the fourth thru seventh grade seem to have the hardest time with anger and competitiveness, but some people just never grow up. On television, you have probably seen tennis players who get upset and throw their rackets down in anger or baseball players who shout at the umpires or other players. These are adults who do not know how to handle competition in a Godly way.

An Opportunity to Be Like Christ

Every time you play a game, you need to know that how you handle this competition will be a test of your character. What can you do before you play to help you pass this test? The answer is to *pray*, and pray with others. Pray for protection, and pray for your attitude to be just like Jesus Christ so that when the game is over, others will still want you to play with them. If you are sacrificially a leader and are helping others, then everyone will enjoy being with you, but they will not like it if you are always trying to be the best or bragging about yourself. Bragging about yourself is not a characteristic of real love.[2] Now, everyone has their up days and their down days. There will be days when you get every basketball thru

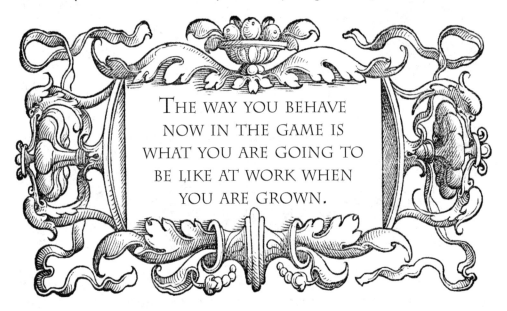

THE WAY YOU BEHAVE NOW IN THE GAME IS WHAT YOU ARE GOING TO BE LIKE AT WORK WHEN YOU ARE GROWN.

the hoop… and then other days when you do not make a single shot. But your goal is to show the characteristics of Christ no matter how you are playing that day.

What is inside of a person that makes them angry and allows them to throw the ball down or get into an argument? Most of the time, it is embarrassment. Maybe they tripped while jumping rope, and they want to blame someone else for the way they were

---

2   *Love is patient, love is kind. It does not envy, it does not boast, it is not proud.* I Corinthians 13:4

swinging the rope. They want to point the finger at someone to try to get the attention off themselves. Or they may have a high expectation of themselves in basketball, and when they miss the shot, they get upset and embarrassed because they did not live up to their own expectation, and they wanted others to see how good they are.

We can end that today. We are going to end this behavior because we are going to tell ourselves the Truth: that a game is there for enjoyment; it is there for fun. Games are there so we can learn to laugh at ourselves, and we are there to make every situation better. We are to be the salt of the Earth,[3] and when you are the salt, you make the game better. First of all, you should not even expect to be able to play in the game at all, but if you do get to play, your goal is to be the salt in that game and make that game better and more fun for everyone.

How do you make a game better? First of all, remember to pray! But after praying, there is one question you ask yourself every time: Would you want someone to do that to you?[4] This will give you the answer to everything that you are supposed to do in every situation. Ask yourself: Do you want someone to bump you when they are playing soccer? No, so do not play too rough toward others. Do you want someone to scream loudly, "You are out!" when you probably already know that you are out? I know I would rather them say something like, "Good job! Okay, next person up!" Then the attention is off of you, and they have said something positive. Getting an out is hard enough, but hearing someone tell you "good job!" is so encouraging and makes the situation better because you do not feel so bad about yourself. In games, we know that we are all going

---

3   *You are the salt of the earth. But if the salt loses its saltiness, how can it be made salty again? It is no longer good for anything, except to be thrown out and trampled by men. Matthew 5:13*
4   Please see more about "Do Unto Others" on page 157.

to make mistakes and lose at times. It is something we all expect of ourselves and each other, so we do not want someone yelling out for everyone to hear, "Hey, you messed up!" and we definitely do not want to treat others that way.

Remember, it is just a game, and games are just a mirror image of what we are doing in life. We are always learning thru these games, and the way you behave now in the game is what you are going to be like at work when you are grown. If you keep up the bad attitude, you will likely not even be able to find a job. If you do manage to get a job and you still have a bad attitude whenever you mess up—being angry and blaming others—then you will not be able to keep that job. God is trying to teach us all how to have a good attitude when we make a mistake.

A Test Set Up Just for You

The main thing we have to understand in life is that everything is screened by God. God knows everything that is going to happen and everything that is happening. Maybe it was not your day to win at foursquare. It was not your day on that video game. It was not your time to hit the home run; instead, you made three strikes and you were out. It was just not your day for winning, and there are going to be more of those types of days than there will be home-run days. Every time you play a game, you are praying, "O God, help me to expect that I may not hit the basketball hoop. I may not hit the home run. God, help me to know that there are going to be other days, and if I do not have a bad attitude, my friends might ask me to play again." They will want to play with you because you are a good sport. There will be more days to have fun.

What if the situation really seems to be unfair? Maybe you were called out, and you are sure that you were not out. Remember that

God is a God of justice. You simply have to walk away from the situation and know that there is going to be another day and another time, and it is all up to God. If you speak up and argue back, then even if you are correct, you are actually making things worse. You are no longer being the salt—in fact, you are being the opposite, and that is not being like Christ. In the end, who cares about the game

WHAT REALLY IMPRESSES PEOPLE IS GOOD CHARACTER, CHRISTLIKE CHARACTER.

anyway? What really impresses people is seeing someone handle a difficult situation in an encouraging way. That is impressive. Most people are not really impressed if you made a basket or ran fast... in fact, they probably will not even remember it. What really impresses people is good character, Christlike character. Do you really think Jesus Christ would be arguing back with someone over something so small? No! So be prepared for that test. Expect it. Put that into your training program. Instead of doing one-hundred physical pushups for training every day, do one-hundred spiritual pushups in humility. Every day you should expect someone to say something like that to you so that you can be ready to walk away from it and say, "Oh, I guess you are right. I was out."

What about when you are playing a board game and you have to go back three spaces? Maybe you were almost to the point of winning a game, and then someone sends your piece all the way back to Start. Do you get mad or upset? No! First of all, you need to have prayed before you even started the game; that puts your heart on the right track before you even begin. Then you tell yourself, "I am going to lose this game, and I am going to make everyone laugh when I do." You make it fun! You say, "Oh, man!" but you are not really mad when you say it, so it makes everyone laugh. A game is meant to be fun and to make the time spent with friends better—it is not for you to show off or to win every time. It is really there for you to be like Jesus Christ and for you to lose. You actually look forward to losing!

> GAMES ARE ALL ABOUT LEARNING TO LAUGH AT YOURSELF WHEN YOU MESS UP, BUT THEY ARE ALSO ABOUT ENCOURAGING OTHERS WHEN YOU WIN.

You know that there is a just and fair God out there, and your day is coming. When it is your turn and you are winning, then you want to make sure you are a good sport. Games are all about learning to laugh at yourself when you mess up, but they are also about encouraging others when you win. Get the attention off yourself quickly by saying, "Wow, you came in second!" or "You are great at this game!"

It is just a game. It should not have anything to do with your ego or making you feel better because you won. How could you feel better about yourself just because you rolled the dice and got some numbers that allowed you beat your opponent? That is the kind of game where even a monkey could win!

A Chance to Bring Joy to Others

Sports and games are there so we can interact and have fun. Who wins or who loses does not make any difference. Your self-esteem must come from having the Fruits of the Spirit. The Bible does not include basketball, foursquare, athletic abilities, musical talent or being the best at a game in the list of the Fruits of the Spirit in Galatians 5. Our goal in life is to make it into eternity with God. This goal is not based on our ability to perform at any game or sport, but it is about having the characteristics of God's Holy Spirit and imitating His personality in every situation. What you want to excel at is being good at copying God's personality and the personality of His Son. We are copying the best person we can think of, and that is Jesus Christ. He was in love with God, and he would lay his life down for everyone else so that they could also find God and make it to Heaven.

That is the characteristic you want to excel at. Work on winning at being Christlike by looking for the needs of others. Does a teammate need a drink of water? What can you do to help your friends? Be the salt everywhere you go. Encourage others. "You are so good at jumping rope!" "I just love the way you play the piano!" "You are a good soccer player!" or "The way you sing is beautiful!" That is the salt, and the next thing you know, everyone is enjoying time together and no one is throwing a ball down or walking off in a huff.

Therefore, since we are surrounded by such a great cloud of witnesses, let us throw off everything that hinders and the sin that so easily entangles, and let us run with perseverance the race marked out for us. Let us fix our eyes on Jesus, the author and perfecter of our faith, who for the joy set before him endured the cross, scorning its shame, and sat down at the right hand of the throne of God. Consider him who endured such opposition from sinful men, so that you will not grow weary and lose heart. Hebrews 12:1-3

This Scripture will help you to slow down and recognize the testing and remember that God is doing everything for a reason. If you find yourself getting out of control, stop and pray. This is not about the game. This is a test of your heart and your character. This is about

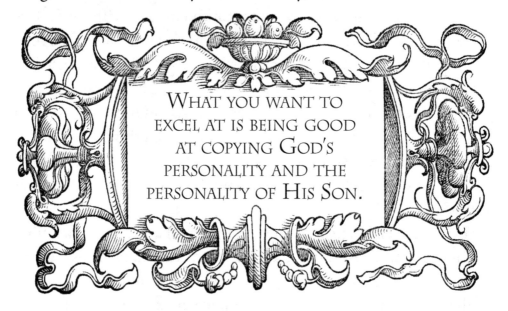

WHAT YOU WANT TO EXCEL AT IS BEING GOOD AT COPYING GOD'S PERSONALITY AND THE PERSONALITY OF HIS SON.

being the salt and making the situation better, making everyone else happy, and knowing it is not your day today. You will have another day.

Do not lose heart. Make every game enjoyable for everyone else and pray more. Consider what you are doing. Think about what a game really is…just a game. I am praying in the name of Jesus Christ that all of us learn to do this with our competition and throw our competitive drive into our character, copying Jesus Christ and being more like our Heavenly Father each day.

PRAYER

Father God, you are the maker of sports and athletes, and you are the one who is the most coordinated of all. You can do all of it a million times better than any of us. You are better at basketball, knockout, foursquare, soccer, football, video games and every game on the planet. You are the Great Athlete, and you know how to act when you are playing a game. You know that the greater laws of love are so much more important than any game. We need your wisdom. We need you, God, so that we can be extraordinarily different—we can be the salt. And I pray for your Spirit to come down on these children so that they can all learn to play a game, enjoy it, and be just like Jesus Christ. In Jesus' name we pray this, Amen

David dared anyone to defy God's armies.

You should look for people who are genuinely Christlike, then emulate their examples. When I was young and read about King David, I was envious with a Godly jealousy when I saw that God said David was the apple of His eye. I prayed, "O God, would You please make me the apple of Your eye? Teach me what to do so that I can be the apple of Your eye." I wanted God's approval, and that is what you need to emulate. You must seek God's favor. Page 198.

Chapter 15

How can a young man keep his way pure? By living according to your word. I seek you with all my heart; do not let me stray from your commands. I have hidden your word in my heart that I might not sin against you. Praise be to you, O LORD; teach me your decrees. With my lips I recount all the laws that come from your mouth. I rejoice in following your statutes as one rejoices in great riches. I meditate on your precepts and consider your ways. I delight in your decrees; I will not neglect your word. Psalm 119:9-16

King David wrote this Psalm, and it is one of my all-time favorite passages for guiding children. King David is an example of someone who sought God. In fact, this Psalm says he sought God with *all* of his heart. As a young man, King David did not have a lot of recreation and entertainment equipment. He was out by himself in a field with sheep that could not talk to him. He was in God's Word every day and memorizing Scripture. Every day, he sought God as he was tending the sheep, taking them to green pastures, and protecting them from wolves and bears. From his experience shepherding animals, he became one of the best shepherds of men who has ever lived, next to Jesus Christ, because he shepherded the people to a love for God.

When I was a child, I remember reading my Bible, and all I had when I was very young was just the New Testament. We were told a few of the stories from the Old Testament, but no one actually read the whole book. Obviously, all that King David had was the Old Testament—the Law and the Prophets and some of the writings of the Prophets who came before him. He did not have the Proverbs, but he taught them to his son Solomon, who later wrote them down. So David did not have as much as you and I have.

However, it is not about memorizing Scripture simply to repeat the words or to show other people that you can memorize it. Memorization is not even required; the Bible does not say anything about Jesus memorizing it, or that they sat and quoted long memorizations of Scripture. No, Jesus followed the Spirit of God and lived it out—that is what he was known for.

What did David do? He put Scripture to song so that he could remember, and he wrote down his own experiences. He put his poetry to music or had a music director put it to music, and they sang it. Merely reading those words does not make you righteous. You could be a young person and not even know how to read and still be like Christ. So it is not about just reading or memorizing; rather, it is letting these words hit your heart so that you *change*, and it is about letting the Holy Spirit teach you and guide you.

THE APPLE OF GOD'S EYE

You should look for people who are genuinely Christlike, then emulate their examples. When I was young and read about King David, I was envious when I saw that God said David was the apple of His eye.[1] I prayed, "O God, would You please make me the apple of

---

1   *Keep me as the apple of your eye; hide me in the shadow of your wings. Psalm 17:8*

Your eye? Teach me what to do so that I can be the apple of Your eye." I was jealous, but it was a Godly jealousy. I wanted God's approval, and that is what you need to emulate. You must seek God's favor—otherwise, when you are older, you will look for the approval of man. The girls will look for the boys' approval, and the boys will look for the girls' approval. If you are not strong in your focus on seeking only

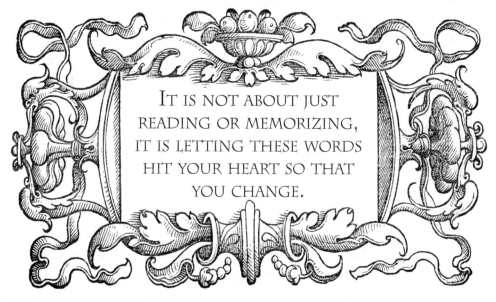

It is not about just reading or memorizing, it is letting these words hit your heart so that you change.

God's approval, a boyfriend or girlfriend may pull your focus off of God instead of you leading that friend to worship God *with* you.

When my children were young and making friends, they were not about to abandon the focus on God first. If you wanted to be friends with Michael or Elizabeth, you had to go where they were going. Do you really think King David would leave his religion to be friends with someone who did not want to focus on God? No, God was everything to him! God answered his prayers. King David wanted to be strong, so he prayed that he would be, and God answered that prayer and made him strong enough to kill a lion and a bear! When he was young, he took a stone and killed Goliath. He was ready to take on enemies of God who defied and insulted God and His Kingdom. It would be like someone insulting a Godly leader, and you are ready to say, "You are insulting one of our Godly leaders, one of our mentors, and you are making fun of someone. We do not do that. We uphold those who uphold God."

God has rescued us from having the wrong focus and allowed us to have a blessed life, but it is not just for fun and games. Do not be so prideful that you go your own way and then realize at the end of the day that you did not follow God at all. Or perhaps you do not even feel Him guiding you, leading you, waking you up in the night. The reason you do not feel the Spirit guiding you may be because you are prideful. You may have the attitude that you are not going to let some other spirit guide you or someone else tell you what to do. Please, never be like that! The irony of the prideful is that they are so unwise. Prideful people are the exact opposite of wise—the Bible refers to the prideful as foolish.[2] This life is not about being prideful. This life is about finding God.

There are children who disobey their parents; and it may be sweetly done, but they always get their way. Think back to your own parents. Down deep, do you feel like you are able to whine or stomp your feet or shed some tears or pout and finally get your way with your parents? Do you know down deep that if there is something you really want, you are able to talk them into it even though they do not want it? As you get older you may think, "I know that I will obey a little and do some things to gain the praise of my parents, but if I really want something, I can trump them. I know what to do to avoid doing something they want me to do. I know how to get my way." Parents may be fooled, and parents can easily spoil you as children. However, the Word of God does not spoil you. If no

---

2   *A fool's mouth lashes out with pride, but the lips of the wise protect them. Proverbs 14:3*

one ever tells you that you are doing something wrong, then you should turn to the Word and let God redirect you and guide you all He can, because it is a sign that you are truly loved. If you are going the wrong way, Godly parents, loving Shepherds and kind mentors will tell you the right way to go. This means that God loves you and that your parents love you.

THE LIVING WATER

Notice that as you get older, various recreational activities are not as thrilling as they once were. While being outside in the water is great, the Water of Life and the Streams of Living Water are better. In John 4, Jesus said to a Samaritan woman, "Come to me, and I will give you living water, and you will never be thirsty again." "Give me that drink," the woman cried. He said, "I am that drink." When you look for Christlike people, know that they have access to that Living Water. Those are the people you should imitate. You could copy all kinds of people and characteristics, but there is one most important thing to copy, and that is a relationship with God. You should be someone who is desperate for God's lead. King David was desperate for that lead from God! How *can* a young man keep his way pure? How can a young woman keep her way pure? The answer is by absorbing the Word, knowing the Word, and then living the Word. The Word is a living thing. We can imitate others as they imitate Christ.[3] You look for those who have the Spirit of God in

> GOD'S SPIRIT WILL FLOW OUT OF SAINTS LIKE A FLOWER BLOOMING EVERYWHERE THEY GO—IN THEIR SPEECH, THEIR KINDNESS, AND THEIR GENTLENESS.

---

3   *Follow my example, as I follow the example of Christ. I Corinthians 11:1*

them—look for love, joy, peace, patience, kindness, goodness, faithfulness, gentleness and self-control.[4] That Spirit will come out of Saints like a flower blooming everywhere they go—in their speech, their kindness, and their gentleness. If you ever see these people angry, it is because someone is hurting God's Church, His Kingdom, but even in those situations, you will see long-suffering attitudes from these Spirit-led people.

The gentleness and self-control of God-led people is God's personality coming thru them. Christ was never prideful. David was never prideful. King David danced in the streets when God's Word came back to His people. He danced to God and wrote songs. He prayed to God and read the Word. He searched for God and sought His lead. He kept God's precepts in his heart and repeated them over and over—all the words, all the thoughts, all the activities. That is what you are to be doing. You should *want* to be like King David. You should *want* to be like Christ, who by the age of 12 could teach about the Words of God and could discuss the Scriptures.[5] He actually could take on some of the arguments and interpret the Bible. He knew God, and he knew what God meant in the Word. You should never want to imitate those doing the wrong things, people being arrogant, disobedient or boastful. Never copy the children or youth who are pulling away and not following their authorities, but copy those who seek out their parents and authorities

> YOUR LIFE WILL HAVE PURPOSE, AND YOU WILL FIND THAT LIVING WATER WHEN ALL YOU WANT IS TO BE LIKE CHRIST, WHOSE ONLY FOCUS WAS TO SEEK GOD AND DO HIS WILL.

---

4   *But the fruit of the Spirit is love, joy, peace, patience, kindness, goodness, faithfulness, gentleness and self-control. Against such things there is no law. Galatians 5:22-23*
5   See Chapter 16, "Age of Accountability," for more about this story.

and obey joyfully. Never imitate the ones who wiggle around and do not pay attention to lessons, but instead copy the ones who are listening, taking notes and putting the lessons in their hearts.

May we all emulate Christ. May we find others who are imitating Christ and copy them. Your life will have purpose, and you will find that Living Water when all you want is to be like Christ, whose only focus was to seek God and do His will! We should all beg in our hearts to be the apple of God's eye like King David. Do you want to have a purpose? Do you want to have a blessed life? Or are you just focused on the here and the now, grabbing what you want but never getting answered prayers? We are here to find God. I pray in the name of Jesus Christ that other activities do not dominate your days, but instead, your days are dominated with seeking after God. Then when God grants you fun recreation time and great meals, He will make the recreation incredible and the food delightful. If you seek the recreation and the food first—before seeking God—it will not be fun, and the food will not taste good, and you will have a disappointing day. But if you will seek God first, then you will have an amazing, blessed, beautiful day.

PRAYER

Father God, we adore you. This is your world. This is your Universe. This is your day and your way. O God, You are the One who causes the world to spin around. You are the One who brings the sun around. You are the One who brings the stars and the light. O God, I pray for these young people. They are going to need to be strong. They are going to have to seek you on their own and imitate the right examples that you have put before us. O God, we want more of you and less of ourselves. Father, I pray in the name of Jesus Christ that these words will sink deep into the hearts of the children and that they will seek to be the apple of your eye. We pray that everyone will realize that if they do not seek you, the day will not be blessed. We pray that you will lead us to people we can imitate, lead our conversations and our actions, guide our feet. All of this we pray in the name of the beautiful Jesus Christ, our perfect example, Amen!

One time when Jesus was 12 years old, his family went to Jerusalem for Passover, and they left without realizing he was not with them. When they returned to search for him, the Bible reports, "After three days they found him in the temple courts, sitting among the teachers, listening to them and asking them questions. Everyone who heard him was amazed at his understanding and his answers. When his parents saw him, they were astonished. His mother said to him, "Son, why have you treated us like this? Your father and I have been anxiously searching for you." "Why were you searching for me?" he asked. "Didn't you know I had to be in my Father's house?" Luke 2:46-49

The Age of Accountability

Chapter 16

I have taken an oath and confirmed it, that I will follow your righteous laws. Psalm 119:106

BABY DEDICATION

The children of old, starting with Israel, Moses and Abraham, had hearts that were given over to God. Hebrew parents would bring a child to the Temple, and the child would be dedicated to God. In Luke 2, we read about Jesus being brought to the temple. *Joseph and Mary took him to Jerusalem to present him to the Lord (as it is written in the Law of the Lord, "Every firstborn male is to be consecrated to the Lord")... Luke 2:22b-23* At dedication, parents are making a public declaration that they themselves will honor God and do whatever it takes to make sure that their children are brought up knowing how to love God with all their heart, and then love each other.

Baby dedication is a beautiful time, but the parents are the ones dedicating the child. It is quite another thing when the children themselves are dedicating their own lives to God and have shown that they are full of the Holy Spirit.

Baptism

Typically, the first step that the child makes is to choose to be baptized. They are making a confession before God and the world that they are dying to their own will and living for the will of God from that point forward. Romans 6 tells us…

What shall we say, then? Shall we go on sinning so that grace may increase? By no means! We died to sin; how can we live in it any longer? Or don't you know that all of us who were baptized into Christ Jesus were baptized into his death? We were therefore buried with him through baptism into death in order that, just as Christ was raised from the dead through the glory of the Father, we too may live a new life. If we have been united with him like this in his death, we will certainly also be united with him in his resurrection. Romans 6:1-5

We are committing to be baptized into this death, going under ALL the way… and then we can be united in this resurrection if we are *united* in the death. *The world and its desires pass away, but the man who does the will of God lives forever. I John 2:17* The thought of living forever and ever is exhilarating! This is a religion of loving God with all of your heart, and all of your soul, and all of your mind, and all of your strength, and then loving others as yourself. It is a tremendous occupation.

Confirmation

Confirmation is a very special time when a child has the opportunity to express before the Church that they are personally dedicating their lives to God. Before being confirmed, the child should be baptized with a public testimony of their faith and love of God. Then, when the child is at the age of 12 or 13, on the day of Pentecost, they may be ready to be confirmed and make a public acknowledgment that this is not just the parents' choice, but also the child's own choice to have an eternal covenant relationship with God. Confirmation is just one more way to publicly express your dedication to God alone.

Pentecost is traditionally the time for Confirmation because of its deep symbolism for our lives. It is one of the biggest events in history that must be correctly communicated to the following generations. It was on Pentecost, approximately 3,300 years ago, when Moses ascended to God, and then God descended to man to give the precious Covenant thru the Ten Commandments. It is one of the most important historical events ever recorded in the life of mankind; however, most Christians do not recognize this event as a Christian event—even though about 1,300 years later on that very same day, God poured out His Spirit on all those who were waiting past the time of Christ. Both events are central to their salvation *and* to our salvation.

> SINCE A CHILD'S HEART AND PERSONAL DEDICATION TO GOD IS EVERYTHING FOR THE PARENTS, THE PREPARATION OF THE CHILD FOR THIS PERSONAL RELATIONSHIP IS OUR MOST IMPORTANT AGENDA IN LIFE.

Understanding this deeply symbolic event—the gift of the renowned Ten Commandments and the Holy Spirit—gives us the tools that we need to establish a relationship with God and an understanding of how to obey and receive the Holy Spirit so we can please God. This is our very life. With these tools, you can sense His lead, and it allows you to step back and give up control and let the Spirit lead so you can walk with God the rest of your days.

Since a child's heart and personal dedication to God is everything to the parents, the preparation of the child for this personal relationship is our most important agenda in life. There is something special about the age of 12 and 13. Every year of life should be spent preparing for this most special year and day in which a child makes their own personal decision to serve God for the rest of their life… or not. In most cases up until this point, they have merely followed their family's religion, but now they take personal responsibility for their baptism, their decision and their actions—they prove their baptism of repentance by their deeds.[1] The parents have done their job according to Deuteronomy 6, and now it is time for the child to take responsibility for this walk before the Lord and make sure they are finding God and His Will thru seeking Him in Bible reading and resources that keep them focused on the Commands of God, such as All Access and Weigh Down classes.

Circumcision of the Heart

There have always been levels of accountability, or expectations of responsibility, for children. In the Jewish population, parents would have their child circumcised on the eighth day and then name the child. Although circumcision is not required today, it was a sign that the child's heart was given to the Lord. Remnant Baby Dedication at Pentecost each year is parallel to circumcision, in which the child's heart is given over to the Lord.

Then God said to Abraham, "As for you, you must keep my covenant, you and your descendants after you for the generations to come. This is my covenant with you and your descendants after you, the covenant you are to keep: Every male among you shall be circumcised. You are to undergo circumcision, and it will be the sign of the covenant between me and you. For the generations to come every male among you who is eight

---

1 *I preached that they should repent and turn to God and prove their repentance by their deeds. Acts 26:20b*

days old must be circumcised, including those born in your household or bought with money from a foreigner—those who are not your offspring. Whether born in your household or bought with your money, they must be circumcised. My covenant in your flesh is to be an everlasting covenant. Any uncircumcised male, who has not been circumcised in the flesh, will be cut off from his people; he has broken my covenant." Genesis 17:9-14

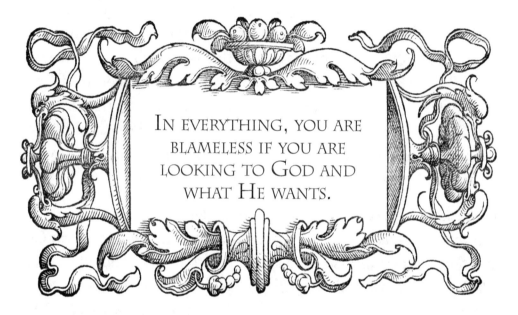

IN EVERYTHING, YOU ARE BLAMELESS IF YOU ARE LOOKING TO GOD AND WHAT HE WANTS.

Then the Bible says, *"All who cross over, those twenty years old or more, are to give an offering to the LORD." Exodus 30:14* This means the 20-year-old is old enough to make his own money and give his own tithe. Between circumcision and the age of 20, the Jewish people have Bar Mitzvah, which means "Son of the Covenant," and Bat Mitzvah, which means "Daughter of the Covenant." For thousands of years, this has traditionally been the age of spiritual personal responsibility. When the boy turned 13 and when the girl turned 12 (because girls naturally mature faster), they publicly testified to their devotion.

Again, from reading Deuteronomy 6, you see that it is totally up to the parents to immerse the child in the Christian way of life at this point, to know the true Bible history and heritage and to have knowledge that is conducive to developing a relationship with the Most Holy Lord.

The age of 12 or 13 is a milestone for children, and a time when something comes from within to want to walk before the Lord God Almighty and be blameless. This relationship is to be an everlasting covenant like a marriage—in this way, each child is married to God, Christ and His Kingdom of Love *before* they have an earthly marriage. When you bring up a child in the way that they should go, they will not depart from it.[2] The Spirit of God given to His people will move the children toward His heart.

> TRUE GOD-CENTERED LOVE IS A RARE LIGHT.

I will establish my covenant as an everlasting covenant between me and you and your descendants after you for the generations to come, to be your God and the God of your descendants after you. The whole land of Canaan, where you are now an alien, I will give as an everlasting possession to you and your descendants after you; and I will be their God. Genesis 17:7-8

When you study circumcision in the Bible, you know that as time goes on, what God was intending with this Covenant was a circumcision of the *heart*. After Christ came, a circumcision group arose and focused on cleaning up the external, but Paul argued that it is the *internal* that truly matters. Whenever anything is done, it is never about the praise of men; it is never about the external. It is always about the heart, a heart that is walking before God and is

---

2 *Train a child in the way he should go, and when he is old he will not turn from it. Proverbs 22:6*

blameless.[3] In everything, you are blameless if you are looking to God and what He wants.

When you are blameless before your parents, you are always willing to see them, and when you are blameless before your boss, you can look them in the eyes. But if you are guilty, then it is difficult for you. You will hang your head in shame. Your goal is to wake up every day with no shame and to go to bed at night and not be awakened with memories of things that are embarrassing. The Holy Spirit works at all ages, but by 12 and 13 years of age, the conscience is strong within a child. When we live to raise each child to be blameless before God, there is no shame, and anyone who trusts in the Lord will never be dismayed.[4]

There will always be a spirit of legalism that tries to enter the Church and turn this "Confirmation" covenant with the Lord into a test of knowledge. Information that makes you fall more in love with God is the knowledge we will present to our children, and it comes from our own genuine relationship. If you feel like you have more to go, you can always guide your children to be around those who have a deep relationship with God and Christ. You can read about Christ and Paul and King David, who adored God with all their heart, soul, mind and strength. When you have dedicated your child at birth and put this age of 12 and 13 as the highest achievement in life, you will meet your goal. However, if academics, sports, talents, popularity, or career goals are more important to you, this day will be empty. Jesus Christ raised the bar from the behavior of those in the Old Covenant. In the New Covenant, it is a superior Covenant with

---

3   *I am God Almighty; walk before me and be blameless. Genesis 17:1b*
4   *So this is what the Sovereign Lord says: "See, I lay a stone in Zion, a tested stone, a precious cornerstone for a sure foundation; the one who trusts will never be dismayed." Isaiah 28:16*

a superior High Priest, and therefore it is the calling of a superior relationship with God.

In My Father's House

The age of 13 is not too early to make that choice. In Luke 2, we learn about the example of Christ:

Every year his parents went to Jerusalem for the Feast of the Passover. When he was twelve years old, they went up to the Feast, according to the custom. After the Feast was over, while his parents were returning home, the boy Jesus stayed behind in Jerusalem, but they were unaware of it. Thinking he was in their company, they traveled on for a day. Then they began looking for him among their relatives and friends. When they did not find him, they went back to Jerusalem to look for him. After three days they found him in the temple courts, sitting among the teachers, listening to them and asking them questions. Everyone who heard him was amazed at his understanding and his answers. When his parents saw him, they were astonished. His mother said to him, "Son, why have you treated us like this? Your father and I have been anxiously searching for you." "Why were you searching for me?" he asked. "Didn't you know I had to be in my Father's house?" But they did not understand what he was saying to them. Then he went down to Nazareth with them and was obedient to them. But his mother treasured all these things in her heart. And Jesus grew in wisdom and stature, and in favor with God and men. Luke 2:41-52

There are several amazing concepts in this passage. First and foremost are Jesus' questions, "Why were you searching for me? Why did you have to look around to find me? Did you not know that I had to be about my Father's business, that I would be in the House of God?" They did not find him in the restaurants, in the marketplace, or at a friend's house. He was found where they should have known he was going to be.

Children, do your parents have to search for *you*? Or do they know where to find you? Are you seeking out God, searching thru His Word, studying and learning? Are you asking questions of the Shepherds? Are you seeking to understand meanings and to consider what the early Christians were doing? Are *you* studying Christ? You are never too young to start that pursuit.

Parents, you should know that is where your child should be. Does your child have a heart like that? Would you know where to find them?

By this age, youth can publicly state what is in their heart and make a decision that they are choosing True Christianity. "This is my religion. I am laying my life down and living for God and investing in the hereafter. This is what *I* want to do. *I* personally want to take on the responsibility. *I* need to make sure that I am going to Heaven, and that I am doing what God wants."

> YOUR MAIN FOCUS WILL ALWAYS BE YOUR RELATIONSHIP WITH GOD, BECAUSE IF YOU HAVE A RELATIONSHIP WITH GOD, YOU HAVE EVERYTHING…

You have reached a level of maturity when you have a fear inside of you, a fear of losing God—He is your *Everything*. He is your Banker; He is your Financier; He helps with your relationships. He is your Healer and your Comforter when you are hurting; He controls everything. He gave you breath, and He is the One you will face when you leave this earthly life.

Again, 13 is not too young to make this choice. At that age, I was in love with God, and in my public-school setting, I was seeking out those who would want to talk about God. By this age I was pulling together groups of others who wanted to sing and share about God. And at 13, I could tell that there was more out there—more to seek, more to understand about this relationship with God. I evangelized and brought other people to Church because I believed that there needed to be a *response* to God. This next generation in the Remnant of Believers can do all of these things and so much more, because they have adults guiding them who know this Truth and honor this relationship with God.

If Jesus at age 12 was debating in the Temple and giving good answers, our children, too, can get into the Word of God, understand it, and help other people understand it. This is a beautiful goal of an evangelistic and powerful relationship with God. These will be 13-year-olds who are going to grow up to lead the Church with power. When someone is looking for them and asks where to find them, we will know that their business will be about God's House. They will be taking care of His House and His people and concerned about His Kingdom.

ONE FOCUS

Your main focus will always be your relationship with God, because if you have a relationship with God, you have *everything*. You have the Triangle and answered prayers.[5] You can know that if you have a relationship with God you are going to make it thru life, and then you are going to make it into eternal life. I recently told my granddaughter Grace that for her to graduate from school, the world will have one set of hurdles for her to jump over; however, I will have another. I will ask all of her siblings and cousins this simple

---

5   See Chapter 9, "Connected to the Heavens," for more about the Triangle and answered prayers.

yet telling question: "Do you know that Grace loves you?" If all the siblings and cousins answer "Yes," then she can graduate in my book!

It all comes down to one focus, and parents who work with their children and teach them this focus end up with children who are secure and Godly, with the beautiful characteristics of Christ and a deep relationship with God.

It is time for a new life. It is time for serious decisions. It is time to read about this life and self-denial that Jesus Christ is calling us to. It is time to read about resolve and what it means to be resolved. Daniel was a great example of resolving to obey God. *Daniel resolved not to defile himself... Daniel 1:8a* This is an exciting challenge and opportunity for you to be even more dedicated to God and to be baptized into Christ.

In the end, parents, there is no greater joy than seeing your children come to the Lord.[6]

Prayer

Father, God, we just praise you so much for Pentecost, this amazing event when your Spirit came down, you touched history, and then you touched the direction of all mankind. Thank you for giving us your Son and showing us how directed he was by the age of 12. We pray for this age of Confirmation, that our children understand this responsibility. They are going to need to cling onto you, but we pray that they will utilize the tool of your Holy Spirit and the Ten Commandments, which we appreciate so much. May they use those wisely. May they take all those Commands to heart. God, we pray for all the parents who are raising their children up and helping them to see that this age of accountability is so important. Father, may you pour your Spirit out on our children as they are obedient. May they know that they get access to your Spirit only thru obedience. All of this we pray in Jesus' name, Amen.

---

6   *I have no greater joy than to hear that my children are walking in the truth. III John 1:4*

"Can we find anyone like this man, one in whom is the spirit of God?" Then Pharaoh said to Joseph, "Since God has made all this known to you, there is no one so discerning and wise as you. You shall be in charge of my palace, and all my people are to submit to your orders. Only with respect to the throne will I be greater than you." Genesis 41:38b-40 Page 221.

The Story of Joseph

Chapter 17

The story of Joseph in Genesis is one of the most amazing examples of "flipping it," which means changing our perspective off of ourselves and seeing things from God's perspective. This true story is better than any movie ever made. Joseph was a young man, just 17 years old, when he was sold into slavery. Can you imagine leaving your parents and your brothers and sisters and being sold off as a slave in another country at the age of 17? Yet he was so close to God and so sensitive to His Spirit—so capable as a worker, so able to take care of an entire estate—that in everything he did and everything he touched, his hand was blessed.

The Lord was with Joseph and he prospered, and he lived in the house of his Egyptian master. When his master saw that the Lord was with him and that the Lord gave him success in everything he did, Joseph found favor in his eyes and became his attendant. Potiphar put him in charge of his household, and he entrusted to his care everything he owned. From the time he put him in charge of his household and of all that he owned, the Lord blessed the household of the Egyptian because of Joseph. The blessing of the Lord was on everything Potiphar had, both in the house and in the field. So he left in Joseph's care everything he had; with Joseph in charge, he did not concern himself with anything except the food he ate. Genesis 39:2-6

Can you imagine being that in tune to God? But this did not just start when Joseph was 17 years old. It began even when he was a young child. He had dreams from God as a young boy, and he was honest and good. God does not put his Spirit into young men who are not upright. Joseph's brothers, however, were not as upright. Joseph had a dream that they would bow down to him one day.[1] He was exactly right.

IT IS THE SPIRIT OF GOD INSIDE OF A PERSON THAT MAKES SOMEONE SUCCESSFUL.

Think about your life today. Your daily goal should be to get everything right. You will be honest with your parents, and you will do everything they ask you to do. If they ask you to do a task, you pay careful attention to them and do the work requested. You put your teachers and parents above your friends and your playtime. When a teacher walks into the room, you stop and listen to the teacher. When your parents walk into the room, you turn away from your computer or your technology, turn your games off, turn your phone upside down—basically, you stop whatever you are doing so you can focus on them and listen for their voice.

---

1   Genesis 37:1-11

This is the type of uprightness that Joseph had. His father said, "Go, find your brothers."[2] And he went and did exactly what his father told him to do. Joseph was blessed. Do you think it was because he started at a very young age? Was it because of special training he had? Did his parents try to make him a successful businessman capable of managing any kind of organization in the world? Did they drill him for hours daily with math and science and computer skills? Or... was it because he was so upright that God's Spirit dwelt in him, and therefore, he was successful? Was it because he studied academics... or was it because he studied the righteous laws of God and lived them out? It was because Joseph was *righteous*.

It is the Spirit of God inside of a person that makes someone successful. Joseph was remarkable. You can go to Harvard, you can go to Oxford, or you can go to any of the top schools in the world... but without the Spirit of God in you, you cannot do anything that is remarkable.

FAITHFULLY ENDURING PERSECUTION

In Genesis Chapter 39, Joseph was faced with the test of Potiphar's wife flirting with him, but he knew what to do. He knew not to look to the left or right. The Bible says to flee that type of situation.[3] He did not defile himself in any way or consider anything that was lustful at all. He was very upright in how he handled the situation and how he responded when he was falsely accused by Potiphar's wife and then by his master, Potiphar, after he had been so beloved by him. That is why Potiphar was so mad—he had loved Joseph so much and expected so much of him. How could Joseph

---

2   *Genesis 37:12-17*

3   *I Corinthians 6:18*

have done this? But did Joseph retaliate and say, "Your wife is lying"? No, he accepted the accusation and went to prison.

Joseph's master took him and put him in prison, the place where the king's prisoners were confined. But while Joseph was there in the prison, the Lord was with him; he showed him kindness and granted him favor in the eyes of the prison warden. So the warden put Joseph in charge of all those held in the prison, and he was made responsible for all that was done there. The warden paid no attention to anything under Joseph's care, because the Lord was with Joseph and gave him success in whatever he did. Genesis 39:20-23

The prisons at that time were dungeons. But even in that environment, Joseph was lifted up. Again, was it because of his advanced studies or highly-rated university background that the warden trusted him so much that he did not even have to show up for work because he knew Joseph was taking care of all the prisoners? No, it was because the Spirit of God was in Joseph. Look at his life and the fruit! Did Joseph get the Spirit of God because he had made a mistake at Potiphar's house or forgot to do his duties? No, he was so diligent to please his boss and so diligent to please his authority that he was lifted up wherever he was…even in a prison.

From a Prisoner to a Ruler

Joseph was so upright in prison that he was able to help Pharaoh's officials and interpret the dreams of the cupbearer and the baker when they were in prison.[4] Later, the cupbearer told Pharaoh what had happened, so Joseph was brought before Pharaoh. Pharaoh then used him to interpret his dreams because the Spirit of God was in

---

4 Genesis 40

him. *Pharaoh said to Joseph, "I had a dream, and no one can interpret it. But I have heard it said of you that when you hear a dream you can interpret it." "I cannot do it," Joseph replied to Pharaoh, "but God will give Pharaoh the answer he desires." Genesis 41:15-16* Joseph had many opportunities to take credit for his skills and the ability to interpret dreams and claim it was because he was so intelligent or had a high IQ, but he did not. He brought glory to God in everything he did. Pharaoh recognized this and said:

Can we find anyone like this man, one in whom is the spirit of God?" Then Pharaoh said to Joseph, "Since God has made all this known to you, there is no one so discerning and wise as you. You shall be in charge of my palace, and all my people are to submit to your orders. Only with respect to the throne will I be greater than you. Genesis 41:38b-40

    A leader can recognize that the Spirit of the Most High God is in someone. It stands out. There is no other way to get the Spirit except for you to do *everything* that is right. You cannot do half of what you are asked or do only 9 out of 10 things that your authority requests. When your parents ask you to do something, you need to write it down and check with them to be sure you understand what they want, and then do it all. Then you report back that you have done it, with no bragging. That way, you can get the Spirit of God in you, too.

    Joseph was not only lifted up, he was lifted high up. He might as well have been the Pharaoh of the entire land, because Pharaoh said, *I am Pharaoh, but without your word no one will lift hand or foot in all Egypt. Genesis 41:44b* And Joseph was given a beautiful wife and eventually had beautiful children. *Joseph named his firstborn Manasseh and said, "It is because God has made me forget all my trouble and all my father's household." The second son he named Ephraim and said, "It is because God has made me fruitful in the land of my suffering."*

Genesis 41:51-52 All the pain from his past was taken away from him. He was given all these blessings because the Spirit of God was in him due to his right living.

As you read Genesis chapters 42 thru 45, you see that Joseph was able to not only save Egypt from the famine, but he also saved the Hebrews, and that was the launch of the Hebrew nation. From Abraham to Joseph, righteousness was where the Spirit of God would remain. And from that, the Hebrews settled in Goshen in Egypt for 430 years. After that, they would form their own nation. An amazing launch to a nation, starting from one incredible man willing to go thru so much suffering.

Is 17 years of age too early for such testing? Would someone blame God for having to go thru that much suffering so young? The main thing Joseph did that was right was that he never blamed God. And in the end, he never took revenge on his brothers, instead saying, *You intended to harm me, but God intended it for good to accomplish what is now being done, the saving of many lives. Genesis 50:20* And indeed, it did. Regardless of what had happened, Joseph had such deep love for his brothers.

He tested his brothers in Genesis 43 and 44 to see if they still had jealousy in their heart for Benjamin, because it was jealousy that made them almost kill Joseph and sell him into slavery. But they passed the test and showed that they had no jealousy for Benjamin. Joseph tested them to see whether they were willing to give up their own lives so that Benjamin would remain free for the sake of their father. He saw that they had repented and reformed and were now upright. They were willing to be slaves the rest of their lives for what they had done.

What a wonderful story. I pray in the name of Jesus Christ that all who read this will follow in the footsteps of Abraham and Joseph, men who were *full* of the Spirit of God. The Spirit of God can only be given by God Himself. What did Jesus do? The Spirit of God lit on him like a dove when he was baptized and went all in, saying "I am giving you everything."[5]

PRAYER

Dear God, we want your Spirit. We want to be the apple of your eye. God, I pray in the name of Jesus Christ for all of the young people who are in this Remnant of Your Kingdom. May we raise children who are full of your Spirit, and may they seek out righteousness daily. May they put everything into it. May they dive into your Word to find out what you want us to do, how to please you. May these children be so upright that they shine throughout the land. And all of this, O God, we pray in the name of Jesus Christ for your glory. Amen.

---

5   *As soon as Jesus was baptized, he went up out of the water. At that moment heaven was opened, and he saw the Spirit of God descending like a dove and lighting on him. Matthew 3:16*

Sing to him a new song; play skillfully, and shout for joy. Psalm 33:3 God has gifted His children in so many ways. The most important gifts are the ones you give to the Church. These are the gifts that will really give back. All over the world people seek ways to aid humanity. They create foundations and cross the world to look for new projects, but there is nothing more important, nothing that will change the world more, than God and His Kingdom, His Business.

Chapter 18

Many people marvel at successful businesses, high ACT scores, college degrees, Olympic gold medals, or wealth and riches; however, when we meet our Maker on that Great Day, none of those man-appointed accomplishments will ever be questioned. God will not ask you how much money you made or what you scored on a test, nor will worldly accomplishments be considered for the entrance examination of Heaven…but rather, you will be asked about your characteristics of Christ—a pure life—having one focus, that of loving and pleasing God above all else.

When you turn to God the Father and Christ, His Son, in determination to make God your everything—your Leader, your Mentor, the Manager, the Organizer of your mind, your soul and your will—you are given a Spirit that draws you even closer to God. This Spirit is full of necessary information that is given to you. *We are witnesses of these things, and so is the Holy Spirit, whom God has given to those who obey him. Acts 5:32* In other words, when you are baptized head-to-toe into Christ, into imitating the life of Jesus Christ, you receive this beautiful, powerful, unbelievable Spirit. When you are filled with God's Spirit, that means you are filled with His personality.

It is hard to believe that God would even send forth His characteristics—His Spirit, His attitude—and allow them to enter the mind and heart of man…that we get to be anything like the Creator who has been here forever and ever! That this is something that even children and youth can aspire to achieve!

What is the Spirit of God? As you know from the Apostle Paul in Galatians 5, the fruits of God's Spirit are love, joy, peace, patience, kindness, goodness, faithfulness, gentleness and self-control. These characteristics are neither male nor female—they are God-like. It is the Spirit from above. God has always portrayed Himself as male, therefore young men should realize that they are likewise to be gentle, kind, and patient, altogether good—the perfect gentleman. These characteristics might be deemed effeminate by some people in our society, but not by the Heavens. God is not effeminate—God is amazing, and He is love. God is patient; He is endearing. Jesus is the humblest of all who walked the face of the Earth, and Moses is said to be next—having all personal goals based on God and His Church. Notice the attitudes that Christ applauded in the Beatitudes…

> WHEN YOU ARE BAPTIZED HEAD-TO-TOE INTO IMITATING THE LIFE OF JESUS CHRIST, YOU ARE GIVEN THIS BEAUTIFUL, POWERFUL, UNBELIEVABLE SPIRIT.

Blessed are the meek, for they will inherit the earth. Blessed are those who hunger and thirst for righteousness, for they will be filled. Blessed are the merciful, for they will be shown mercy. Blessed are the pure in heart, for they will see God. Blessed are the peacemakers, for they will be called sons of God. You are the salt of the earth. But if the salt loses its saltiness, how can it be made salty again? It is no longer good for anything, except to be thrown out and trampled by men. You are the light of the world… In the same way, let your light shine before men, that they may see your good deeds and praise your Father in heaven. Matthew 5:5-14a,16

So true Saints, true seekers of God—young and old alike—are those who are putting on the attitudes of Christ and of God. They are the merciful, the meek, the peacemakers. They are righteous, and they are joyful even in persecution—the salt or the joy of life. Satan is the king of this world, and the world always takes and always hates. No wonder there is the need for *light*—because the rest of the world is increasingly dark. The world is full of envy, anger, hate, rudeness, keeping records of wrong, rejoicing in evil and always smiling to your face but projecting and judging behind your back. True God-centered love is a rare light. It is salt that makes this bad-tasting evil in the world much sweeter and easier to be around. This salt makes the hate toward you from the world easier to swallow and digest. When you get the Holy Spirit, you follow the Son—you take up your cross and walk in this delightful denial—and then you will have the selfless characteristics of Christ.

Gifts for the Church

But to each one of us grace has been given as Christ apportioned it. This is why it says: "When he ascended on high, he led captives in his train and gave gifts to men." Ephesians 4:7-8

The most important gifts are the ones you offer to the Church. These are the gifts that will really give back. All over the world, people seek ways to aid humanity. They create foundations and travel the world to look for new projects, but there is nothing more important, nothing that will change the world more, than God and His Kingdom, His Business.

The Body needs each person, and this also includes the children. The youth are so gifted and talented, but in today's society, they often end up bored, empty and purposeless because they are not given responsibilities and opportunities. By the time they are 13 years old, youth are ready and wanting to take on responsibilities based on their gifts and abilities. It is such a special honor and joy for the children to be able to serve in God's House and be a part of the Body. When they are younger, they start as apprentices. Then by 11, 12 or 13 years of age, they are ready to do more. They understand tithing and responsibility for caring for God's Church. And with every age, the responsibility and opportunity grow more and more. As they enter their late 20s, they are able to shepherd and to lead and to do more speaking and assisting with the Assemblies. Their gifts are known—everyone would be part of a ministry team; everyone would know that this is not a part-time job, but this is their calling to serve the Kingdom and to put God first.

Finding these gifts that God has given you for His Kingdom is an important part of growing up. As you mature, you and your parents are continually identifying gifts and abilities that God has placed in your heart and mind, narrowing them down so you can focus. Some of these gifts will be abilities that He has given you to use for the Church, and it is usually something that the world does not compensate you for, such as art, music or decorating. If you are encouragers and evangelists at heart, you may want to try foreign languages—you could become foreign ambassadors, representatives for Jesus Christ, taking the message over to other populations. We need these children to be highly skilled in the Word and knowledgeable about resources and Truth, building their own catalog of information so they can share with others and bring Truth to people who are hurting.

Gifts for Careers

Then there are gifts that you can use to earn a living. To find these, you start by praying, asking your parents, getting guidance from Godly Leaders, taking feedback on your abilities from other adults around you, and studying what businesses need or want—looking at the careers and employment needs in the workplace long term. Pay attention to the words that teachers and other adults use to describe you. If they say you are loving and outgoing, that can give you clues to your gifts and area of service. Someone who is loving and outgoing is out front, meeting others. They are greeters; they are good at sales; they are good at encouraging. Or they may say that you are a good student—you are good at reading or at math. Take that information and keep asking and searching to see what it is you are going to be doing, and then it makes learning more fun.

Parents, you can tell if your children are more social or more studious. Do they like books? Are they good at verbal communication, or are they good at written communication? Are they better at taking something apart and putting it back together than they are at reading? You need to spend time with your children, helping them hone in on their interests and skills as much as you can, taking them to the library, piling them up with the books of their choice of interest. You will know if something is their interest because they cannot put it down...they want to do more and more and more! Now, I know that sometimes the thing that turns out to interest them is a computer game or a sport, but look to see *why* that particular computer game or sport is of interest. Is it because they are building or creating in it and they have engineering minds, or maybe they have a creative mind and like that aspect of the game? Or is it because they are social and want to play whatever game the other children are playing so they can build a connection with them?

> TRUE SEEKERS OF GOD—YOUNG AND OLD ALIKE—ARE THOSE WHO ARE PUTTING ON THE ATTITUDES OF CHRIST AND OF GOD. THEY ARE THE MERCIFUL, THE MEEK, THE PEACEMAKERS.

This preparation takes time and focus. Traditionally, the Jews did not spend a lot of time on sports or extracurricular activities. Everything is purposed. Consider putting money into buying the equipment or material they need to advance in their field instead of taking another vacation.

When considering occupations, prayerfully look down the road to see what skills will be needed in 10, 20 or 30 years. What is something that everyone has or needs? Use the Internet to search for how many actual job openings are in that field. Once you and your parents determine the subject matter, you can start studying for that field. Go to the library, search it out on the Internet, talk to Saints who work in that area. You can learn the vocabulary of that subject, because every career has its own set of jargon, acronyms and vocabulary, and you have to learn it. Then you can start working and apprenticing in that occupation by working under someone who is in that industry, or if there is a ministry in that field for the Church, you can start serving in that area. For example, if you have a desire to go into law, you could start watching shows and documentaries about law and legal cases. You will learn the vocabulary of jury, prosecutor, plaintiff and more. For most occupations, it all comes down to vocabulary. So by the age of 12 or 13, you know where you are heading, and you start learning the vocabulary specifically for that career, and then by the time you are 14 or 15 years old, you are way ahead in that particular area of study and

> WHATEVER GOD LEADS YOU TO DO, BEING SKILLED, LEARNING EVERYTHING YOU POSSIBLY CAN ABOUT IT, EXCELLING IN YOUR WORK AND BEING UNDER AUTHORITY WILL PUT YOU WAY AHEAD.

are reading deeply in that field—honing in on your future career. Suddenly, school becomes fun because it has a purpose!

In general, you want to aim for the top. If your chosen field requires advanced education, plan for the longest education from the outset. Tell yourself that you are going to get two Ph.D.s in engineering or medicine or programming. In reality, you may only wind up with one Ph.D., or a master's degree, or just a bachelor's degree; but in the beginning, shoot for the long-term, and do not think of

Success is about narrowing things down and having one focus.

yourself ending school until you are done. The further in school you go, the more you are compensated, and you are able to pass that down to your children.

There are other routes to good employment than just advanced degrees, however. The type of higher education that we have today is odd because it is so broad that no one seems to end up being proficient at anything specific. In the past, children would start apprenticing and learning a trade by the time they were 10 to 12 years old, so that by the time they were 15 years old, they were highly skilled.

With the degree programs today, many of them are so general that even when you graduate, you still do not really know what you are going to do.

Another option is seeking technical jobs with certifications and trade-school training programs. People with training in trades such as plumbing, electrical work, infrastructure and other skills are going to move quickly up the ranks, and they may end up making more money per hour than a person with a postgraduate degree in a field where there are few jobs.

Whatever God leads you to do, being skilled, learning everything you possibly can about it, excelling in your work and being under authority will put you way ahead. Work as if you were working for God and Jesus Christ. Give the most you can and the best you can.

A Narrow Focus

Success is about narrowing things down and having one focus. When you get overwhelmed in life it is often because you have too much going on. Narrow it down. All life becomes crystal clear when you have a single focus—when it is God first—and then you take the gifts that God gave you and give back to Him. He is the One who created and programed inside of you every single gift and ability that you have. You have the opportunity to give back to God and His Kingdom first, and then build onto your career—in that order. You are taking care of God's House first, and then you are taking care of your house—and that is fulfilling the Laws of God. And when you have a spouse and children, you have to make sure that your family is always first before your career as you continue this beautiful cycle of building God's Kingdom.[1]

---

1   To record your child's spiritual gifts, please get your copy of the Remnant Fellowship Child's Dedication & Memory Book.

As you put on the characteristics of Christ, learn how you can use the gifts God has given you to serve His Church and build His Kingdom, grow in your relationship with God, and continue to make His agenda first in your life. Your agenda needs to be *God's* agenda: who God would want you to marry, where God would want you to work, and what gifts God has given you. Do not look sideways at the abilities and relationships others have. Find the gifts that God has given *you*, and do not compare them with others.

There are amazing examples of grounded youth throughout the Bible. Daniel and his three friends are examples. Obedience to the Laws of God is what made Daniel and his friends ten times wiser than all the other young men, and he was promoted to second in the land of the world power at the time. Daniel sought zero praise of man and was only looking all of his life, from a young age to old, to please God. Page 237.

Motive of the Heart: A Lesson to the Graduates

Chapter 19

Since the creation of man, every generation under the sun has searched for excellence in the education of their children and the development of their gifts. The drive to win and the competition for excellence in academics, the arts and sports is universal and unanimous—crossing various nations, races, creeds and backgrounds. There is an innate agreement on the definition of top beauty, athletic prowess, intelligence, coordination and public speaking talents. For Believers, it is instinctively understood that children who have excelled have been touched by God. There is a Connection, and this Connection has been so impressive that it has turned pagan kings to worship The One True God, such as in the days of Joseph in Egypt or Daniel in Babylon.

What is not universal—and what is not agreed upon—is ***how*** one arrives at accomplishing these goals. With all the different nations, races and creeds, there is absolutely no uniformity or standard for how to bring about the best in children. This controversy has even led to denominational and religious splits, relocations and immigration, and perhaps is responsible for many divorces. The formula ranges from extremely liberal anti-authority protocols to extremely rigid, dictatorial environments. When there is talent in isolated situations, people attribute this to university education. But note that when a university maintains the highest entrance qualifications, the student granted admission was the rare superior student in the first place. The university is simply capitalizing on the best that was available.

At Remnant Fellowship, however, members are granted admission by God—there are no standardized tests to pass—and the children have all come from various academic levels and backgrounds. Yet mysteriously, we consistently witness an extremely high percentage of excellence in school performance, skills, careers and marriages. We especially witness long-term superior character overall, which rewards the child more than any other endeavor. Therefore, we have deep confidence in God that our graduates will do even better in life because God has shown us how to raise our children with a focus on Him, His Church and His Kingdom.

Parents strive for this secret. The standards, scores, character and job performance for children in this country have continued to decline so that now, America is ranked far below other countries. According to Pew Research in a recent survey, the U.S. placed an unimpressive 38th out of 71 countries in math, and a sad overall rating of 30th.[1] The once uncontended bar of excellence has evaporated in front of our very eyes.

How did the U.S. at one time have the highest records in academics and achievements but now it has been replaced with despondency and loss of drive? Whatever America is trying is not working…we

---

1   Pew Research, "U.S. students' academic achievement still lags that of their peers in many other countries," 2017

Motive of the Heart: A Lesson to the Graduates

are going backwards fast. Something needs to be done quickly due to the increase in suicide rate, especially among youth. Tragically, the number of middle school students who have committed suicide has doubled in the last seven years.[2]

How many times have you seen children who have been driven by parents to succeed, but they instead wind up unhappy and unsuccessful? People may not know it, but they instinctively rank a person's character as being less important than their gifts, yet it is the basic *character* that is the driving force and the source. For example, one could be an A student, a great athlete and a hardworking person, but also full of pride—and therefore miserable and unpopular. They could excel for the praise of man but also be a smart aleck, disobedient to their parents, anti-authority or addicted to drugs. They might find short-term success at a young age but come to a miserable end. There is nothing more heartbreaking.

If American standards are not working for our youth, what *is* the training that will ensure long-term success and happiness? What can parents do to make certain that their child finishes the race of life with joy, peace, purpose and salvation?

There are amazing examples of grounded youth throughout the Bible. Daniel and his three friends are examples. King Nebuchadnezzar had ordered the chief of his court officials to bring in specific Israelites from the royal family: young men without physical defect, handsome, showing aptitude for every kind of learning, quick-witted, well-informed, swift to understand and qualified to serve in the King's palace. The King wanted the best. Daniel and his three friends excelled. In fact, the King found none equal to these young Hebrew men. They were ten times wiser than all of the magicians

---

2   National Public Radio, "Middle School Suicides Reach An All-Time High," 2016

and enchanters of Babylon, which created jealousy. The King—the head of this world power—lifted them up, and Daniel rose to the top to be second in command. Without their parents around, what was the driving force behind these excellent young men that would lift them to the top of the world over other Babylonian children who had more money and more advantage?

There is a constant out there...there is a Rock that never changes, with reachable, achievable goals.

THE DIFFERENCE

The answer to this question is found in Daniel 1:17a, *To these four young men God gave knowledge and understanding of all kinds of literature and learning.* God was the source. It was the object of their devotion. Is the object of *your* devotion God...or man? This is fundamental and essential, because it is from whence comes your drive, your source of life. Most drives, whether good or evil, come from within. The true motive of the heart has to be tested. One motive will drive you to the finish line with God and eternal life, and one motive will stop you short. One brings happiness and contentment—one brings disappointment and misery. The Apostle Paul had it right:

*Those who live according to the sinful nature have their minds set on what that nature desires; but those who live in accordance with the Spirit have their minds **set** on what the Spirit desires. The mind of sinful man is death, but the mind controlled by the Spirit is life and peace; the sinful mind is hostile to God. It does not submit to God's law, nor can it do so. Those controlled by the sinful nature cannot please God. Romans 8:5-8*

What is your mind set on to glorify? For that is what gives you the power and the Spirit. If parents have raised their children to succeed so that the parents can live vicariously thru the children, then the drive will die out in the teen or young adult years. If the parents have trained the child to merely please them and other people—to live for the praise of man—the child will rebel, or God will block their success. What is your motive? Is it for the praise and glory for self? Is it for money or for power? Did that play a part? You say that your motive is for God, but were you tempted to cheat? Why? Did you put others down to get your child ahead? Is your child doing the same thing he has seen you do? What have you taught your children?

Our goal is complete obedience to glorify God, for it is the person having the best attitude that glorifies, despite maybe having the lowest grades or being the athlete that comes in last. Those who can let go of selfish ambition completely mystify the world. **The victory is in your daily attitude in any endeavor.** Your motive and your drive have to be for the good of God and His Kingdom alone. In this, you are investing in the eternal.

A Moving Target

Merely being selfless is not the key. You could be a servant and appear selfless but still be unhappy. Why? A selfless person who lives for the wrong cause cannot keep it up. Parents need to realize that teaching your child to be selfless for the wrong motive is only setting your child up for a woeful, pitiful end. That upbringing will promise the world to the child, yet it only robs and starves the child, deprives the soul, paralyzes the will, and demoralizes the heart, bringing the child anger and depression and unrealized expectations. But why? Why is it so drastic? Why is that the result? It is because if pleasing men is the goal, then that goal is a moving target. You may have instilled good character, good morals and a servant's heart in your child, but to please a moving target is impossible.

> Your motive and your drive have to be for the good of God and His Kingdom alone. In this, you are investing in the eternal.

Humans are naturally trying to please. You wonder why your child is miserable? Well, he was given the goal to please man, whose whims and goals never stay the same. When you are brought up to please man, the target shifts so that you can never make the mark. It is like a company that changes the goals of its quota—it is completely depressing and demoralizing for those trying to reach the quota. People become desperate, exhausted and hopeless when they see that even with all their efforts, they cannot hit the quota for the boss, therefore they cannot please that boss, and they cannot get the praise of man or get a raise to help with finances. This could be parallel with teachers at school, professors, or worldly churches where the morals are fluctuating with ever-changing political correctness and endless ever-changing guidelines from the government about how we are to perform and act. Capricious, ungrounded parents will never be pleased, because the child cannot do enough. It is like changing the

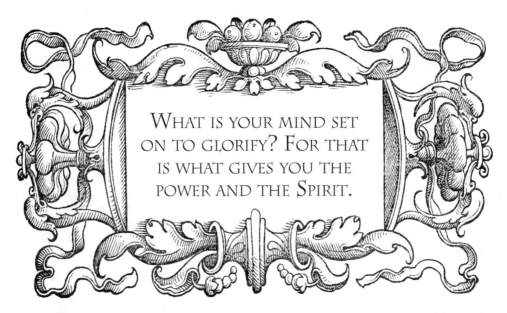

WHAT IS YOUR MIND SET ON TO GLORIFY? FOR THAT IS WHAT GIVES YOU THE POWER AND THE SPIRIT.

goal line for runners, so they give out trying to reach the end—the goal line is elusive, an illusion, and they never get the praise. All of this has bred confusion, exhaustion and insecurity in the world's children because they feel like failures. No wonder there is rebellion.

THE ONE CONSTANT GOAL

There *is* a constant out there. There is a Rock that never changes, with reachable, achievable goals. When a child is given *one* goal—to please God—they are grounded on the Rock of morals—God's morals versus the ever-changing, shifting sand of morals based on what pleases man. This child will be able to stay steady on the course, and even in challenging situations such as in Daniel's case, or in the stories of Joseph or Christ, they stay grounded and focused on God. Yes, I proclaim, there is a constant, and grounded parents can daily reinforce reachable, achievable goals so that the child becomes spiritually healthy, secure, mature and happy at a very early age.

Countries, governments, and companies change their morals constantly—they live on shifting sand. But the True Church founded on the Rock of God is never-changing; it is the same consistent reachable goal, producing children who defy the statistics with peace and happiness and maturity. Christ showed us the way. Christ is that Rock, and his words are that Rock, the capstone of the Church. Those grounded on the Rock will always be at peace in any circum-

Do not quit, do not give up, but *CHANGE*.

stance because their goal has not shifted or changed. Their skill level to live out these morals and this goal only increases as they age—so they are more and more successful every day.

Misplaced Devotion

In I Samuel 3, Eli was a Prophet who had two sons who had misplaced devotion—to themselves, their sensual desires and their sensual lusts. When you are devoted to man or to yourself, you are never satisfied because this lust is always wanting more.[3] Man's heart is always changing, and you cannot keep your lust from growing. This lust will always want more, so the goal is never reached, and you are empty, miserable, unhappy. Eli's sons even put their lusts above the desires of God—misplaced devotion—and God became upset. The Bible says, *His sons made themselves contemptible, and he failed to restrain them. I Samuel 3:13b* The parents failed to restrain the children, and as a result, their two sons were unpopular with God. Not just unpopular, but "contemptible," which means loathsome and disgusting.

Parents, when you fail to restrain your children, you are only making them unpopular with God. It may be making them popular with a few children in the world, but it is making them unpopular with the Creator Who holds your salvation! How selfish for you to seek to get in good with God yourself but fail to restrain your children. *The LORD declares: "Far be it from me! Those who honor me I will honor, but those who despise me will be disdained." I Samuel 2:30b* That day, Eli lost both sons in war and lost his own life; he fell back and broke his neck because the Ark of the Covenant had been removed. How we raise our children is a serious job. It is a beautiful opportunity and a big responsibility.

Romans 8 says that the person who is not focused on God's Will will be hostile to God.[4] *Hostile* is a strong term. Why not just say "neutral," because that is what it looks like they are? Why not just "unbiased"? No, "hostile" is the correct term because when God's

---

3   *Having lost all sensitivity, they have given themselves over to sensuality so as to indulge in every kind of impurity, with a continual lust for more. Ephesians 4:19*
4   *The sinful mind is hostile to God. It does not submit to God's law, nor can it do so. Romans 8:7*

Will is not your will, God Almighty turns out to be not your Creator but your competition.

Parents who look for honor from man for themselves and their children are wasting God's time, money and energy. Daniel sought zero praise of man and was only looking, all of his life from young to old age, to please God—the God Whom I love because He has never changed His expectations…His reachable, achievable Commands, written in stone. It is false religion that tells you that you cannot please God or even meet His demands. The Truth is that man is the one who has the capricious, unreliable, erratic and fickle target, changing the quotas, the goals, the expectations.

> DO NOT LIMIT YOURSELF BY PLEASING YOURSELF…PLEASE GOD AND ACHIEVE SOMETHING THAT IS BEYOND YOUR WILDEST DREAMS.

All satan and his forces do is put that false accusation on the Heavens, but I have found that the only achievable security is pleasing God alone and staying focused on that, and the reward has been great. Obedience to the Laws of God made Daniel and his friends ten times wiser and promoted to second in the land of the world power at the time. Only with God is a human capable of being ten times wiser than the already super smart. Paul said in Galatians, *You were running a good race. Who cut in on you and kept you from obeying the truth? That kind of persuasion does not come from the one who calls you. Galatians 5:7-8* That is coming from the dark side, throwing you off. Think about it: you could win a gold medal but still stand in contempt of God by pleasing men instead of following His Commands.

There is a difference between self-glorification (and therefore, competing with God) and doing everything for the glory of God.

One makes you depressed because with greed you can never get enough glory for yourself. However, if it is done for God...to glorify His name...to prove and justify *His* existence, then you will have fulfillment, success and joy.

Do not think this is going to be an easy task to figure out your true motive. The heart of man is very deceitful.[5] Do you really know why you helped a Saint move or took food over to a sick person? Every good deed must be done in secret. Do not let the left hand

know what the right hand is doing—if for no other reason than to test your own heart for its motive.[6]

All Honor and Glory to God

The Lord's Prayer, as we have read earlier in this book, is a beautiful foundation. It starts off, *This, then, is how you should pray:* "Our

---

5   *The heart is deceitful above all things and beyond cure. Who can understand it? Jeremiah 17:9*

6   *Matthew 6:1-4*

Father in heaven, hallowed be your name, your kingdom come, your will be done on earth as it is in heaven." Matthew 6:9-10 We have prayed this prayer all our lives, but did we really pay attention and genuinely mean the first line in this prayer? It is addressing GOD Himself, with all the attributes of His Divine Nature—His power, wisdom, justice, mercy…acknowledgement that God is omnipotent and His Kingdom and His Will are above all. But there is something deeper here—so much adoration that we give all attention to God just like His Angels do in Heaven. **It is giving honor.**

In other words, "Dear Heavenly Divine Father and Creator, may everything I do and everything I say today be to HONOR YOU…may it be a glory and tribute to You alone and credit and recognition to make You and Your ideas, Your Kingdom and Creation, Your ways and commands and everything about You look great!" All glory and honor belongs to God.

> TRUE JOY-FILLED CHRISTIANS GET UP EVERY DAY FOR A LIFETIME TO RUN NOT TO JUSTIFY OR EXALT THEIR EXISTENCE BUT RATHER TO USE THEIR GIFTS TO JUSTIFY GOD'S EXISTENCE AND HIS GOODNESS.

It is not about a particular name; it is that this omnipotent God of Love is way above all. I simply do not have the words to express the inequity of credit given to men who do not deserve it versus God and Christ who deserve a Universe of credit more.

We honor the youth who have embraced the total character of God and Christ. I believe we are born with gifting and a light of brilliance from God…each gift is strategic and needed. May each young adult find his or her gifts and then develop them to their fullest capacity—and that means with following Christ, obtaining his characteristics—and striving to be the best in God's eyes. Then you will also receive God's Spirit. But this combination of power and light of a gift from the Heavens mixed with the powerful Spirit from the Heavens must be given back to God.

True joy-filled Christians get up every day for a lifetime and use their gifts not to justify or exalt their own existence…but rather to justify God's existence and His goodness. Any selfish use of this divine mixture will bring pain, shame, curses and disappointment. Loving and crediting God will bring you His essential, embellishing Holy Spirit, which gives you the fruits of love, joy and patience, and that sees you thru to the end—so that no life is cut short from the disillusionment created by false grace. There is a great pain out there in the world without God. You must purpose to endorse, foster and glorify the Kingdom of Love. God brought you here to be hired by His Business and to build it and promote it above all other businesses in the world.

JOIN IN THE RACE

Make God your Rock and your only goal. Do not quit, do not give up, but *change*. Make sure there is no desire for the praise of man in you. Check your motives. One will bring true lasting happiness and success, and one will bring misery. Do not just sit on the sidelines and watch the race of life—join in the race. Go for the gold. Life has an eerie way of slipping by, and as has been said before by the Roman poet, "Seize the day." Fulfill your destiny. Seize this Connection, and glorify the One and Only True God!

Let me embolden you to develop your gift to the top of your class and let no power or opposition deter you from your task—then let me encourage you to use it ingeniously and consistently to glorify God and Christ and the Church. May each generation never forget that God's generous gifts are not here to fulfill your dreams; they were not given to exalt you; they are not here to justify your existence. The generous gifts from the Heavens are distributed among us all to justify and to prove and to exalt the existence and the goodness of THE One and Only True God of the Universe! That is your purpose. In doing that, you find fulfillment and joy for your dream—believe it or not, beyond what your dream was, knowing that it is a bigger and better dream that God has for you. Do not limit yourself by pleasing yourself—please God and achieve something that is beyond your wildest dreams. *God glorified* is the achievable goal realized—and with success in this, you find respect, peace and joy.

Do you not know? Have you not heard? The Lord is the everlasting God, the Creator of the ends of the earth. He will not grow tired or weary, and his understanding no one can fathom. He gives strength to the weary and increases the power of the weak. Even youths grow tired and weary, and young men stumble and fall; but those who hope in the Lord will renew their strength. They will soar on wings like eagles; they will run and not grow weary, they will walk and not be faint. Isaiah 40:28-31

Not only seize the day—but continue to seize and cling to the rock-solid goal of pleasing God. Keep this motive in your heart forever, and you will hang onto this Rock, you will rise up, you will soar with wings like eagles, and you will run and not be weary.

SEIZE THE DAY…SEIZE THE UNCHANGING ROCK!

Motive of the Heart: A Lesson to the Graduates

In history, Jewish families arranged marriages, and they knew the match would work when both were idol-free, true children of Abraham. Both young adults would be selfless, and they had been taught how to be a wife, how to be a husband, how to live for each other, help each other—be helpmates, and work together to launch the institution called the "family" for the glory of God. When you do that, the interest and purpose of the young adults will be one, so that they will be totally in love with the other person, and this love will grow every year. Page 256.

Chapter 20

Flee the evil desires of youth, and pursue righteousness, faith, love and peace, along with those who call on the Lord out of a pure heart. II Timothy 2:22

Before any courting relationship can be considered, a foundation of purity must be clearly established. Purity is to be cherished, but how in this day and age is it possible? In fact, purity seems rare and elusive. It was applauded and valued 50 years ago, even being the expectation on popular television shows, but now you will find that even the "upright" characters on TV are so corrupt that their actions are unspeakable.

You are not born pure or impure—you have to make the *choice*, commit to it and work on it for the sake of God and His Kingdom. God's agenda is purity: *You were taught, with regard to your former way of life, to put off your old self, which is being corrupted by its deceitful desires; to be made new in the attitude of your minds; and to put on the new self, created to be like God in true righteousness and holiness. Ephesians 4:22-24*

We are commanded to be like our Father in true righteousness and holiness.[1] Today's Christianity tells you that "you are only human" and that "you should try, but know that you can never achieve purity." But in fact, all of Creation obeys God—the animals,

---

1   *To put on the new self, created to be like God in true righteousness and holiness. Ephesians 4:24b*

the elements, the mass and matter all obey the laws set forth by God. We count on the Earth spinning each day on its perfect axis, so we never get too cold or too hot. We take obedience of physics for granted—to a fault. The Universe naturally obeys the laws set forth by God, but for humans, it is a choice—but it is a choice of *love*. Why? Because **the purpose of creating man was to find true love.**

> When you make the choice to follow Christ, you are daily cleaning up, making everything right, and fulfilling the calling of holiness, which means "set apart."

Who may ascend the hill of the Lord? Who may stand in His holy place? He who has clean hands and a pure heart. Psalm 24:3-4a Purity is a command, a law, for the happiness of man. It is a choice to be pure. The choice is made when you realize that your God-given personal responsibility and personal accountability were put there to show love. Purity proves your love for God and then for your spouse. Pure feels better than all other choices! We are commanded to purify ourselves. *Now that you have purified yourselves by obeying the truth so that you have sincere love for your brothers, love one another deeply, from the heart. I Peter 1:22*

When you make the choice to follow Christ, you are daily cleaning up, making everything right, and fulfilling the calling of holiness, which means "set apart." You are holy, set apart, to love only God. *Blessed are the pure in heart, for they will see God. Matthew 5:8*

Why is purity so powerful? Because it proclaims to the world that you are putting your own selfish agenda to the side and doing what God wants. It shows a choice of a relationship with God over man. Purity shows love for God, and when you have a relationship with God, this is everything and gives everything. You will be a light for the world because you have no worries. It is a light to salvation, and it automatically brings joy and happiness because there is no guilt or shame. The calling of Christ and a death to your own agenda is ironically thrilling, for pure feels better than all other lifestyle choices.[2] God is not looking for your skill set, but He is looking for the love of your heart. God wants your love and purity before Him and before others around you, which means you have found this relationship, and the benefits are immeasurable.

APPROPRIATE TIMING

Once a young person has firmly established purity in their heart, and they have built a solid relationship with God and are maturing, then their hearts naturally begin to long for Godly relationships with friends and then into consideration of Godly courtships. All parents of older children should keep this natural progression in mind, but do not wake up this desire too early in a young person.[3] If it does appear when a youth still seems too young, then lovingly redirect them back to their personal relationship with God, their academic studies and preparation for a career so they could even begin to consider starting a family later. Help them stay focused on building up the Church and serving God's Kingdom, knowing that this courtship opportunity for them will come as time passes. As the parent, be prayerful about when they are, in fact, ready. It may be sooner than you think for those youth who are spiritually mature.

An internal drive for marriage is programmed deep inside the soul of both man and woman. God created opposites and gave internal

---

2   *Please see Weigh Down Works! Chapter 19, "Free From Unwanted Behaviors and Substances" for more about purity and morality.*
3   *Daughters of Jerusalem, I charge you: Do not arouse or awaken love until it so desires. Song of Songs 8:4*

feelings of satisfaction and desire in order to secure that His Will will be followed. Notice that young people in today's world are getting married later and later—or not getting married at all—because this drive for marriage has been suppressed. Even though psychologists and studies will tell you that the predominant age for this internal drive is 18, 19 and 20 years old, and the majority of the world has embraced that over the centuries, modern American society does not accept that. American parents often push for their children to finish their higher education first…but after that, sometimes the desire is gone. God should be the guide. In Malachi 2:14, the Bible references *"the wife of your youth,"* indicating that the Jews were marrying young. People who have waited for a while and marry when they are older often find themselves already set in their ways, and they have a harder time with marriage and establishing a household with another person.

With the right priorities, however, you will see more marriages and blessed marriages. *He who finds a wife finds what is good and receives favor from the Lord. Proverbs 18:22* Marrying is a good thing, and it does not necessarily interfere with higher education. In many cases, marriage actually helps the young adult become a better student than they were before because the spouses can help one another.

Lasting Relationships

What is involved in this process of building a relationship that will last? What are the factors for Godly courtship and dating? Consider…have you ever started your own business or know anyone who has? How much time, focus and energy are needed to launch a business? With dating and marriage, you are launching a *whole family unit* that is of huge importance to God—to glorify God and to glorify His Church—and it should take even more time, prayer and consideration.

Aside from putting God first overall, the most important element in building a Godly marriage is helping the young adult to find the right person. In many cases, God will put this on the hearts of the parents. They will see the characteristics of the other youth, and they are looking for *righteousness* above all in a potential spouse. I do

AN INTERNAL DRIVE FOR MARRIAGE IS PROGRAMED DEEP INSIDE THE SOUL OF BOTH MAN AND WOMAN.

believe this is part of a family's responsibility and that you should help your child with this. You need to be involved in the youth events, getting in behind the scenes, learning who is out there so you can help your child. Parental involvement is essential. In almost every case where you encounter a successful young person, you can be sure that they had parents who were actively involved in their life. I cannot say enough about it—it is that important. You cannot be lazy in this—you need to consider it carefully. And it starts early in life, as you are making sure that your child is presentable—making a good impression and making the best of their appearance—and that all their behaviors are beautiful and royal.

I do believe God puts people together, but it is not as complicated as finding this one serendipitous person out there, like the movies would have you believe—that you just have to keep going until you find that "one soulmate." True soulmates are people who are idol-free, and *that* is the foundation of a lasting, peaceful relationship. It is not always just about feelings—life is short, and it is not about us—it is about marrying for righteousness.

> With dating and marriage, you are launching a whole family unit that is of utmost importance to God—to glorify Him and to glorify His Church.

In history, Jewish families arranged marriages, and they knew the match would work when both were idol-free, true children of Abraham. Both young adults would be selfless, and they had been taught how to be a wife, how to be a husband, how to live for each other, help each other—be helpmates, and work together to launch the institution called the "family" for the glory of God. When you do that, the interest and purpose of the young adults will be *one,* so that they will be totally in love with the other person, and this love will grow every year.

Righteousness is Alluring

Youth need to be brought up to understand that they want to marry **righteousness**—God-fearing women, God-fearing men—no matter what they look like. It is not about physical attractiveness first—it is about what God wants, a born again relationship with God and wanting to serve Him with all their heart so they wind up in the same places and doing the same things, right in the middle of Church, and that is when attractiveness for one another grows. In fact, every year they are going to look even better and better to one another! The woman is going to become more beautiful and the man more handsome as they grow in righteousness. The characteristics of Christ are what are attractive. Young men and women who are even-tempered, kind and gentle to everyone are the ones who are alluring. Only with righteousness comes the beauty and the handsomeness and the attractiveness.

Your young adult should be looking for someone who is in love with God. If you bring your child up the right way, they will find that person among the righteous. Then you will have two people together who are both in love with God, and they will be getting their prayers answered. That is real life, and it is truly delightful!

You can read in Genesis that Isaac was sent back to Abraham's people to find a wife.[4] Godly people look only among the righteous for a spouse, even if it means traveling to find a righteous woman or righteous man. Where you position your children during those important years will completely change the outcome of their relationships. If you position them far away from the righteous, it is very difficult. If you make sure they are around other Saints—those who have the same purpose—it is magic, and it will happen.

> TRUE SOUL-MATES ARE PEOPLE WHO ARE IDOL-FREE, AND THAT IS THE FOUNDATION OF A LASTING, PEACEFUL RELATIONSHIP.

When the couple starts off with the determination together to be pure and focused on God first, it will make all the difference. In addition to being sure your young adults are around other youth who are seeking God, parents can help with guiding activities and making suggestions on ways they can get to know each other. There are many

---

4 *Genesis 24*

things young adults can do to keep God at the center of their relationship. "Dating" does not have to just mean two people spending time with one another going to a movie or a dinner. Many young Saints find that serving the Church is a wonderful way to connect and see how God is leading in the relationship. Dating includes participating in youth events, reaching out to encourage others, helping out at Church, attending worship services and Church events together and checking in regularly with parents. Praying together every day is such a beautiful goal. All of this is easy to do if God is your everything.

> ONLY WITH RIGHTEOUSNESS COMES THE BEAUTY AND THE HANDSOMENESS AND THE ATTRACTIVENESS.

These young people need to be so careful and kind with each other. They must be sensitive to the feelings of others and never hurt the other person if they are approached about dating. Help them to see that it is an incredible honor that any person would consider seeking their company and want to know more about their relationship with God! We must have such respect for each other. There should never be any jumping around from person to person or gossiping about who is dating whom. This is a Spirit-led process and should be done with much graciousness and sensitivity, being very careful. Otherwise you will find yourself distracted and lose your focus off your goals and your relationship with God, and someone will wind up with hurt feelings.

At this age it is also important for young adults to start thinking in terms of finances. Part of the process of launching a new family unit is having both of them, as helpmates, be able to financially support a household. Young adults should learn from an early age to understand finances and consider employable careers, building a strong foundation for a household. Parents can help their children start saving money and gathering things that they can use to establish a home. There are times when parents can help with some of the major purchases when possible, while teaching their children how to establish good credit and how to make sure that whatever they buy is a lasting investment.

A Blessed Result

Does it work? It absolutely does work. It is how I raised my own children, and they have been so blessed with their own marriages, and their children are being blessed. Michael and Elle, and Elizabeth and Brandon are closer every year. Because of my relationship of selflessness with them, they know that I would never want to use them but only want to help them, so they desire my company. We are all helping each other and loving each other daily. We cannot wait to get together; it is fun and delightful because it is a group of selfless people helping each other, and the children are growing up to learn the same thing. We are growing closer and closer.

In the same way, all these righteous families in the Church are marrying into other righteous families. And if purity and the glory of God are the goals, then all the families will grow closer and closer, uniting the whole Church together to where it becomes a mighty fortress! There is no telling where this will all go. It is a powerful dream of a Kingdom of Priests, a Holy Nation. My prayer for this Remnant Revival is to pursue total purity in our relationships and marriages—purity of the mind, body and soul of all involved—so that we all will be a light and that we will be blessed in all we do for the Glory of God.

Marriage has deep meaning and significance to those who are seeking a relationship with God. It is symbolic of our relationship with Him—symbolic courting, symbolic engagement, symbolic marriage of a man to a woman as man is to God. It is an institution that deserves much consideration, analysis, deliberation and prayer. Page 262.

Chapter 21

The Lord God said, "It is not good for the man to be alone. I will make a helper suitable for him." Now the Lord God had formed out of the ground all the beasts of the field and all the birds of the air. He brought them to the man to see what he would name them; and whatever the man called each living creature, that was its name. So the man gave names to all the livestock, the birds of the air and all the beasts of the field. But for Adam no suitable helper was found. So the Lord God caused the man to fall into a deep sleep; and while he was sleeping, he took one of the man's ribs and closed up the place with flesh. Then the Lord God made a woman from the rib he had taken out of the man, and he brought her to the man. The man said, "This is now bone of my bones and flesh of my flesh; she shall be called 'woman,' for she was taken out of man." For this reason a man will leave his father and mother and be united to his wife, and they will become one flesh. Genesis 2:18-24

In the very beginning, God ordained this sacred holy union where two would become one. God has indeed made and encouraged the institutions of marriage and family, and it is the strength of the Church when it is done as commanded or directed by God. How beautiful is this genius idea of God to make male and female, and then to make them attracted so they will be married for life. Jesus reaffirmed this in Mark:

But at the beginning of creation God "made them male and female." "For this reason a man will leave his father and mother and be united to his wife, and the two will become one flesh." So they are no longer two, but one. Therefore what God has joined together, let man not separate. Mark 10:6-9

You see, down deep in mankind there is a moral compass that draws you from within into the Will of The Creator. The institution of marriage is one of those internal drives, and it transcends every continent, country, race and language. In fact, it is the biggest institution of all institutions. Because it is an institution created, designed and ordained by God, it is a glory to God. He did not create universities or graduate schools. He did not create Harvard or Yale or Oxford. He may have allowed these to be established, but *His* institution that He created is marriage. It is the marriage of two people who will love each other and stay together, starting a home, having children and continuing this beautiful Kingdom of God.

Marriage has deep meaning and significance to those who are seeking a relationship with God. It is symbolic of our relationship with Him—symbolic courting, symbolic engagement, symbolic marriage of a man to a woman as man is to God. It is an institution that deserves much consideration, analysis, deliberation and prayer.

Opposites Attract

It is obvious that in marriage God is uniting two humans who have things in common, but a man and a woman are just different enough. Why did God create these differences, and how do opposites attract? God made matches that are suitable with much in common, yet different enough to be attracted—to create the mutual admiration that is a glue to hold them close.

Each human should know—unless blocked by pride—that we have weaknesses, so people automatically look for those who have strengths in the areas where they themselves are weak. When you have a fear of crowds and groups, it is intriguing to see someone who is outgoing and socially comfortable. The other person might know they talk too much and are impressed with someone who can control their tongue. It is a desire to be more outgoing on the one hand and quiet on the other, so these opposite characteristics will be watched and incorporated, and in the end, both partners are complete. Two halves make a whole. Remember, the Lord God made a woman from the rib He had taken out of the man, and He brought her to the man, and then the man was complete. He was missing something that was found in the woman, and he had what she did not have. God creates this relationship that is beautiful and compatible and helpful—one that has no competition, as the boy does not want to be pretty, and the girl does not want to be masculine. Together, you have the whole person. When this union is done correctly, it is formidable.

> GOD IS CEMENTING A STEEL FOUNDATION THRU GENERATIONS OF DEEPLY RIGHTEOUS GRANDPARENTS, PARENTS, CHILDREN AND GRANDCHILDREN, WHO THEN BECOME RELATED BY MARRIAGE WITH OTHER GROUNDED FAMILIES. THE RESULT IS BREATHTAKINGLY BEAUTIFUL.

THE UNITY OF MARRIAGE

The unifying effect that marriage has on families involved continues to be an increasing joy within the Remnant Fellowship Churches. Marriage is a glorious victory for God, the union of two precious young adults who have esteemed and admired each other, and now God has allowed them to come together. It is delightful to watch God draw them together—all of these powerful Christlike characteristics now being unified into one package. By unifying two people who put God first, the new family unit is now ten times more blessed than they were as individuals. They are exponentially more powerful for each other, for God's Church and for the Kingdom of God.

It is also a marvel of how unifying it becomes for the parents and families of the couple. The extended family and community become extremely tight knit and interwoven so that it is hard for satan to breach the walls. God is cementing a steel foundation thru generations of deeply righteous grandparents, parents, children and grandchildren, who then become related by marriage with other grounded families. The result is breathtakingly beautiful. It is rare today to see such a structure built upon wholehearted vows—an awesome, fearsome groundwork to behold in the midst of a world of disunity, discord, division and half-hearted marriages and vows. We must realize its value and praise God for it in a day and age of uncertainty, where morals are evaporating, and people do not know up from down.

> DO NOT ENTER INTO MARRIAGE WITH EXPECTATIONS FROM YOUR SPOUSE TO MEET YOUR OWN DESIRES. RATHER REVERSE THIS AND ENTER INTO MARRIAGE AS AN OPPORTUNITY TO BE REFINED AND TO ENHANCE THE LIFE OF YOUR SPOUSE.

A Strong Foundation

How do these marriages stay strong with continually growing love for one another? It is not just based on living in a house together or merely existing together; it is *growing together* in your relationship with God. You must be born again of God, which is based on selfless love.

To the young generation I say this: do not enter into marriage with expectations from your spouse to meet your own desires. Rather, *reverse* this and enter into marriage as an opportunity to be refined and to enhance the life of your spouse. *As iron sharpens iron, so one man sharpens another. Proverbs 27:17* Marriage is perfect for refinement because it helps to round off all the rough edges. We should have no expectations except fine tuning, enhancement and improvement of our own character, the purpose of our life, to be God-like, Christlike…the opportunity to be a living, walking source of love. We must consider the opportunity of marriage for self-improvement—rather than self-indulgence.

Competition in life can divide and separate close friends, but redirecting competition toward exuding the Fruits of God's Spirit is fascinating and amazing and marvelous. Do you not want to be the most humble, the most selfless, the most charitable and the most respectful? Why not outdo one another in showing honor, practicing patience, displaying kindness, and turning the other cheek? Why not allow yourself to be wronged and then have the opportunity to give love in return? Why not tame the tongue and allow God to speak to your spouse—for God's correction and redirection is so perfect and so effective, whereas a human correcting a human has to be very skillfully, carefully and wisely done to ever have an effect. Be quiet and allow God's Spirit to help in the transforming of anyone you are close to.

Let No Man Separate

As you are building this relationship, it is essential to keep in mind what matters most to God. What is important to Him? Well, if you are in the Will of God, you might drop out of college with no moral judgment because He does not say anywhere that this is something you will be judged about. However, God *does* say very clearly that His intent with marriage is for it to be a sacred union.[1]

When I was a child, divorce was extremely rare, but now it is increasingly normal. Both inside and outside the worldly church, the separation rate has risen to 50 percent—the church is the same as the rest of the world. This data does not include the statistics of breakups among cohabitants who never married. If that were considered, the actual separation statistics would be much higher.

What has changed in the last five decades that would lead to the increased rate of divorce? It is the lack of solid, moral teachings. By just listening and putting into practice the teachings of Jesus Christ, this divorce rate drops. The answer is following the footsteps of Jesus Christ from birth on. When these teachings and standards are based on the heart, and when the morals are high and the bar is raised for both husband and wife, couples have such a better chance at a lifelong union. We must take Philippians 2 to heart, because the good times and the bad times will come.

Do nothing out of selfish ambition or vain conceit, but in humility consider others better than yourselves. Each of you should look not only to your own interests, but also to the interests of others. Your attitude should be the same as that of Christ Jesus: Who, being in very nature God, did not consider equality with God something to be grasped, but made himself nothing, taking the very nature of a servant, being made in human likeness. And being found in appearance as a man, he humbled himself and became obedient to death—even death on a cross! Philippians 2:3-8

---

1 *For more about marriage and divorce, please see Chapter 24.*

LOVING WITHOUT EXPECTATIONS

All honor will be given Christ because he humbled himself, and he is now lifted up. It is giving *without expectations* every day. A human's tendency is to give to others whatever you want to give them (instead of what the other person actually wants), and then to expect them to be happy about it.

We must not expect appreciation for what we give. If you could just understand this concept, you would not believe how happy you will be. When you give like Christ with no expectations, looking only to the Father, your life will stand out—*so that you may become blameless and pure, children of God without fault in a crooked and depraved generation, in which you shine like stars in the universe... Philippians 2:15*

People marvel at those who can serve and love and get nothing in return—so many of Hollywood's movies are made from that theme. Not thinking of yourself as better than your boss or parents but putting their needs before yours and being under authority—I do not have a better word to use in this day and age than *magic*. It is unbelievable. It opens doors, and all who follow this Truth are blessed.

If you think about growing up and learning all your life that marriage is not about you—if God's selfless will is your everything—it would be almost impossible for you to separate from a Godly union. "Difficult" and "easy" are a matter of the chosen goal of the heart.

Our lasting Remnant marriages consist of a husband and wife who share the foundation set on the example of Jesus Christ, who said, *The world must learn that I love the Father and that I do exactly what my Father has commanded me... John 14:31a* That is love! Since

Christ put his Father first, our young people are following in those footsteps, and they have been so blessed as a result. No doubt there will be troubled times; but keep God first and remain unified in His Spirit.

Unity is the key to staying married. You are born again to love with God's attitudes and God's characteristics and God's Spirit. Add to this the characteristic of perseverance in never losing that child-like love for God and for your spouse. This is the love that you had at first—this free and anxious respect you have that makes you want to protect each other's reputations. Never lose the desire to spend time together and talk about the real meaning of life, which is knowing God and doing His will. Never lose the desire to remain best friends, being able to keep company all day without tiring. Expect nothing going into this marriage but to give—marriage is an opportunity to give, to practice self-denial. If you do this, everything else will be added unto you, because love never fails.[2]

To Add, You Have to Subtract

It is irony… the world's logic says if you deny yourself—if you give up your desires—you are going to be unhappy. But it is the opposite; you find you get more back with each passing day that you just keep giving and giving, and you find that you are happier, and you are better off. It is a Truth lived out by Christ all the way to his death on the cross. He gave it all, but he rebounded all the way to the highest place… to eternal life. This concept revolutionizes the world. It is a revelation, and it revitalizes. No matter what age you are, this concept makes you younger year after year. It is an incredible mystery. It completely builds up relationships, marriages,

---

2   *Love never fails. But where there are prophecies, they will cease; where there are tongues, they will be stilled; where there is knowledge, it will pass away. I Corinthians 13:8*

family; it blesses all those who touch even the edges of this amazing revelation.

In a world where marriages are becoming rare, Saints are volunteering to reduce and go from two separate people—two separate lives, two separate paths, two separate goals—to becoming one. Transforming from two to one—with one God, one path, one goal, one Lord, one faith, one baptism. Although it seems like it would reduce, this union is actually prolific in so many ways—increasing in happiness, joy, and life itself. This reduction is the only way to increase…amazing! Subtraction gives you more—when two become one, it can produce three, then four, or maybe even more in the family unit. So subtraction gives you more—mathematically, it is impossible, right? It makes no sense to the world that when you give up, you get even more—less is more. If you try to save your life, you will lose it, Jesus said, but if you lose your life with each other, you will save it.[3] That is how you save a marriage. You lose your separate life by joining with another and seeking God's path together, unified on this journey.

A whole book could be written just on the superiority of altruism—the principle or practice of unselfish concern for, or devotion to, the welfare of God first and then others—even in a world that has adopted self-centeredness and self-indulgence. People have closed their eyes to the dreadful fact that false Christianity has permeated so much of this Earth and has only produced second-rate marriages…unions separated back from one to two. It is so sad. Sometimes even while they are choosing to live in the same household, the separation is still in there in the heart, bringing bitter

---

3 *Whoever finds his life will lose it, and whoever loses his life for my sake will find it. Matthew 10:39*

days and argumentative, angry subsistence living—relations that are lonely. It is painful—relational lowliness, emptiness, financial ruin, emotional depression. Without the consistent diet of strong teachings on the true cross-driven, blessed Christianity, the church becomes weak and sick and asleep, while satan leads every soul into the black hole of self-focus. It is a miserable, hopeless existence.

Open your eyes; there is true Christianity out there—there is self-denial for God, which is love. Only true love could cause two different people—a man and a woman—to come together, changing to one name, bound so tightly that they dissolve into one being…united in love for a lifetime. Genuine love is patient and kind. Authentic love creates relationships that last forever.

Saints who continue in this path of righteousness will never be shaken, no matter what comes their way. Their lives will continue to glorify the great beloved Almighty Creator, for it is by your actions that you give your sacrifice to God. The way you live your life is your true act of worship and adoration of God.

The young couples in Remnant have found this true love that leads to a blessed, royal, beautiful union. They have found purity, they have found humility, and they are not ashamed of it. They have found this transforming message, and as a result, they have transformed from darkness to light for the glorification of God and His Church. Thru their selfless unity, they have been—and will continue to be—blessed and lifted up. What God has put together, may no man put asunder—all for the love of God. Read on to learn more about how this foundation will make these young people even more attractive to each other and more united with every year that passes.

Two Become One

Ruth made herself beautiful with her humility, love and devotion. Boaz said to her, "I've been told all about what you have done for your mother-in-law since the death of your husband—how you left your father and mother and your homeland and came to live with a people you did not know before. May the Lord repay you for what you have done. May you be richly rewarded by the Lord, the God of Israel, under whose wings you have come to take refuge." "May I continue to find favor in your eyes, my lord," she said. "You have given me comfort and have spoken kindly to your servant—though I do not have the standing of one of your servant girls." Ruth 2:11-13

How to Make Yourself Beautiful

Chapter 22

People all over the world long for love and beauty, and these concepts have been a part of fairy tales and stories for hundreds of years. However, in the past century, we have evolved into a society that has redefined beauty and redefined love in such base ways that it can be hard for people to find their way home to *true* love and *true* beauty. There is a world of expectations and fantasies that grows every year, and as we read earlier, with unmet expectations, many people are getting married later in life or even not at all. For those who take a chance and do get married, no doubt these couples spend a decade or two in shock because of unmet expectations. Many resort to drugs and alcohol to bridge expectations and reality; affairs and workaholism are used to get out of a house filled with arguments, and worship of children is used to ease the disappointment of the underperforming existence.

The world justifies such behaviors by declaring that this is just how it is…this is life. However, it is not the life lived by the early Christian families. No, these underperforming relationships are a result of believing the great delusion while ignoring the Truth in the Bible.[1] When you grow up with Barbie dolls and dream houses,

---

1 II Thessalonians 2:7-12

dream cars and dream clothes, with Ken dolls that are quiet with a permanent smile on their face, and then you get married to someone who is not "perfect"—it is painful and depressing. Many people jump from relationship to relationship…their marriages end in divorce, only to marry again where they find themselves right back in the same situation.[2]

The latest surveys indicate that recently the divorce rate is lower than in previous decades, but they have not factored in that many young people now avoid divorce by never marrying in the first place.

INWARD PEACE IS ONE OF THE ESSENTIAL FOUNDATIONS OF GENTLENESS.

A focus on *self*-fulfillment in both husbands and wives is high… self-centeredness is the culprit. Professional athletes have one of the highest rates of divorce—60 to 80 percent among the athletic elite.[3] The fact that a professional athlete fails at marriage should surprise no one. An astute commentator proposed that this rate

---

2   For more about divorce, please see Chapter 24, "Divorce and Remarriage."
3   New York Times, "Taking Vows in a League Blindsided by Divorce," 2009.

was high because these athletes suffered from "me-itis" and "got-rich-too-fast syndrome." With the exception of the elites and movie stars, the divorce rate is generally higher at the bottom of the income scale, but this does not mean money is the glue that holds marriages together. Curses from sin show no favoritism, but that is not how the tabloids make it look. It does not take long for the lost lambs of the world to start believing that God is unjust and life is unfair, and they begin desperately seeking how to keep their marriage together. The confused world gets back up each day in the hopes that things will be different, somehow, some way.

A Gentle and Quiet Spirit

Anyone who has lived for some time on this Earth has experienced that there are beasts in this world, for obviously this world is owned by satan. On the other hand, there are also kind, beautiful people in this world. While I am not referring to outward appearances, what girl does not have moments of dreaming to be beautiful and attractive? But how is beauty defined by the Heavens?

Wives, in the same way be submissive to your husbands so that, if any of them do not believe the word, they may be won over without words by the behavior of their wives, when they see the purity and reverence of your lives. Your beauty should not come from outward adornment, such as braided hair and the wearing of gold jewelry and fine clothes. Instead, it should be that of your inner self, the unfading beauty of a gentle and quiet spirit, which is of great worth in God's sight. For this is the way the holy women of the past who put their hope in God used to make themselves beautiful. They were submissive to their own husbands, like Sarah, who obeyed Abraham and called him her master. You are her daughters if you do what is right and do not give way to fear. I Peter 3:1-6

There are many misconceptions of marriage and roles, but God, who has the most refined, educated taste, describes beauty as an inward quietness…inward gentleness.

What is a Christian man? So many husbands believe it is their job to get their wife in line, and they fail to see that they themselves are nothing like Christ, who laid his life down for his Bride, the Church. Christ was the best husband as he spent his energy on setting the example, instead of judging and projecting. Those who project will never transform—indeed, they become the beast. It takes all of our soul, mind and strength to change, all of it…not a moment can be wasted on projection. It is a complete waste of your precious limited time. Why have some husbands been so unaware of who Jesus really is? *Take my yoke upon you and learn from me, for I am* **gentle** *and humble in heart. Matthew 11:29a* Gentlemen who are Christlike are the most powerful entities on Earth. Christlike, Heaven-bound men have power. Unfortunately, in this generation, being gentle is often associated with weakness and fragility.

There is so much fear associated with the prospect of marriage—fear of losing your agenda for the sake of someone else. Likewise, in their jobs, men fear being submissive to their bosses—because who is there to support you and your dreams? If you were to lay your life down for someone's salvation, what would become of your time? To submit yourself and to be supportive of others' agendas takes great reserve and self-control and a selflessness that is becoming extinct.

The true Christian family is beautiful…it assumes that those who are sacrificial are void of physical and verbal abuse. Christian children are raised in gentleness. Goodwill and unity in the home should be the family's daily and supreme pursuit. **Inward peace is one of the essential foundations of gentleness.** We should remove sin and the selfish ambition that causes us inner turmoil. When this is removed, you can be gentle.

It is not beyond your reach to have your family transformed. We have the choice to do as the Scripture says and make ourselves beautiful. It is how the women of old made themselves beautiful. It is easier to be gentle if you are genuinely undisturbed in your heart and if your mind is free of selfish ambition and greed for self. Peace from within comes from living right before God so that you have confidence with God.

How does staying quiet, giving in, keeping the peace, bowing out of arguments and not insisting on your way work? It transforms not just husbands and bosses, but all who are present. The power of the prayer of the submissive person is supernatural and gives you the peace that you are being taken care of. The gentle word turns away wrath.[4] To be gentle requires a quiet strength that results from spiritual intelligence. Gentleness is more of a **praying** and **thinking** way of life rather than the world's way of making things happen by brute force, control, moods, anger or the silent treatment. When you communicate with unthreatening body language and calmness, you have conquered the spiritual realm of demons. To accomplish this, you must consider the other person's thoughts and feelings. That takes time and spiritual intelligence. It is this intellectual meditation of consideration that sets the Saints apart from the world of needy, greedy, grabbing, angry, controlling humans who are destined for trouble all their lives. Oh, for manners to come back to the youth and to be the defining characteristic of the Saints!

If there were no purpose or power in this submissive way of life, it would be less intriguing and more excruciating—but as it is, there

---

4   A gentle answer turns away wrath, but a harsh word stirs up anger. Proverbs 15:1

are instant, incredible results that I have noted from all those who have tried it and let me know about answered prayer after answered prayer, incredible turnarounds that I have witnessed for more than 30 years. God is the Genius behind it all. There is a purpose behind

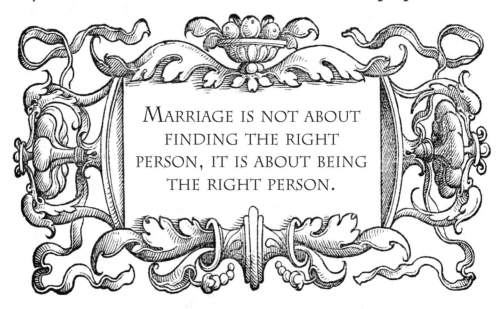

MARRIAGE IS NOT ABOUT FINDING THE RIGHT PERSON, IT IS ABOUT BEING THE RIGHT PERSON.

being gentle and placing yourself under authority. It is a superior way. Again, *Wives, in the same way be submissive to your husbands so that, if any of them do not believe the word, they may be won over without words by the behavior of their wives... I Peter 3:1* It is a beautiful concept...to be won over without words. Remember, you are the special daughters of the holy women of old if you do what is right and do not give way to fear for yourself.

GOD LIFTS UP THE HUMBLE

Yes, the beasts abound, but God is in control and knows how to humble the prideful. Once you have that quiet and gentle spirit, God steps in. Once you lay down the directing, the correcting, the teaching, and the dominating role and choose the role given as the wife, God then does an amazing work and brings out the best in all of us. The testing can seem dreadfully unfair, but the great Prophets of old teach us that revenge is the Lord's.[5] We are not to take revenge but to overcome any evil spirits with gracious spirits, good spirits.

Chapter 4 of the Book of Daniel tells of the arrogant Babylonian King Nebuchadnezzar. Because of this king's arrogance, God cursed him to become a beast for years—he grew claws and feathers and lived in the wild among the animals. To break his pride, it took losing the status of a human, a being that should be far above the animal. Nebuchadnezzar's pride did not break in a day. It took years before he could see that he was a beast, that he was not a god, that he could not change a thing without God. He could not transform until he could do things God's way—acting with kindness and gentleness until he was able to say, "Heaven rules." From a human to a beast, and now from beast to human, and he was even royalty. No doubt we have seen this story lived out in husbands and in prodigal children—from rebellious beast to a gentleman. It is not always the husband, however, for there are many cruel wives or rebellious teenagers.

A foolish son is his father's ruin, and a quarrelsome wife is like a constant dripping. Proverbs 19:13

Houses and wealth are inherited from parents, but a prudent wife is from the Lord. Proverbs 19:14

Better to live on a corner of the roof than share a house with a quarrelsome wife. Proverbs 21:9

---

5   *It is mine to avenge; I will repay. In due time their foot will slip; their day of disaster is near and their doom rushes upon them. Deuteronomy 32:35*

Better to live in a desert than with a quarrelsome and ill-tempered wife. Proverbs 21:19

A quarrelsome wife is like a constant dripping on a rainy day. Proverbs 27:15

Neither husband nor wife is to be quarrelsome; this is referencing anti-authority. The wife is not to be quarrelsome but rather brilliantly quiet and most careful with all words in the home—she is there to build bridges, not break them down.

A Picture of Beauty

Most likely inspired by the Bible story of Nebuchadnezzar is the novel *Beauty and the Beast*, a traditional fairy tale written in 1740 by French novelist Gabrielle-Suzanne Barbot de Villeneuve. Although the story has been revised several times, the original version is this: A wealthy, widowed merchant lives in a mansion with his six children: three sons and three daughters. All of his daughters are very beautiful, but the youngest, named Beauty, is the most lovely. She is kind, well-read and pure of heart, while the elder sisters, in contrast, are wicked, selfish, vain and spoiled. The sisters secretly taunt and threaten Beauty, treating her more like a servant than a sister because they are jealous. The merchant eventually loses all of his wealth and ships in a storm at sea. He and his children are consequently forced to live in a small farmhouse and work for their living. After several years, the merchant has hope as he hears that one of the trade ships was found. Before leaving, he asks his children if they wish for him to bring any gifts back for them. Thinking their father's wealth has returned, his sons ask for weaponry and horses, and his oldest daughters ask for clothing, jewels and the finest dresses possible. The youngest daughter, Beauty, is satisfied with just a rose from her father. The merchant, to his dismay, finds that his ship's cargo has been seized to pay his debts, leaving him once again without money to even buy his children their presents.

While returning to the farmhouse, the merchant becomes lost in a forest during a storm. Seeking shelter, he enters a dazzling palace. A hidden figure opens the giant doors and silently invites him in. The merchant finds tables inside laden with food and drink—left

POWER IS GIVEN TO THE GENTLE.

for him by the palace's unseen owner. The merchant accepts this gift and spends the night there. The next morning as the merchant is about to leave, he sees a rose garden. Upon picking the loveliest rose he can find to bring home to Beauty, the merchant is confronted by a hideous Beast who condemns him to death for stealing after accepting his hospitality. The merchant begs to be set free, arguing that he had only picked the rose as a gift for his youngest daughter. The Beast agrees to let him go with the condition that the merchant return to the palace as his prisoner.

The Beast sends him on his way with wealth, jewels and fine clothes for his sons and daughters. Beauty, sensing something is wrong, pries the truth from her father. Her brothers threaten to fight the Beast, but the father dissuades them, knowing that there is no chance against the monster. Beauty sneaks away and makes a deal with the Beast to substitute her life in place of her father's life. In an attempt to make her happy during her stay, the Beast gives her lavish clothing and food, and she eventually tolerates his company. Their relationship grows, and the Beast becomes a gentleman.

In time, Beauty trusts the Beast and asks for permission just once to visit her father and family, all on the condition that she return to his palace. The Beast gives her a magical mirror and ring—the mirror allows her to see what is going on back at the castle, and the ring allows her to return to the castle in an instant when turned three times. Once she gets home, her jealous older sisters are surprised to find her well-fed and dressed in finery. In their envy, they try to trick her into not returning, but Beauty uses the mirror to see the Beast back at the castle. She is horrified to discover that the Beast is lying half-dead from heartbreak near the rose bushes, and she escapes her sisters by using the ring to return to the castle.

> EVEN WHEN IT IS NOT RETURNED, GIVE MUCH, MUCH MORE THAN YOU EVER RECEIVED.

Beauty weeps over the Beast, and her loving tears drip on him. In an instant, the Beast revives, and what is more, he further transforms into a very handsome Prince. At this point, his true history is revealed: long ago, a fairy had turned the Prince into a hideous beast after he refused to let her in from the rain, and only true love could break this curse. He and Beauty are married, and they live happily ever after together.

BEING THE RIGHT PERSON

If any brother has a wife who is not a believer and she is willing to live with him, he must not divorce her. And if a woman has a husband who is not a believer and he is willing to live with her, she must not divorce him… How do you know, wife, whether you will save your husband? Or, how do you know, husband, whether you will save your wife? I Corinthians 7:12b-13, 16

TO GIVE WHEN OTHERS DO NOT GIVE IS BEAUTY!

People who jump from relationship to relationship looking for just this "right person" will never find Heaven's love. You are not to simply go from person to person. Indeed, significant emotional pain lies in the wake of any other view. Do not look behind you or ahead; rather, focus on the present—making the relationship given to you the most beautiful ever.

Marriage is not about finding the right person; it is about being the right person. God encourages marriage to provide the opportunity to birth, grow and embellish eternal qualities. Success is dependent on a commitment of accepting God's Will in our God-given circumstances. Our personal transformation from a beast to a beauty comes from this driven determination to persevere so as to make a victorious success of the job, the marriage, the financial status that

God gave us—regardless of the circumstances. Selfishness has led to division, but now selfLESSness—God-focus—will keep marriages together. Peace will be achieved, and then, who knows, oh wife… who knows, oh husband, if you are not going to be used as Heaven's glorious instrument as an evangelist.[6]

How short-sighted to be concerned with your own needs and protecting your pride, yet how brave are those who say "I'm sorry." Being the first to give in, the first to embrace humility—a small change on our part makes for a great change in the unbelievers in the end. Seeing beyond the surface, removing yourself, and loving the unlovely constitute the purpose and the sway and the influence for transformed lives—even if the only life transformed is your own. There is nothing to fear, but rather an ironic joy in shedding your pride. Pride is useless for those who cling to it—destroying both self and the family.

What if you gave up your ambitious dreams for different circumstances and turned your circumstances into the dream? Make this commitment to transform your family into royalty, the Holy Priesthood. God blesses this approach, wanting Godly marriages, wanting generosity and kindness from the husband and gentle submission from the wife so that the two can become one. It is in your hands…

A gentle answer turns away wrath, but a harsh word stirs up anger. Proverbs 15:1

Through patience a ruler can be persuaded, and a gentle tongue can break a bone. Proverbs 25:15

---

6   *How do you know, wife, whether you will save your husband? Or, how do you know, husband, whether you will save your wife? I Corinthians 7:16*

Do not tell me there is power in brute force. The power is given to the gentle.

GIVING WHEN OTHERS DO NOT GIVE

Here is the challenge: look for the good in your spouse, in your job, in your circumstances, with the parents that you have; look for the good while giving even just a little more. Even when it is not returned, give much, much more than you ever received. God will provide for you. Does it matter if you are always the one giving, and *God* provides you with everything? How could you make it in Heaven if you expected other heavenly Angels or subjects to provide for you? We must start now to depend on God for all needs: emotionally, spiritually and physically. GOD is everything. However, *you* are to give—*So in everything, do to others what you would have them do to you, for this sums up the Law and the Prophets. Matthew 7:12.* To give when others do not give is beauty, extraordinary beauty! Who knows… what if you saved your spouse for eternity?

Is returning evil with good too great a price to pay? It has the power to transform. Just the smallest act of respect and admiration might cause a huge transformation in the arrogant. What a purpose in life! Do not fall short of your purpose and expect the spouse to change before you do, for such an expectation is the way of the base world… the idea that if the husband does not bend or respond to your kindness, you will not give again. Most humans expect only to be slightly more giving than the spouse, slightly less prideful, slightly less defensive. Why do humans tend to lower ourselves to the lowest common denominator? If there is one bad child in a class, by the end of the school year, the whole class has lowered themselves to the most basic, least sophisticated level of taste, sensibility or behavior of the group.

Notice that having true inward beauty is of great worth to the glory of God—it is to make *Him* look good. It is more than suffering or turning the other cheek at the hands of a beast. It is more than merely facing adversity in living with personalities that are beastly. God is calling the extraordinary to give *more* love in return. In fact, these difficult situations are given for our exquisite training to test if we can see beyond the surface and into the windows of eternity; yet it is even more. It is a mysterious adventure thru the Kingdom of God. It starts with suffering like Christ for the salvation of another, but until there are tears of love for the beast, there is no transformation. The beast would forever remain a beast and die as a beast. Lives that are void of this true love only make the beasts of this world more reclusive and bitter and cruel in each home. How many beasts are out there slowly dying? But how rare are the beauties—those who look beyond the surface and deeper into the potential of the human soul—from an animal to a human.

> DIFFICULT SITUATIONS ARE GIVEN FOR OUR EXQUISITE TRAINING TO TEST IF WE CAN SEE BEYOND THE SURFACE AND INTO THE WINDOWS OF ETERNITY.

As Saints, we must not take negative behavior personally and instead must see the pain behind the insults, the negativity, the self-centeredness, the insecurity. We must not look at the evil but rather at the *potential* of those caught up in sin—using **love** to surface the good in others. We must reach out to the unlovely and give love in return.[7]

To those who have been called out—the Ecclesia, who have been called to be like Christ—why not take the challenge of the

---

7   *For more on Loving the Unlovely, see Chapter 22 of* The History of the Love of God. *Find out how to get your copy in the Appendix.*

Heavens? Take my challenge to not lower your behavior. Do not compare yourself to those who give less, who are more prideful or more defensive—but instead, rise above in such a calling, to be as far apart as Beauty was from the base Beast. Transform from a dragon to the divine, from a witch to the worshipful, from the antichrist to an adoring angel—then you will have the power to help transform those around you.

Selfless love transforms. If it were just for this life, perhaps the sacrifice would be too much. However, it is not just for this life but for *eternal life*—to help give eternal beings a glorious life! The true beauty is a choice made by the beholder of God and His Holy Spirit. Praise God that we can apply God's Will to be transformed and then help others transform. Be as gracious and as kind and as loving on a scale that spans the distance between that of a beauty from a beast—that much love, that much giving. May we rise to this royal calling—not to be just slightly different—but to behave far beyond the mundane base world and be *extraordinarily beautiful*, Heaven's beauty, for the needed glorification of the Beautiful God of the Universe.

Your goal as the leader of the household is to allow no idols in the house, and then to bring the family to Church, to Christ, as every unit in this Royal Priesthood is being refined. Godly men are following in the footsteps of Christ so that the children know and the wife knows that they worship and adore God. Page 294.

A Christian Husband

Chapter 23

Teach the older men to be temperate, worthy of respect, self-controlled, and sound in faith, in love and in endurance. Titus 2:2

We all long to be closer to Christ, the Apostles and their examples, which show us how we are to live and what we are to be doing—a picture of the behavior of God-fearing men and God-fearing families. The depictions of the Christian men in the Bible are not there as merely a historical record. They are there for us to emulate and imitate and incorporate into our lives in every way. Our goal is to imitate these Godly examples. In Ephesians, Paul laid out for us the foundation of being a husband and a father.

Husbands, love your wives, just as Christ loved the church and gave himself up for her to make her holy, cleansing her by the washing with water through the word, and to present her to himself as a radiant church, without stain or wrinkle or any other blemish, but holy and blameless. In this same way, husbands ought to love their wives as their own bodies. He who loves his wife loves himself. After all, no one ever hated his own body, but he feeds and cares for it, just as Christ does the church, for we are members of his body. Ephesians 5:25-30

"To make her *holy*" is quite a mission. Think about this vision—every husband investing time and energy into his wife, like a man invests time and energy into his most beloved, treasured hobby. When you see this lived out, it is such a light. Can you imagine this light in every household—where there is complete compliance inside the home and unity with the Church and the leadership, with everyone walking shoulder to shoulder in the same direction for the Kingdom of God?

Now, what does this look like on a practical level? A Godly man assures the wife of his love and commitment to God first and then to her. These men are free to let the world know that they love their beloved partner for life above all other humans—that this woman is who they have been put on Earth to take care of. They have no hesitation in letting others know about their deep devotion to God and how much they love and adore their wife. At home, they spend time troubleshooting anything that blocks attendance at Church so that the whole family is in place sitting in the Sanctuary and ready to worship God. Attending the assembly is the focus of the whole week, and everything that happens throughout the week is directed toward that goal. All efforts are directed toward guiding and purifying the hearts so that the parents' and the children's minds are ready for the Sabbath. The father lets the children know that he is excited about going to sing and to pray before God Almighty with a host of other Saints.

> THINK ABOUT THIS VISION: EVERY HUSBAND INVESTING TIME AND ENERGY INTO HIS WIFE, LIKE A MAN INVESTS TIME AND ENERGY INTO HIS MOST BELOVED HOBBY.

Making Prayer a Priority

The early Christians were devoted to prayer, to the teachings of God and the Apostles, to the fellowship, to evangelism and to baptism.[1] They were *full* of the Holy Spirit. They were so devoted to prayer that in almost every book in the Bible you will see that anytime something happened, they were in the middle of prayer.

On their release, Peter and John went back to their own people and reported all that the chief priests and elders had said to them. When they heard this, they raised their voices together in prayer to God… After they prayed, the place where they were meeting was shaken. And they were all filled with the Holy Spirit and spoke the word of God boldly. Acts 4:23-24a, 31

We need to slow down and take the time to get down in prayer before our God while we have the chance. If God really is your first love, then why would you *not* talk to Him all the time? If you really believed that your prayer will be answered, then why would you not pray without ceasing?[2] Are you leaving that impression on your family? Are your children familiar with seeing their father down on his knees in prayer? Nothing in our lives should be half-hearted, mundane or aimlessly done… no aimless meals, no aimless times getting together, no aimless time spent without prayer.

Here is the question to ask: What does your home look like? The home is a reflection of you, and you are going to be responsible

---

1   *They devoted themselves to the apostles' teaching and to the fellowship, to the breaking of bread and to prayer. Acts 2:42*
2   *Be joyful always; pray continually; give thanks in all circumstances, for this is God's will for you in Christ Jesus. I Thessalonians 5:16-18*

as you work out your own salvation.[3] In your home, do your children know you as a man of prayer? Do you have calluses on your knees? As they all wake up, does your family know that this new day is about prayer? Do you have just one prayer time during the day, or do you have many times of prayer throughout the day? The Jewish people had three times a day of prayer, but again, we also see the early Christians praying throughout the day. In Acts 10, we read that Peter went to his roof to pray and received a vision and revelation from God.[4] How do you expect revelations to come if you are not praying? For the sake of your family, you need to be sure you are praying throughout the day, both praying over your family and praying with them.

ATTENTION TO THE NEEDS OF THE FAMILY

Kind instruction is on the mouth of Godly men as they gently remind their children of the behavior that is expected in the presence of the Lord. "Kind" is the key word. At home, these men are not self-focused or self-seeking; therefore, they are not moody or manipulating with silent treatment, anger or slamming doors. These men encourage the wife and have respect for her intellect and her gifts—always including the wife's gifts in managing the household. This union is not a dictatorship; this is a partnership.

These great men do not just leave housework up to the wife; they help out when needed. They spend time with the wife and time with the children, teaching the right way to live, both in work and in play. A lot can be learned in play, such as how to be a good sport and how

---

3   *Therefore, my dear friends, as you have always obeyed—not only in my presence, but now much more in my absence—continue to work out your salvation with fear and trembling.* Philippians 2:12
4   Acts 10:9-23

to be Godly in play time and not selfish or greedy or competitive to a fault.[5] There are family times of reading the Bible, and then, most importantly, individually checking on each member's prayer life and their time with their Creator.

This teaching should not be left only up to the wife; it is the father's role. The fathers get to be professors, instructors, kind teachers; and as you are teaching, *you* are learning as you share with your family everything about their behavior, their mindset, their interac-

WE NEED TO SLOW DOWN AND TAKE THE TIME TO GET DOWN IN PRAYER BEFORE OUR GOD WHILE WE HAVE THE CHANCE.

tions, their character, and how they approach God—the things one should do and the things one should not do. There is so much to learn! The family knows what you love, and they will see your love for God first. It is instinctive; you do not have to say it with words. They know it by your actions. They will know if your first love is really self. They will know if it is food, alcohol, money or your job. They will know if it is sports, hobbies or womanizing. They can see right thru you!

---

5 *Please see Chapter 14 "Godly Competition…The Pefect Athlete" for more on this topic.*

They know if your heart is filled with pride—they can tell by the time you spend with them and by what comes out of your mouth.[6] You cannot hide what you love. A righteous man loves God—you should be known by your family for loving God first and worshiping God above all things.

The Godly Man

Your goal as the leader of the household is to have no idols in the house, and then to bring the family to Church, to a Body of Believers, as every unit in this Royal Priesthood is being refined. A Godly man is willing to bow down before God in submissive prayer so that his wife and children know that he worships and adores God. You long for purity in your home, where the words are gracious and there is no gossip. You cannot ignore things anymore. You will want to have a finger on the pulse of the conversations in your home. You cannot tune it out or turn the television up louder. You need to listen to what the children are saying, what your wife is saying, and what is in their hearts so that you can encourage and advise them and help with their needs. Are you listening to your family, to what is in their hearts, to what is in your house? The family knows *you*—do you know *them*?

> THE FATHERS GET TO BE PROFESSORS, INSTRUCTORS, KIND TEACHERS... AND AS YOU ARE TEACHING, YOU ARE LEARNING.

Are you more concerned about the praise of man over the praise of God? Your family will know this because you will never help your wife or child go all the way to true self-denial and putting God first.

---

6   *The good man brings good things out of the good stored up in his heart, and the evil man brings evil things out of the evil stored up in his heart. For out of the overflow of his heart his mouth speaks. Luke 6:45*

You might correct them initially, but you do not follow up on it, or you overlook it, and you let it go. You do not hold the line. Children will know when you care more about their approval than about the approval from God, or when you care more about making them happy than you do about having unity with your spouse, and they will use this knowledge to control the whole family. A Godly man will kindly maintain the line of authority, but not to make his own life more comfortable or so that everything will be perfect for him. No! He is making sure that every direction is for the Godly direction of the family so that they will have a better relationship with God.

The selfish man will control his children and wife for his own reasons. He will manipulate the family to make sure that it is easy on the father, so that there is no noise to bother him, nothing to interfere with his television show, nothing that might interrupt his evenings. He will make sure that those children grow up to be "independent" so that they will not seek him out for his time or advice in the future. Another form of selfishness is seen in the father who gives the children whatever they want, hoping that his child will be his best friend and always be there for him to meet his own emotional needs. Both situations are sick. It is selfishness…loving things and using people for his own gain. A royal man of God will use things and love people; it is the opposite way of life.

A good, righteous father will think only of God first—God's need for righteousness and God's need for righteous offspring—and he will consider the needs of his child so that child will be able to access the Kingdom of God and build a personal relationship with God Almighty. That is all that matters to the Godly man; it is his only worry. It is the reason that Godly men help their families and guide them, strengthening the wife's relationship with God and the child's relationship with God. There is no other purpose but this

Connection with God Almighty. The father is teaching the family about self-denial, living out self-sacrifice, and helping them learn how to pick up their cross, showing them thru his own example that this focus is lovely. As a result, Godly men are never self-focused or self-seeking, and their families will follow their example. These men will kindly, gently, longsufferingly direct the family, with *all* patience, knowing that if the father has to gently repeat himself over and over, that is just what God's kind Holy Spirit does for us every night. They are ready to give gentle, thoughtful, daily instruction of the same idea over and over if needed, almost expecting it not to sink in, and ready to repeat it when necessary.

This Royal Remnant Revival was not founded on selfishness but on self-*less*-ness. The men of Remnant are to love their wives, as we read from Ephesians earlier, just as Christ loved the Church and gave himself up for her to make her holy by cleansing her by the washing with the water thru the Word. But what does that mean? As the father, *you* are taking the time to study God's Word. You are up in the middle of the night seeking out God, and then you are with your family during the day, studying God's Word, looking to see if there is anything else hidden in your heart. Are you giving enough of your time to this responsibility? Are you washing the entire family thru this Word?

THE DRIVING FORCE FOR THE FAMILY

Near the end of Ephesians, the Apostle Paul continues:

For this reason a man will leave his father and mother and be united to his wife, and the two will become one flesh. This is a profound mystery but I am talking about Christ and the church. However, each one of you also must love his wife as he loves himself, and the wife must respect her husband. Ephesians 5:31-33

A Christian Husband

This is a beautiful, powerful, unbelievably amazing picture. It *is* profound—a mystery, as Paul says—and it is worth fighting for. It is worth getting up every day and living for this objective. It is the number one purpose of your life, your very being, why you are where you are, why you are married to whom you are married. There is no place like the Church in being able to implement this God-given authority line in the home. In fact, I would say the world is the opposite—in this world, it may seem impossible to implement God's authority line. They are not going to back you or support you on the idea of upholding authority, but the True Church will support Godly authority.

Having this authority does not mean you are the source for everything. For example, you may have a wife who is a talented accountant or bookkeeper, and you want to use that gift in your household. You do not have to be the one who knows it all, but you need to know where to find that information. You need to be involved at Church. You need to know how to counsel and encourage. You need to seek what God wants and how He wants it implemented. You need to be in the Word more and more every day. If you do not know as much about an issue and your wife knows more, find out what she has learned, but your position is the one who implements it in the family. You are the driving force for your family.

> ARE YOU LISTENING TO YOUR FAMILY, TO WHAT IS IN THEIR HEART…TO WHAT IS IN YOUR HOUSE? THE FAMILY KNOWS YOU—DO YOU KNOW THEM?

You have everything you need for a beautiful, peaceful household, letting your family know that your focus is to serve God. Your children should have confidence that everything you are asking them to do, every task—whether it is cleaning their rooms, doing homework, helping their mother or siblings, going to Church, or any other request—will be prayed over and is only there so they can have a relationship with God Almighty and live forever with Him. That is your only goal for them, and that is how they will know that you truly love them. It is about their relationship with God so that God's Kingdom can grow.

Authority in the Workplace

Everyone must submit himself to the governing authorities, for there is no authority except that which God has established. The authorities that exist have been established by God. Consequently, he who rebels against the authority is rebelling against what God has instituted, and those who do so will bring judgment on themselves. Romans 13:1-2

Where many men stumble in this faith is committing to their authority line at work. Most men believe their problems all stem from their boss. These men have expectations for what they think they deserve or how they should be treated. You may feel you have been given more responsibility with less pay. Perhaps people who are less productive than you are receiving more favor at work. You see yourself as the one doing the lion's share of the work but not getting salary increases. You are the one who is put down or not invited to committee meetings. You believe you are entitled to a better job because of your skills, your creativity; you deserve more attention. But it is just the opposite. It is the men and women who humble themselves and are grateful—who feel they do not even deserve a job or recognition or bonuses—who are the ones who end up being honored and upheld in the workplace. They are the same ones who build up the True Church.

The New Jerusalem, the City of God, was founded on the suffering Christ. The Remnant of the Kingdom of Love and Weigh Down is a message of Christlike pridelessness and selflessness that starts by eating less food, because the Truth is you do not deserve more than what your body needs.[7] In fact, you deserve a lot less of anything that you have. I cannot think of a better medicine to make the soul happy and content than to take this concept to heart and know that it is true.

PROVIDING FOR THE FAMILY

As we read earlier, *He who loves his wife loves himself.* You love yourself and feed yourself and take care of yourself, so you are loving your family as yourself and providing food and housing, meeting their needs every day, working to provide for them as the Lord has commanded. The amount makes no difference because it is as the Lord blesses—everyone has a different lifestyle, and that is all for the glory of God. If there is a need in your family, you bring it into the Church. That is God's joy! Within the Church, every person is cared for, and even every animal is fed; there should be no needs within the Church. No one has too much, and no one has too little, and therefore we can praise God together as one unit and as one family.[8] Not that everything will be equal, but we will all be able to give to one another using our different gifts, and those who are able to be generous can be generous.

Most of all, providing for the family means providing the spiritual food they need, making sure they fill up on Truth… having time

---

7 To learn more about how to overcome overeating, see *Weigh Down Works!* Find out how to get your copy in the Appendix.
8 As it is written: "He who gathered much did not have too much, and he who gathered little did not have too little." II Corinthians 8:15

in the Bible, being able to get on All Access[9] and being at Church on time with their minds and hearts ready, even arriving early to give the family time to prepare and be in prayer before the service begins. This is important. It also means being prepared for demonic attacks and knowing how to focus only on God. What father would not give food to a child who asked for it? Who is going to turn their child away when there is a need?[10] In the same way, what father would not feed *spiritual* food every day to a hungry family?

Homes in this beautiful, Royal Revival are to be different than homes in the world. If each man has a relationship with the most powerful Being of the Universe and then passes on this relationship to their families—if they do everything to ensure their own relationship with God for the sake of their wives and their children—then the whole family will be connected to God, and the beauty will be mind-boggling. You must continue to read on, for there is more to learn…

Prayer

Dearest Father in Heaven, the most Royal of Royals, the King of Kings, the Lord of all Lords, you are the Alpha and the Omega. You are most amazing, and your crown is higher and more glorious than any crown. Your clothing and your robes are royal, and your subjects are royal. We praise you for gathering together love and generosity and patience—all the men who are mighty, who are strong enough to be patient, who are the most gentle men. God, those are the muscles that are amazing. Christ had all of those muscles to be able to face a world of angry, hurting people, and then to love them and then die for them while asking forgiveness for them because they did not know what they were doing. It is a power beyond power. It is a peace beyond peace. It is a stamina that is unbelievable. Christ is so worthy of our praise and our imitation. I praise you, God, for the men of Zion, the New Jerusalem. Father, I pray for

---

9   For more about All Access, visit www.WeighDown.com
10   Which of you, if his son asks for bread, will give him a stone? Matthew 7:9

their homes to be completely healed and to become gorgeous, beautiful examples, a light on a hill. I pray for these families to unite and to come together and make a united Remnant. I pray for this Kingdom to last until Jesus comes back. May you tie this Church family together; may it be the tightest bond, tighter than any molecular bonding from any substance that has ever been discovered. Father, I pray that it will be so clear to the world. May this message shine out like a beacon, and may we teach this to our children so that they can follow you all the rest of their lives. In Jesus' name we pray, Amen!

No one was more sympathetic to the oppressed, the downhearted, or the abused than Jesus Christ. Christ was neither condemning nor judgmental when he talked to the woman at the well who had five husbands and the one she was living with was not her husband, but he was gentle and he led her to righteousness.

Divorce and Remarriage

Chapter 24

As we have read, in the beginning God created man and woman and He launched His glorious concept of marriage where the two will become one, and what God has put together let no man separate. Where there was no genuine marriage between the two, however, He allowed for divorce and remarriage.[1][2] God himself divorced Israel, His Bride, for her unfaithfulness; God used the term "adultery," but this was adultery of the heart.[3][4] This has long been debated, but I believe that when God gave Israel a long time to get things right and then finally divorced, He set the example for earthly marriages. Man is the one who has distorted the Scriptures, leaving oppressed people

---

1   So God created man in his own image, in the image of God he created him; male and female he created them. Genesis 1:27
2   "For this reason a man will leave his father and mother and be united to his wife, and the two will become one flesh." So they are no longer two, but one. Therefore what God has joined together, let man not separate. Mark 10:7-9
3   I gave faithless Israel her certificate of divorce and sent her away because of all her adulteries. Jeremiah 3:8a
4   "You have heard that it was said, 'Do not commit adultery.'" But I tell you that anyone who looks at a woman lustfully has already committed adultery with her in his heart. Matthew 5:27-28

in burdensome situations, or if allowing divorce, has shamed those involved to an extent where they are once again oppressed. This is not the intent of God. When God divorced Israel, He then remarried, creating a new covenant with a forever faithful Bride.[5]

God's Example of a Faithful Marriage

God made His first offer of marriage to His chosen people and sealed it with the Ten Commandments. Heartbreakingly, the people turned away and were repeatedly unfaithful with recurrent idolatry and adultery of the heart. This was described in the Book of Hosea, where God had Hosea marry a prostitute who left him time after time for other men, even bearing children from adultery.[6] After this repeated and particularly appalling and disgusting rejection and disrespect, God warned that this Covenant marriage would end in a divorce. He spoke thru Jeremiah and was quoted by the Apostle Paul in Hebrews 8…

"The time is coming," declares the Lord, "when I will make a new covenant with the house of Israel and with the house of Judah. It will not be like the covenant I made with their forefathers when I took them by the hand to lead them out of Egypt, because they did not remain faithful to my covenant, and I turned away from them," declares the Lord. "This is the covenant I will make with the house of Israel after that time," declares the Lord. "I will put my laws in their minds and write them on their hearts. I will be their God, and they will be my people. No longer will a man teach his neighbor, or a man his brother, saying, 'Know the Lord,' because they will all know me, from the least of them to the greatest. For I will forgive their wickedness and will remember their sins no more." By

---

5 To read more about this, please see Chapter 8, "Conditional Love" and Chapter 11, "Let No Debt Remain" in *History of the Love of God, Volume II—A Love More Ancient than Time*
6 Hosea 2

calling this covenant "new," he has made the first one obsolete; and what is obsolete and aging will soon disappear. Hebrews 8:7-13

This is clear—the fault was not with the contract or the required Covenant itself; it was with the response of the people to this contract. What was obsolete and aging was the behavior of the *people*. Something had to change, for God had extended His hand only to be rebuffed time and time again, but His long-suffering was at an end. God started over with a new marriage contract, a forever-faithful Covenant with the new Bride of Christ. Humans can be faithful to a spouse; how much more so to their Creator? But there would be something very distinctly different—this Covenant would be for a new people, so not just any Gentile or Jew could enter into this new Covenant under Christ. They had to have an incredible quality…the quality of *faithfulness*—the faithful people. To be saved by faith would take on a whole new meaning. It cannot be mere intellectual knowledge. Faith does not mean saved by intellect. No, we are saved by faithfulness—by having no idolatry or adultery of the heart, no revolving doors, no flirting eyes, no looking to the left or the right.[7] Only the faithful evermore could come to this new community, this New Covenant with God, created for those who have love written in their heart. Opening up the doors to any heart from any nation or any race, this Covenant contained words engraved deep in the hearts and minds that God would be their God. God has not changed, and the words written on stone have not changed, but the

> FAITH DOES NOT MEAN SAVED BY INTELLECT. NO, WE ARE SAVED BY FAITHFULNESS— BY HAVING NO IDOLATRY OR ADULTERY OF THE HEART.

---

7 For more on this topic, see www.RemnantFellowship.org "What We Believe" section for "Saved By Faithfulness."

people had to change and respond to this unbelievable opportunity of a proposal of marriage to the Heavens.

Breaking God's heart is what is obsolete. God is love; He is social and wants a people of His own. It is symbolic that God wants a wife—this marriage where you share everything. God is inviting the heart of man to walk with Him with no pride and in a faithful-evermore relationship.

The Meaning of a "Faithful Spouse"

The Remnant affirms the sanctity of marriage. A Remnant marriage by definition is one where a man and a woman are both believers; therefore, they have put God, Christ and His Church first. Both are idol free and truly believe in putting others above themselves, and as a result, they are never egocentric, always looking inward, and never projecting fault onto others, which creates a marriage that is full of peace, tranquility, love and respect. Unity and harmony are expected as God's will is first in both the husband's heart and the wife's heart.

The definition of a true Christian husband is a man who keeps his vows and responsibilities. Likewise, the definition of a Christian wife is one who keeps her vows and responsibilities. Both definitions are based on love and mutual consent. The man's vows define a husband's role, and the woman's vows define a wife's role. The definition of a husband in the Old Testament, which was continued into the New Testament, was specific. It is summed up in Ephesians 5:25-33 by the Apostle Paul, as we have read earlier…

Husbands, love your wives, just as Christ loved the church and gave himself up for her to make her holy, cleansing her by the washing with water through the word, and to present her to himself as a radiant church, without stain or wrinkle or any other blemish, but holy and blameless.

In this same way, husbands ought to love their wives as their own bodies. He who loves his wife loves himself. After all, no one ever hated his own body, but he feeds and cares for it, just as Christ does the church—for we are members of his body. "For this reason a man will leave his father and mother and be united to his wife, and the two will become one flesh." This is a profound mystery—but I am talking about Christ and the church. However, each one of you also must love his wife as he loves himself, and the wife must respect her husband.

So to love your wife as Christ loved the Church—this is an all-encompassing standard of excellence. Jewish law requires a husband to be mature and control himself physically, and it forbids any attractions outside the marriage. For the wife or the husband not to satisfy the spouse's emotional needs was grounds for divorce in Jewish law.[8] The husband puts God and His Church first, and he demonstrates all the Fruits of the Spirit.[9] As we have read, he must be kind, compassionate, humble and forgiving, which would make him a gentle man.[10] Obviously, he must work and provide for his wife and his family or he would be considered an infidel. I Timothy 5:8 says… *If anyone does not provide for his relatives, and especially for his immediate family, he has denied the faith and is worse than an unbeliever.* The definition and strict adherence of "husband" from God thru Moses and the Prophets, Christ and the Apostles, has had a positive impact on all cultures and religions.

Before marriage these vows and roles are taught, then are publicly declared at a Covenant ceremony and upheld by the Shepherds and entire Church Body, holding people accountable. If any party is in

---

8   *Jewish Divorce Ethics, 1992*
9   *Galatians 5:22-23*
10 *Colossians 3:12-14 and I Thessalonians 5:14-15*

breach of their Covenant or their Vows of Responsibility and refuses to repent and fulfill their vows, then there are grounds for divorce.

When you see a human being in distress you have an obligation to help him. Judaism mandates positive behavior, which is a unique innovation in law. In many legal systems it is not a crime to be a bystander. In Judaism, however, social consciousness is a legal obligation, as the Torah states, *Do not stand by your neighbor's blood. Leviticus 19:16* Being a good person requires taking action—you are either part of the problem or part of the solution. The Jewish people teach a message that extends beyond family…that as a people, they should take care of the world around them. That is why they have always had obligations toward helping the poor and supporting the community, which became the basis for their social welfare programs. Being responsible also included being kind to animals and taking care of the environment. In Jewish law you cannot eat before your animals eat—you are not allowed to be cruel as Proverbs 12:10 states, *A righteous man cares for the needs of his animal, but the kindest acts of the wicked are cruel.*

Again, the husband is to love the wife, and the wife is to respect and love the husband. The wife is a helpmeet to her husband. Disagreements can be resolved quickly and peacefully by seeking God's will first and refocusing on the Covenant Vows that were taken at marriage. Remnant Leadership and wise Shepherds are always a good source for seeking out God's will and His Word about specific situations. This provides a lifelong and lasting environment where the God-fearing couple grows closer together every year. So by definition of a husband and wife, it was forbidden to be lazy, indulgent, self-centered, neglectful spouses, nor were they allowed to be controlling, manipulative, angry, raging people.

As we read in the previous chapter, there are many definitions of a husband's role. A husband supports and protects his wife, working hard to provide for his family's needs. He is honest and worthy of respect and sound in faith.[11] A God-fearing man encourages his wife and has respect for her intellect and her gifts—always including the wife's gifts in managing the household. This union is not a dictatorship; it is a partnership. A Godly man is a companion, spending time with his wife and time with their children. Colossians 3 tells us that a husband should be gentle to his wife and never provoke or embitter his children. He is to bring happiness to his wife and provide for his family's spiritual needs.[12] A Godly husband and father will take time to teach his children about the beautiful commands and Word of God.[13]

Paul encourages two moral believers to be thankful and stay in their circumstances and to not divorce. If these two moral believers cannot learn the way of peace, they may separate and then get back together. They need to realize that they have found a rare situation of purity and morality and learn to look at the positives in their relationship by visiting some pagan marriage situations.

THE UNBOUND UNBELIEVER

There is a difference between a "pagan/infidel" and an "unbeliever." In theory an unbeliever could actually have been a very moral spouse as described above and could possibly be a convert—one who does not mock God or the righteous. In studying the Scriptures, you will know that you are interpreting correctly when the

---

11   *Teach the older men to be temperate, worthy of respect, self-controlled, and sound in faith, in love and in endurance. Titus 2:2*
12   *If a man has recently married, he must not be sent to war or have any other duty laid on him. For one year he is to be free to stay at home and bring happiness to the wife he has married. Deuteronomy 24:5*
13   *These commandments that I give you today are to be upon your hearts. Impress them on your children. Talk about them when you sit at home and when you walk along the road, when you lie down and when you get up. Deuteronomy 6:6-7*

request of God in the Old Covenant and New Covenant parallel and yet the requirement of man is corrected and redirected. In the Old Testament the Hebrews were warned to not intermarry with a pagan, a non-believer, because they would corrupt the community and corrupt the offspring.[14] In isolated cases, there were pagan conversions, but when the community, in a broader sense, began intermingling and marrying into a pagan society, the Jewish community's existence was in danger of extinction because of the strong persuasive influence of idolatry over monotheism. After the Jews returned to Jerusalem at the end of the Babylonian captivity, the men married pagans and had children. When Ezra found out, he begged God for forgiveness and then rectified the situation by divorce and separation from the foreign wives and their children—sending them all away and thus purifying God's people.[15] I Corinthians 7:15 gives the related principle; Paul wrote... *But if the unbeliever leaves, let it be so. The brother or the sister is not bound in such circumstances; God has called us to live in peace.*

Now, if someone converted to Christianity and their spouse did not—they were unequally yoked—and if the moral unbeliever wanted to stay and allow the spouse to fulfill every command and obligation to the Heavenly Father without persecution, including the raising of the children in the Lord, then Paul says stay together... *How do you know, wife, whether you will save your husband? Or, how do you know, husband, whether you will save your wife? I Corinthians 7:16* This is the opportunity to practice all aspects of love with extending grace, using longsuffering, patience, thinking the best, with the intent to encourage each along this journey to the Heavens.

---

14 *Do not intermarry with them. Do not give your daughters to their sons or take their daughters for your sons. Deuteronomy 7:3*
15 *Ezra Chapters 9-10*

With reverent submission, the stony heart can fall in love with God. When both are attending God's Church, the unbelievable power of the Spirit of God is available to convict.

But what about the opposite situation? What if the unbeliever is a pathological antagonist, always mocking the Church and the Saints? What if the unbeliever does not allow the spouse to fulfill the commands of the Heavenly Father? What if they have an aversion to being around any Saints at all? What if this unbeliever uses anger to control the spouse and children, or the unbeliever grows increasingly immoral? In this situation the believer has grounds for divorce due to abuse, oppression and persecution.

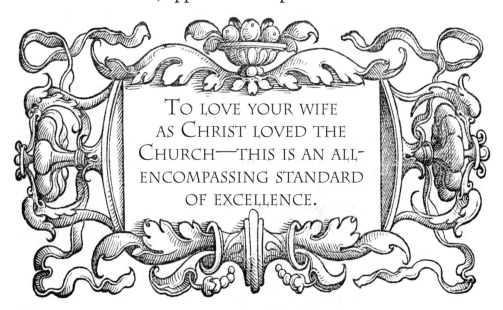

To love your wife as Christ loved the Church—this is an all-encompassing standard of excellence.

God is a God of peace and is building a New Jerusalem.[16] Remember, "Jeru" means city and "Salem" means peace…City of Peace. This pruning is all a part of protecting God's dream of a Bride that has a whole heart for God. Any marriage situations in question

---

16   *For God is not a God of disorder but of peace. I Corinthians 14:33a*

should be brought before the wise and sage Church Shepherds. There have been occasions where those who have previously mocked God's Church have been converted and are now strong examples of loving God wholeheartedly; but when each year gets worse and the situation becomes increasingly demonic, it is time to seek Godly counsel. What happens in marriage situations with mockers of God's religious system is that they will use the very system that they mock to keep their spouse oppressed under their use and abuse. It is ironic that they uphold nothing else of the law.

Legalism Versus God's Truth

Scripture clearly relays God's intent for marriage to be between two God-fearing believers. Marriage is intended to reflect our heart to God...the Bride of Christ...and therefore marriage would be for life and be forever. Jesus described the relationship between husband and wife in this manner in Matthew 19:6... *They are no longer two, but one flesh. Therefore what God has joined together, let no one separate.* When Jesus had a trick question from the pharisees, who were always challenging him to see if he was following Moses or not, Jesus skillfully answered by taking it to a pre-Mosaic time—in the beginning, God joined God-fearing men and women together intending for them to be "one flesh" for life.[17]

I tell you that anyone who divorces his wife, except for marital unfaithfulness, and marries another woman commits adultery. Matthew 19:9 This Scripture has been debated over the centuries, and some Bible translations interpret Jesus to mean only sexual sins. The other half of the translators render this to be broader unfaithfulness to the marriage contract; it is any violation of God's intentions for a lasting, faithful "one-flesh"

---

17   *Genesis 2:19-24*

union and any breach of the definition and/or vows of a husband or a wife. This could include any of the above-discussed responsibilities and obviously include rage, malice, anger, folly, envy, slander, arrogance, theft, lewdness, drunkenness, heartlessness, deceit or other traits found in Matthew 7:21-22, Romans 1:29-32, I Corinthians 6:9-10, Ephesians 5:3-5 and Colossians 3:4-10, which are clearly sins of the flesh that define an immoral unbeliever or a pagan. Galatians 5:19-21 says… *The acts of the sinful nature are obvious: sexual immorality, impurity and debauchery; idolatry and witchcraft; hatred, discord, jealousy, fits of rage, selfish ambition, dissensions, factions and envy; drunkenness, orgies, and the like. I warn you, as I did before, that those who live like this will not inherit the kingdom of God.* These are all signs of someone living according to the sinful nature. Spouses in these situations are not bound and are free to remarry. To abuse one's spouse verbally violates that one-flesh union and neglects the Covenant vows. Committing cruelty against the spouse—such as using anger in order to make them conform, cower, shrink back—or showing anger toward offspring is unacceptable. God is peaceful, and we are to live in peace. *Let us therefore make every effort to do what leads to peace and to mutual edification. Romans 14:19*

Again, in Matthew 19, Jesus was addressing two moral, non-mocking Saints, and they were not to use divorce casually just to remarry another woman. Jesus was clearly referring to casually exchanging one wife for a different one, which was prevalent at the time of Christ and has been prevalent since the beginning. Note the translations below for Matthew 19:

New Living Translation
*And I tell you this, whoever divorces his wife and marries someone else commits adultery—unless his wife has been **unfaithful**.*

New American Standard Bible

*And I say to you, whoever divorces his wife, except for **immorality**, and marries another woman commits adultery.*

NET Bible

*Now I say to you that whoever divorces his wife, except for **immorality**, and marries another commits adultery.*

Webster's Bible Translation

*And I say to you, Whoever shall put away his wife, except for **lewdness**, and shall marry another, committeth adultery: and whoever marrieth her who is put away, committeth adultery.*

Weymouth New Testament

*And I tell you that whoever divorces his wife for any reason except her **unfaithfulness**, and marries another woman, commits adultery.*

These translators understood the correct interpretation of "adultery." Unfaithfulness comes in many forms, but it is basically the breach of any of the vows that have been made before God. Keep in mind God divorced His unfaithful Jerusalem and remarried the faithful New Jerusalem—a community that followed the footsteps of Christ. May the teachings of Christ and God become clear…that God Himself called Israel "adulterous," and that is impossible to be taken literally—therefore, unfaithfulness or adultery is when the heart of the offender turns away from any of the vows as stated above.

Many times the spouse is in love with themselves and the whole world centers around self so that the two never became one. No doubt, today, one way the oppressed spouse is abused is when the other spouse makes all decisions to indulge only themselves. These people control with anger, never considering the pain of their helpmeet—only worshiping self and so self-centric that they were never able to be "one flesh," and therefore, the abused spouse is forced into just focusing on the narcissist...with no needs met of their own. In such cases, that is not a marriage.

LIBERTY AND PEACE FOR THE OPPRESSED

When God remarried He painted the picture of marriage that He had intended all along. Indeed, God's own marriage actions of divorce and remarriage showed mankind His full plan, revealing the Bride of Christ—the removal of the impure and the embracing of the pure, creating a delightful community. Again, this misunderstood passage from Matthew 19 is about casually exchanging your spouse for a different one, and this is forbidden. You cannot just want another spouse, simply divorce and easily marry another person. With this in mind, it explains the long-debated and legalistic approach to divorce and remarriage. God remarried to obtain holiness and true love and faithfulness—a beautiful relationship where everything was perfect, growing in love every day with each other, versus one spouse growing in love with themselves more and more with ever-increasing demands. The main rule for the divorced was to either be celibate, giving all service to the Lord, or to remarry an idol-free, God-fearing, "God-first" Saint.

> A GOD-FEARING MAN ENCOURAGES HIS WIFE AND HAS RESPECT FOR HER INTELLECT AND HER GIFTS—ALWAYS INCLUDING THE WIFE'S GIFTS IN MANAGING THE HOUSEHOLD.

The Bible teaches that of all the lawful things, divorce is the most hated by the Heavenly Father.[18] This would be referring to the divorce of two idol-free believers inside the Church. But as we have seen, it was allowed with pagans, abusers, adulterers, etc., because God hates abuse, wants the children to become believers in love with Him, and wants the Peaceful City. Christ allowed divorce in these situations but taught that it should never be done when *your* heart is being given to another—the very thing that brings darkness into the Church and is worthy of the fires of Hell. Anyone who has lived in the past few generations has been adversely affected by this legalistic interpretation. In this world of legalism, when shepherds and Bible translators misinterpreted God and villainized "divorce," it brought shame where God never intended shame to be and left victims in oppression and riddled the church with symbolic violence. This wrong has to be righted, and every marriage in God's True Church should be absolutely beautiful, peaceful and noble.

The Early Christians understood this non-legalistic approach and divorced as needed. However, after Constantine and the birth of Roman Catholicism, a man-made, strict approach was instituted: zero divorce. Even in situations of sin or adultery, marriage became basically undissolvable. (While the Catholics will not divorce, they will, in very limited circumstances, allow an annulment of the marriage.) This demonic approach led to great abuse of both men and women, inciting pagan unbelievers to take advantage of this oppressive arrangement. This has brought great grief to the abused and to the Heavenly Father, no doubt. Many other denominations

---

18 *"I hate divorce," says the Lord God of Israel, "and I hate a man's covering himself with violence as well as with his garment," says the Lord Almighty. So guard yourself in your spirit, and do not break faith. Malachi 2:16*

also wrongly hold a similar legalistic stance, which has only encouraged more sin of just "living together" without lawful marriage at all.

Legalism is devastating to the soul. The school of Beth Shammai (a school of thought founded by a Jewish scholar from the first century) held for "marital unfaithfulness" to mean whoredom or literal adultery in the Hebrew; but the school of Beth Hillel (a competing school of a thought founded by scholar from the same era as Shammai) maintained that it signified any defection or any bad temper that made the spouse's life uncomfortable, saying essentially, "Any of the latter a good man might bear with; but it appears that Moses permitted the offended husband to put away the wife on these accounts, merely to save her from cruel usage."

The Jews have long allowed divorce because they value marriage and the sanctity of this relationship so highly and do not look kindly on mistreatment of either party. It is a sacred union and commitment. The International Academy of Family Lawyers describes it by saying "Jewish marriage is not a creature of the state, and no state action, no state involvement, nor state ceremony is mandated." Orthodox and Conservative Jews do not recognize a civil divorce. A marriage can only be dissolved by a sefer k'ritut (or a scroll of cutting off), which is often called a "get" today. This document does not state the reason for the divorce. It simply allows the parties to remarry. It is even considered a "mitzvah," a sacred obligation, to divorce when it is the only alternative in order to be sure that marriage remains a holy, sacred covenant relationship.[19]

The decision of divorce should never be done quickly, and Remnant Shepherds can guide the believer thru these troubled waters. If abuse continues and the peace does not come, then this is grounds for divorce based on both abuse and persecution. In addition, if the unbeliever is increasingly gravitating to the dark and not the light, and they want to leave, let them. In I Corinthians 7, Paul refers to an unbeliever voluntarily leaving, meaning a moral unbeliever. When the unbeliever is immoral, there is no legalism here. Keep in mind the real initiator of this dissolution is the one who is in breach of their vows, the abuser, the one who refused year after year to lay their life down for their spouse as God did for the Church…the one who made no effort to be "one flesh" or have the same mind (in other words, their actions have indicated that they have no intention to be part of a HOLY marriage). If it is possible, do everything in peace. This is not about divorce and remarriage but a much bigger picture. The whole purpose behind all of God's laws and direction is to build the City of Peace. God is a God of peace…Jerusalem, an eternal City of Peace, Zion.

Another issue to address is staying together because "Who knows if you will convert someone?"[20] There are many criteria that need to be considered if you are to stay, such as deciding what is best for the

---

19 Please note that the Jews take this so seriously that the International Association of Family Law states that "Rabbinic courts are permitted, according to Jewish law, to beat a man or imprison him, take away his driver's license & professional license (as they are authorized to do in Israel) until he "willingly" gives his wife a Get, and this type of "inducement" is not deemed by Jewish law, to be 'coercive.'" International Association of Family Law, and "The Effect of Jewish Divorce Law on Family Law Litigation." Also see WomensLaw.org "Jewish Get Law," Chabad.org "The Get Procedure."

20 How do you know, wife, whether you will save your husband? Or, how do you know, husband, whether you will save your wife? 1 Corinthians 7:16

children, as the non-repentant pagan lifestyle of one spouse is highly tempting and could draw the children in. Another criteria is how long has the Saintly spouse been making an effort to have reverent submission and be respectful? How many years have they been trying? How perfect is the Saint? Finally, what is the real potential for conversion? The potential can be evaluated…does the nonbeliever despise the Scriptures, the Jews and the Remnant of Believers, and are they an enemy or antagonist to the Church? Is there rage in their words and actions? Are there demons present? Do they seem to change quickly in and out of rage, never acknowledging afterward that the rage even occurred? Again, Godly counselors can help determine all this.

Honoring the Covenant

The marriage institution is from God and is to be most beautiful and symbolic. Two converts who have devoted themselves to God are an honor to this Covenant, for it is God's will and also is symbolic of God's marriage to His bride—the New Jerusalem. The New Covenant that we are representing, as we addressed earlier, always painted a picture of a beautiful marriage. But in the end, it is about the purity of the Body of Christ, and that is key.

Again, Ezra and Nehemiah had the Jews who married pagan women send them away. *Now let us make a covenant before our God to send away all these women and their children, in accordance with the counsel of my lord and of those who fear the commands of our God. Let it be done according to the Law. Ezra 10:3*

Jesus said in Matthew 5:17-19, *Do not think that I have come to abolish the Law or the Prophets; I have not come to abolish them but to fulfill them. I tell you the truth, until heaven and earth disappear, not the smallest letter, not the least stroke of a pen, will by any means disappear from the Law until everything is accomplished. Anyone who breaks one* of the least of these commandments and teaches others to do the same will be called least in the kingdom of heaven, but whoever practices and teaches these commands will be called great in the kingdom of heaven. That had been a law all along from Deuteronomy. So now you have not missed what was taught from the Old Testament to the New Testament. This cannot be in contradiction to what Jesus taught.

Just as the Sabbath was made for man and not man for the Sabbath,[21] marriage was made for MAN and WOMAN, not man and woman for marriage. Again, when the pharisees were trying to trap Jesus, they were attempting to trap him on the basis that he was

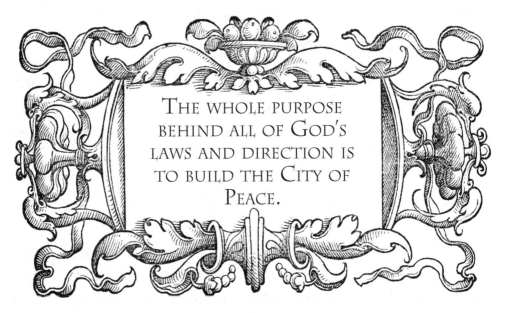

THE WHOLE PURPOSE BEHIND ALL OF GOD'S LAWS AND DIRECTION IS TO BUILD THE CITY OF PEACE.

not following Moses. They wanted to make sure the crowd saw that Jesus was not obeying Moses so that they could pull his following away from him. In several Scriptures, Jesus would be persecuted for healing a man or woman on the Sabbath. Essentially, what the pharisees were saying was, "Why are you helping a human in need

---

21   Mark 2:27

who is oppressed, crippled, lame and blind on a Sabbath? We are here to serve the Sabbath; we are not here to serve the person." Jesus responded by saying, *If one of you has a son or an ox that falls into a well on the Sabbath day, will you not immediately pull him out? Luke 14:5* Not only would he help, but he would come to their aid quickly... *And will not God bring about justice for his chosen ones, who cry out to him day and night? Will he keep putting them off? I tell you, he will see that they get justice, and quickly. Luke 18:7-8*

What are we doing when we leave ANY human being oppressed in order to serve an institution? Man was not made to serve the marriage where there is never the word "divorce," doing everything they can to avoid it. This would be serving the system. In addition, the religious institutions do not want increased divorce statistics, so they send the member back into their difficult, oppressive situation. Bottom line, you have spouses being abused and children being oppressed, yet people are overlooking it and allowing it.

To stay married in any and every circumstance has never been what God, Christ, Moses or any of the Prophets taught, but there are sects of Christianity that have been cruel and left abused people in horrible marriage situations that are oppressive. This is the guilt of that leadership, and the leaders will be answerable to God. Moses allowed divorce, and Christ knew it was allowed when he answered the Jews, who by that point were divorcing their wives if they burnt their toast. No one was more sympathetic to the oppressed, the downhearted, or the abused than Jesus Christ. Christ was neither condemning nor judgmental when he talked to the woman at the well who had five husbands and the one she was living with was not her husband, but he was gentle, and he led her to righteousness.[22] May the next generation know that marriage between two Saints is the most beautiful

---

22   John 4:1-26

institution, but when unfaithfulness (that comes in many forms) occurs, it can be the most abusive and devastating circumstance in the world, and in many cases worse than a prison because the oppression is done in private. Many spouses neither report nor leave the situation due to fears of safety and/or not having the financial resources needed to live on. The Church was intended to intervene and save the oppressed. God is a God of peace, and with no shame, God dismissed Israel whom He had led by her hand and had done all He could for her. But when her heart was more in love with the world and self, He dismissed her, and then He made a new Covenant with a new Bride. How dare legalistic people make a rule and put burdens on people's backs greater than they can bear! That is altogether unlike the phenomenally awesome, stunning, marvelous, loving God that I know.

What God has Made Clean is Clean

In the Book of Acts, the Apostle Paul relays the following...

About noon the following day as they were on their journey and approaching the city, Peter went up on the roof to pray. He became hungry and wanted something to eat, and while the meal was being prepared, he fell into a trance. He saw heaven opened and something like a large sheet being let down to earth by its four corners. It contained all kinds of four-footed animals, as well as reptiles of the earth and birds of the air. Then a voice told him, "Get up, Peter. Kill and eat." "Surely not, Lord!" Peter replied. "I have never eaten anything impure or unclean." The voice spoke to him a second time, "Do not call anything impure that God has made clean." This happened three times, and immediately the sheet was taken back to heaven." Acts 10:9-16

God has spoken... the Remnant has been used by God to continue in the path of Jesus Christ, who laid his life down to confront the legalism and man-made rules of the pharisees. May this clear examination of the Word end the strict conformity to the letter of the law rather than its spirit and the synthetic precepts, which state that we are to stay in oppressive situations under any and every circumstance. May divorce be a *last* resort. When the situation falls under God's parameters, may we follow the footsteps of our God where He was long-suffering with Israel, forgiving and making multiple attempts. But if a marriage is no longer a marriage, if the vows are no longer kept, and if after Godly counsel, you fast and know that God is leading this...you approach this with much prayer and soul-searching, asking God for peace and grace to represent Him well as you **separate with kindness** (not appearing as self-serving, but continually portraying concern for the other person). Both sides' needs are thoroughly considered.

Christ had a strong message, and his words have held many selfish people together and changed both lives and relationships—doing the world a tremendous service. God used all circumstances to help test the heart. However, Christ was the first to rescue the brokenhearted.[23] It is in knowing Christ and knowing God that you can interpret the Scriptures and the will of the Father.

Divorce is allowed in circumstances, but it must be for the pure Church and not for merely selfish reasons. There are those rare times that you are divorced and then remarried—not because you do not value marriage but because you **DO** value purity in God's marriage vows...to set an example that you **DO** value His Holy Covenant... you **DO** believe in commitment and building strong families. But most of all, you **DO** believe in building Zion, you **DO** believe in building the New Jerusalem, you **DO** believe in building the City of Peace. Just as there is no judgment and only empathy/sympathy toward God for His own marriage problems and His divorce, and

---

23 *Psalm 68:5, Malachi 3:5, James 1:27, Psalm 34:18, Psalm 147:3, Luke 4:14-20*

just as there is respect, joy and elation for His beautiful selection of a pure Bride for His second marriage, there should be no judgment toward Saints as they strive to help build a pure Church.

Many people have stayed far too long in abusive situations where the spouse is not meeting the needs or keeping their vows before God, all because of legalistic interpretations. They are serving the institution versus serving what the institution was made for, which is to provide a beautiful environment to live in. God has always intended something beautiful. This is no different than people living in the man-made rules of dieting and never being able to be set free. We have, as a Remnant, been groundbreakers in all legalism. This is the final frontier. Let us confront these old pharisaical, heartbreaking, oppressive situations with the Truth.

May Jerusalem be as it should—the City of Peace, the happiest place on Earth, superior to any civilization that has ever existed. In Isaiah 65, God speaks of a city... *Behold, I will create a new heavens and a new earth. The former things will not be remembered, nor will they come to mind. But be glad and rejoice forever in what I will create, for I will create Jerusalem to be a delight and its people a joy. I will rejoice over Jerusalem and take delight in my people; the sound of weeping and of crying will be heard in it no more. Isaiah 65:17-19* May God's people forever be attentive to the cries and the tears of God's hurting Lambs, and may everyone support and help those who are persecuted and downtrodden. May everyone pray for the captives to be released, for the oppressed to be set free, for the prison doors to open, as in the Year of the Lord's Favor.[24] God, the beautiful Heavenly Architect with the biggest heart, is building the most awesome structures into a perfectly peaceful City of Peace, a City that has no tears.

---

24 Isaiah 61

Divorce and Remarriage

Not only was the Teacher wise, but also he imparted knowledge to the people. He pondered and searched out and set in order many proverbs. The Teacher searched to find just the right words, and what he wrote was upright and true. Ecclesiastes 12:9-10 Page 334.

Chapter 25

A man can do nothing better than to eat and drink and find satisfaction in his work. This too, I see, is from the hand of God, for without him, who can eat or find enjoyment? To the man who pleases him, God gives wisdom, knowledge and happiness, but to the sinner he gives the task of gathering and storing up wealth to hand it over to the one who pleases God. This too is meaningless, a chasing after the wind. Ecclesiastes 2:24-26

We have all seen it, and we have all experienced it—happiness and unhappiness…satisfaction and dissatisfaction. There are people who do not enjoy life. They work hard; they have accumulated much and smile, but underneath they are not content…and certainly not pleased for someone else to have better or more clothes, houses, cars, friends or fun. It is not in their hearts to enjoy with others who have been blessed by God with smarter, prettier offspring or with better marriages. There are those who have, no doubt, been influenced by the teachings in Ecclesiastes, yet they have interpreted them in the wrong way and have ceased toil and sold everything… living as a homeless person, not understanding the tangled meaning of life or how to interpret its difficulties. And they certainly do not know how to help their children, so they just send them out to fend for themselves—to either sink or swim in the sweat and toil of life.

There are many words that come at us every day. We are surrounded by words…many books full of words…but what is the Truth? Many believe there is no Truth. But there *is* Truth.

Ecclesiastes is not the book that tends to draw people who are looking for encouragement. These words are inspired and were penned centuries ago, but parts seem to be contradictory. The Teacher, the writer—King David's son Solomon—repeats over and over that everything is meaningless—work, riches, friendships, promotion, pleasures and youth. *Is* everything meaningless? What is the writer trying to say?

There is a secret, a hidden Truth between the first and last words of this book. *Yet when I surveyed all that my hands had done and what I had toiled to achieve, everything was meaningless, a chasing after the wind; nothing was gained under the sun. Ecclesiastes 2:11*

The writer is saying over and over that everything is meaningless. This is a seemingly extreme critique of this world and this life, and even the word "everything" seems to be too broad… but is it? Have you ever had deliberations along these lines? Do you seem to be spinning and spinning but you suspect that you are getting nowhere—you are gaining nothing? Do you sometimes sit back and wonder about your life and your time and why you seem to despair of life itself?

This Teacher seemed to be repeating "meaningless" in the context of a certain subject, for he starts with this question, *What does man gain from all his labor at which he toils under the sun? Ecclesiastes 1:3* Now re-read it. This is about **man's** gain. Is man achieving anything? Is man getting ahead?

The foolish never stop to contemplate, and they live and die asking nothing. They only follow the generations before them, the crowd, and they accomplish nothing. Wisdom must ask, "Is there anything I can do better? Have I improved?" Look back on the generations before you and ask, "Is my family any better? Have I

The Meaning of Life

accomplished anything? Where did I start? Where did I come from, and where am I going? Where am I leading others?"

This writer says that everything is meaningless under the sun. What does he mean? He is concentrating on *man's* gain alone. The sun comes and goes, but it does not get hotter on Earth…however, that does not mean nothing is gained, for the fruit of the fields are ripe with produce. Water evaporates and then it rains, and the excess runs into the river and then into the sea…but that does not mean nothing is gained, for you would not want gain in the seas—the Earth is two-thirds water and would soon be 100 percent water if there was a gain. Who would want the sea to overflow? Instead, the water has been recycled and used over and over for produce, for food and for life.

The writer says: *The wind blows to the south and turns to the north; round and round it goes, ever returning on its course. Ecclesiastes 1:6* Could the translator have lost that perhaps the writer is implying repetition—it all repeats. In place of "meaningless, meaningless," perhaps he means "repetitive, repetitive"—a phenomenal, everlasting, reusable source of resources? This is brilliant of God. But there is more…the Earth existed and was in balance long before man existed, and it will be rotating and receiving light, sun, heat and water long after a man lives his life. So what is this "useless" or "meaningless" that the writer is addressing?

The author then contrasts this getting nowhere repetition with man's daily toil and work. It is the same deduction, "meaningless." He says that nothing is accomplished by the work—a chasing after the wind. Yet as a rule, mankind, from generation to generation, fights to live and is compelled to labor on this Earth. But for what? Mankind builds civilizations only to watch hate rise up and barbarians come in and destroy, bomb and burn it all—incredible centuries-old structures, burned inside of a day. Millions come to visit Rome only to find columns standing alone in a field…severed from their once architecturally-advanced, useful structures. Fire is something to respect, for it can take something apart instantly that took centuries to build. Think about Egypt with its unique, massive structures. Who would have thought of constructing such mammoth, larger-than-life triangle-shaped buildings called "pyramids"? It is simply amazing. Once the solid, gleaming stone of an advanced society—but now much of Egypt's incredible civilization is practically dust. Think about what has been lost over time. Books have been written but are now destroyed. So the Teacher in Ecclesiastes has a point here. Man does all this work, you do all this work, and then it is destroyed. What are you working for?

When a man spends his life seeking wisdom, the Teacher says he is left with more sorrow; however, he concludes that wisdom with sorrow is better than ignorance and bliss while being a fool. Then he leaves wisdom to test pleasure—anything his heart desires—and he finds himself wearier and filled with boredom and emptiness. So he returns to work as he progresses, and he concludes that work is better, for at least there was some delight in the labor.

This Too is Meaningless

Does the writer really mean "meaningless"? Was his revelation lost in the interpretation? The word "meaningless" must be close to the correct interpretation, because by chapter two the writer despairs of life.

So I hated life, because the work that is done under the sun was grievous to me. All of it is meaningless, a chasing after the wind. I hated all the things I had toiled for under the sun, because I must leave them to the one who comes after me. And who knows whether he will be a wise man or a fool? Yet he will have control over all the work into which I have poured my effort and skill under the sun. This too is meaningless. So my heart began to despair over all my toilsome labor under the sun. For a man may do his work with wisdom, knowledge and skill, and then he must leave all he owns to someone who has not worked for it. This too is meaningless and a great misfortune. What does a man get for all the toil and anxious striving with which he labors under the sun? All his days his work is pain and grief; even at night his mind does not rest. This too is meaningless. Ecclesiastes 2:17-23

Why is the writer so exceedingly jaded by the life of man? If you look closely, it seems to be all wrapped up in the realization of the mortality of man. God makes a man, and then the man dies. Why would God do that? Man comes and he goes in such a short time that all of his work and inheritance is done for the next generation, and death is the same fate of those who are wise and of those who are fools. Now we see that the writer is referencing ALL things in the light that man lives for a few minutes and then dies; generations come and generations go, but the Earth remains forever. The writer is also informing the world that this Earth has nothing to offer of any eternal value. The writer makes these judgments when the man is living solely for earthly personal achievements and personal gain… meaningless. You soon die and give your life's work to children who may have no appreciation of it; they may not understand its value or not know what to do with your hard labor. They may twist it, tear it up, burn it down or sell it—so it gained nothing for the next generation. It is all lost, so it is meaningless. All men die, so why the bother? Would it have been better to sell it all in our few days we are down here on Earth?

One of the most upside-down teachings and confusing, debated Christian concepts is that of Christian wealth, money and investments. Well-known philosophers of the past have said that it cannot be solved, and those who have tried to solve it often determined that each person should just live an ascetic lifestyle. For example, Socrates, Plato, Francis of Assisi, Mother Teresa, Gandhi and Buddha would have you believe that religion teaches the renunciation of all material or physical pleasures to arrive at inner peace. But is that the path? Will having or not having material possessions and money assure anyone inner peace?

Whether you know it or not, man is driven by what he has chosen as priority of his life—his chosen core values. This world and each generation has its own set of priorities. What one values and prioritizes depends on what is deep in someone's heart… is it academics, worldly achievement, financial accumulation, sports success, entertainment, adventure, power or man's approval? What drives you each day? What things turn your head or call your name? Where do you want to be in 10 years? In 20 years? What you desire down deep in your heart is how you make your life's choices—your choices for this year, this month, this day and this hour. Too many choices are made on the basis of getting the approval of man instead of the approval of God.

If your priorities and your life choices do not line up, you will have inner conflict. This conflict can lead to great stress inside and outside of your relationships. If there is stress, it is time to pray. If you feel inner turmoil, it is time that you stop, seek Godly advice, and go to God in prayer. Inner peace is ignored by many—but for the thoughtful person, it turns out to be a guide for your life's choices and priorities.

The Meaning of Life

The heart of man is very complicated because one of its protective drives is to justify man's actions. The heart of man hates to be wrong or to own up to guilt. It will justify all actions with white lies of whitewash. It is complicated, because one might say that you value the simple life, but your "simple life" choice was at the expense of others and the burdensome worry of others. You might be saying you want the simple life, but if the truth be known, it is really because you are

FEARING, FINDING AND FILLING GOD'S COMMANDS IS PLEASING GOD.

greedy for your own time…you crave independence and autonomy so that you can control other people to further your own free time for laziness or for your own extremely complicated hobbies. Thus the motives—the motive of justifying the simple life—is just so that you could live in the complexity of your hobbies and preoccupations. The heart of man can be very problematic because his own desires drive so much of what he does. It is something deep inside… but something deep inside also has hope.

Satisfaction in Your Toil

What is meaningful and what is not? Is the writer of this passage contradicting himself when he writes, "Toil is meaningless?" Then he goes back to say, *Then I realized that it is good and proper for a man to eat and drink, and to find satisfaction in his toilsome labor under the sun during the few days of life God has given him—for this is his lot. Ecclesiastes 5:18* and *A man can do nothing better than to eat and drink and find satisfaction in his work. Ecclesiastes 2:24a*

So not only is it man's lot to work, but it is *good* to work. That feeling may not be automatic, but God leads us to find it—to find satisfaction in our work…a peaceful feeling, satisfied, sated, satiated like after a good meal…gratification, happiness, pleasure, fulfillment. What is this satisfaction in work? This is tied up in the deep meaning of this writing. This should be contemplated and understood and taught to the next generation—teaching our children that God expects work, but then giving them the secret of how to find the satisfaction in it.

So work—is it meaningless, or is it good for satisfaction? Why is this confusing? It is because the writer is making you think, opening up your mind to something much greater, superior…

The final words of Ecclesiastes help us to untangle these writings:

Not only was the Teacher wise, but also he imparted knowledge to the people. He pondered and searched out and set in order many proverbs. The Teacher searched to find just the right words, and what he wrote was upright and true. The words of the wise are like goads, their collected sayings like firmly embedded nails—given by one Shepherd. Be warned, my son, of anything in addition to them. Of making many books there is no end, and much study wearies the body. Now all has been heard; here is the conclusion of the matter: Fear God and keep his commandments, for this is the whole duty of man. For God will bring every deed into judgment, including every hidden thing, whether it is good or evil. Ecclesiastes 12:9-14

Your work and the toil that counts is keeping the Commands of God above all things. Earthly work is not the whole duty, but work has been given as the lot of man and will be a part of your life to get food and shelter, the essentials. God makes it this way—a man who does not work will not eat.[1] Look at the animals; none sleep in, but every one of them gets up and goes to work to get their food. God has created it so that there is no getting around this fact.

Enjoying Life

In this work, God may allow some to accumulate more than others, but all will eat. You could have much wealth and not enjoy it, or you could have little with great enjoyment—enjoyment is the better choice.

I have seen another evil under the sun, and it weighs heavily on men: God gives a man wealth, possessions and honor, so that he lacks nothing his heart desires, but God does not enable him to enjoy them, and a stranger enjoys them instead. This is meaningless, a grievous evil. A man may have a hundred children and live many years; yet no matter how long he lives, if he cannot enjoy his prosperity and does not receive proper burial, I say that a stillborn child is better off than he. It comes without meaning, it departs in darkness, and in darkness its name is shrouded. Ecclesiastes 6:1-4

How fundamental and essential is this teaching. If only we had all been taught very early in life that without enjoyment, there is

---

1 *For even when we were with you, we gave you this rule: "If a man will not work, he shall not eat." II Thessalonians 3:10*

nothing, no meaning. Without enjoyment, it is like living in the dark and dying in the dark—it would have been better had you never come at all. The money earned is simply green pieces of paper in your hand, and it is nothing—no more than water that evaporates. This is deep. How could enjoyment be so important? It is said over and over in the twelve chapters of Ecclesiastes. We are to find joy in work, joy in relationships, joy in material things—otherwise it has been a complete waste. What if you took a fantastical vacation that was very costly and you had saved for, but no one in the family enjoyed it? Then it was meaningless, a waste. Why spend the money…why go? *This too, I see, is from the hand of God, for without him, who can eat or find enjoyment? Ecclesiastes 2:24b-25*

So I commend the enjoyment of life, because nothing is better for a man under the sun than to eat and drink and be glad. Then joy will accompany him in his work all the days of the life God has given him under the sun. Ecclesiastes 8:15

Enjoyment is such a revelation. Do you really think that God made all this to just look down and see evil, jealousy, hate, wickedness, lust, greed and murder? No! God wants to enjoy His creation. Enjoyment is a strategic crossroads. Who has ever told us before that enjoyment is an indicator that you are headed for eternity? But the Truth that rises from the Ancient Text is that this enjoyment is given by God. Without God, you cannot even eat with enjoyment.

PLEASING GOD

Now you see the need for God in all. You could have achieved riches and honor, but only God can unlock the hidden key in your heart and turn on enjoyment. But to whom is it given and why? The writer explains, *To the man who pleases him, God gives wisdom, knowledge and happiness, but to the sinner he gives the task of gathering and storing up wealth to hand it over to the one who pleases God. Ecclesiastes 2:26a*

It may seem like contradictions, "toil is meaningless but work is good," but it is all cleared up with the right motive behind every thought and action, the right heart. The writer is shocking you and trying to make you prioritize before it is Judgment Day. Fearing, finding, and filling God's commands IS pleasing God. Think about this carefully. If pleasing God brings joy and happiness, and doing God's Commands is what pleases God, then when you purpose that everything you do—every move, every word, every action—is to please God, you have risen above the meaningless to THE meaningful life.

Joy accompanies the man pleasing God thru his obedience. But it is not temporary enjoyment or merely having fun, although fun is a part of it, but it is something very deep that eliminates worries and fears and the anxiousness in life. It is not just laughing—it is a wisdom of enjoyment that foresees the future so there is no need to hurry, to be anxious or to have fear. Look at these words…

> IN THESE TROUBLED DAYS WITH UNCERTAINTY AHEAD THERE IS A PLACE IN THE HEART OF HOPE.

He has made everything beautiful in its time. He has also set eternity in the hearts of men; yet they cannot fathom what God has done from beginning to end. I know that there is nothing better for men than to be happy and do good while they live. That everyone may eat and drink, and find satisfaction in all his toil—this is the gift of God. I know that everything God does will endure forever; nothing can be added to it and nothing taken from it. God does it so that men will revere him. Ecclesiastes 3:11-14

In these troubled days with uncertainty ahead, there is a place in the heart of hope. It is all about eternity. That is why the Teacher can say...

It is better to go to a house of mourning than to go to the house of feasting for death is the destiny of every man. The living should take this to heart. Sorrow is better than laughter, because a sad face is good for the heart. The heart of the wise is in the house of mourning, but the heart of fools is in the house of pleasure. Ecclesiastes 7:2-4

The person who lives for the eternal stays more sober and concentrating. It is God who will be here, *always* here. We are so temporary. God is the only Substance that was always here and will always be here forever and ever. We are just a blink in time. A thousand years is a day to God.[2] We live, work and die. We must wake up and prioritize because it is almost over. It is time to get your life in order.

The Teacher takes it all from the here and now—from meaningless to the eternal—judgment and eternal life. All meaning is wrapped up in the term "lasting." You could go back and replace "meaningless" with "un-lasting," "disappearing" or "evaporating." It is leaving, going away. If you make a sandcastle and the waves take it out an hour later, what was its purpose, its use? It is all **meaningless** unless the motive was led by God to build it, led to please Him; then it had a meaning whether it came and left or it came and stayed. Then it mattered. But without that, it is something we are trying to achieve for this Earth for the praise of man or to amuse ourselves... these roads, infrastructures, banks, pocketbooks, houses, this city,

---

2 *For a thousand years in your sight are like a day that has just gone by, or like a watch in the night. Psalm 90:4*

this country, this nation...these are not lasting. Within just a few centuries the landscape can completely collapse and something new can be built over it, or hurricanes, tornadoes, thieves, robbers or wars could all change the face of the Earth that eventually will all burn. This Earth will pass away, but the man who does the will of the Father lives forever.[3] So what is lasting, what is eternal is **God**, and the city of God, the heart. Anything without Him is meaningless, futile and useless because it will disappear forever. It is useless, for it is temporal, and He is forever. Only in partnering—commingling with something eternal—could eternity come into our hearts. Who have you partnered with? What are you co-mingling with? Is it the world or is it God?

> IT IS TIME TO BE QUIET BECAUSE TO OBTAIN TRUTH, IT CANNOT JUST COME FROM OUTSIDE OF YOU, BUT THIS TRUTH WILL BE AFFIRMED *INSIDE* YOU. YOU WILL NOT JUST HEAR IT...YOU WILL FEEL IT.

The truth is, there are many words in the world...books, news, internet. So many words come at you all the time. But no matter what the words are or how eloquently they are spoken, it does not mean that the words are Truth. It is time to be quiet because to obtain Truth, it cannot just come from outside of you, but this Truth will be affirmed *inside* you. You will not just hear it...you will feel it.

Speaking of the end of time, Jesus said: *Two men will be in the field; one will be taken and the other left. Matthew 24:40* On that last day when God comes back and takes everyone, some will stay with the physical, and some will be glued to the eternal. Do you feel

---

3   *The world and its desires pass away, but the man who does the will of God lives forever.* I John 2:17

eternity—this enjoyment, this happiness in your heart—or have you yet to really please God? Live to please God. Two people could be toiling at the same grinding stone, but one will go up with the eternal and one will be glued to the Earth and be destroyed with

Only in partnering—commingling with something eternal—could eternity come into our hearts.

it.[4] The secret is not in the work you do, it is in the heart focused on pleasing God with the labor of whatever you have put your hands to.[5]

Meaning is wrapped up in a feeling called satisfaction or enjoyment…happiness. Enjoyment that those around you have overcome evil and the evil one thru Christ and now live each hour with the purpose of pleasing God. I see a City out there—it is all a vision of the highest joy I can express, a vision where all move and live and breathe to just see God smile. And in the vision in this great City of

---

4   *Two women will be grinding with a hand mill; one will be taken and the other left. Matthew 24:41*

5   *Whatever your hand finds to do, do it with all your might, for in the grave, where you are going, there is neither working nor planning nor knowledge nor wisdom. Ecclesiastes 9:10*

God, I see the loving Heavenly Father joyful, and all surrounding Him are full of peace and love and kindness and joy. It is a joy derived from God's children, His offspring giving Him no trouble, but rather living so above reproach in character and under authority that there are no worries. These children bring sheer joy—making Him laugh as they consistently and constantly live only to put a smile on the face of their Father, of their Authority who is eternal and forever. The desire to please their Father grows the love of God in them—it is given, and then God is in them, and since He is eternal, they cannot help but live forever.

Pursuit of the Eternal

The writer of Ecclesiastes starts with the question and statement: What does man gain? It is all meaningless. The Earth gives nothing. However, if your motive is for God and His glory, though the Earth takes and never gives back to you, God gives abundantly. If your motive is for God, and God is in us, then we live now with enjoyment—it is the seal that you have eternity inside. Simply put, God gives joy. The genuine enjoyment of life is an essential sign that God is in you. Now, having children has a purpose: there are more beings to please the Father. This is all that matters to that child. No matter what they do, what scholastics they are in or what they are doing with their time, it is all to please the Father. You and your children wake up each day, carefully choose your words, pray over heavenly-guided moves and thoughts that are God-driven and directed… all of your giving, your working around the house, everything that you do brings satisfaction because you did it to see the Heavens smile at last, so deserved, so long in coming.

What have you done? Where is your potential to put the smile in the Heavens? Can you picture God walking around and smiling at all of His subjects? And because everyone is so focused on pleasing Him, He has no anxiety or worries. His Creation pleases and obeys Him. O Lord, may we please YOU, our prayer—for the exchange of eternity—is to please God.

Everything is meaningless because everything dies. Replace the word "meaningless" with the words "mortal," "temporary," or "not lasting." The only salvation from this meaningless life would be the concept of the eternal God in us. Do you wonder, "What am I? What is this depravity and evil?" That is true without God in you, without Christ in you. With God in us, we have nothing to fear, because there is eternity and a piece of that eternity is inside our souls. Is there not a voice deep inside your soul that tells you this is the Truth?

> SIMPLY PUT, GOD GIVES JOY. THE GENUINE ENJOYMENT OF LIFE IS AN ESSENTIAL SIGN THAT GOD IS IN YOU.

We are weak; we are fleeting. But there is something inside your soul that is not weak and not fleeting. In fact, it is powerful, and it is eternal. God places eternity inside your fragile life. Man gains nothing by toil and work and wealth accumulation, riches, friends, promotions or material possessions. The only thing that matters is God. I have tried all, and I concur with the Teacher. Nothing from the Earth brings you joy. Joy comes from above and is given. Nothing here can ever bring you satisfaction; satisfaction is given only by God and from Paradise. Nothing on Earth brings you enjoyment; enjoyment is given by God alone. When, and only when, you see that this world is empty and that you are empty and only God can fill you up and unlock it all, you will live to promote God's happiness. Oh, the faithless and selfish, end it now. Stop and please God… prioritize this above all else. Get up every day to live to let God enjoy

His own handiwork, His own wealth, His own children and His own relationships.

This Omnipotent and Powerful Father will enter your fragile and mortal life and place in your hearts a piece of His powerful, blissful eternity with its enjoyment. You will then get up each day with meaningful toil and work to promote God and His day's agenda. Then satisfaction, fulfillment, purpose and enjoyment are given. Everything else is a waste of time and meaningless, yet God and His commands, pleasing Him, is everything. Then meaning and eternity is given back to you. Is not your heart speaking to you from within? Can you feel the hope in you? This is the Truth. What you do in the few days you are allowed with this temporary life matters, so go forth hour by hour to please the Alpha and Omega, the Beginning and the End, God Almighty, so that perhaps you too can get wrapped up into eternity and live forever.

Prayer

Omnipotent and Heavenly Father, the God of all who deserves such a beautiful day and life and eternity, you deserve children dancing around your feet, focused on you. You deserve the vision of everyone striving to do everything to please you. Father, I pray that each soul will look to please you and will train their children that no matter what they are doing—whether they are playing or studying or working—they are communing with you. May their worship, every thought, every minute, every day, every week, every month, every year, may it forever be a choice to please you thru the obedience of your Commands. May we purposely never go against anything you have commanded. May your Spirit come into our hearts as you have told us. May your Spirit come in to these fragile bodies; may the power of you exist and come forth so that you are glorified. And in all that we do, may we make you look good and not worry you, not bring one moment of anxiousness to you. All of this I pray thru the powerful name of Jesus Christ for a perfect response from the Remnant to you, O God. Amen!

Imagine a community that shows great honor to God, Christ, and then to each other! It is a light to all the world, a peaceful, beautiful community built on honor. It is a glimpse of the Kingdom of God, a society worth beholding and fighting for. Page 352.

How to Honor

Chapter 26

Everyone must submit himself to the governing authorities, for there is no authority except that which God has established. The authorities that exist have been established by God. Consequently, he who rebels against the authority is rebelling against what God has instituted, and those who do so will bring judgment on themselves. For rulers hold no terror for those who do right, but for those who do wrong. Do you want to be free from fear of the one in authority? Then do what is right and he will commend you. For he is God's servant to do you good. But if you do wrong, be afraid, for he does not bear the sword for nothing. He is God's servant, an agent of wrath to bring punishment on the wrongdoer. Therefore, it is necessary to submit to the authorities, not only because of possible punishment but also because of conscience. This is also why you pay taxes, for the authorities are God's servants, who give their full time to governing. Give everyone what you owe him: If you owe taxes, pay taxes; if revenue, then revenue; if respect, then respect; if honor, then honor. Romans 13:1-7

There are several elements to accomplishing genuine honor. The definition of honor is the showing of unusually merited respect, a feeling of appreciation, and courtesy—always being gracious, like Christ, no matter how we are feeling, no matter what the situation. To honor is to esteem or to value someone. So the question is, since we are commanded to honor, *whom* do we honor? We know that we must honor God and Christ first, but is honor due to anyone, no matter their behavior? Any leader, no matter their request? What about unmerited behavior?

America claims Christianity as its religion, but in the past four or five decades it has been a society of increasing *dishonor*. No one is exempt from anti-authority and degradation in this society today. This is a time when political and religious cartoons and editorials routinely criticize, satirize, and even lampoon our top leaders. Radio talk shows discuss leaders in a way that destroys their reputations but gathers a large audience for the talk show because it reflects the thinking of a growing segment of this world. Television talk shows are even harder to watch, not only because of the dishonor they show leaders and others around the world, but because of the humiliation that they show one another as they sarcastically talk over each other. This reflects a highly uneducated mindset and narrow-mindedness when it comes to what is going on around the world.

This type of behavior is easily passed down. It is difficult to keep the honor going in the next generation, yet it is very easy to pass down sarcasm, hate and self-focused moods, especially as children are continuing to watch cartoons and popular children's movies that portray even more self-pride and general disrespect for every level of authority. Again, no one—no matter their position—is exempt from dishonor in this society today. But this is not so in God's Law, nor is it the case in most other world religions.

Most people are unaware that America's proud display of dishonor and anti-authority is shocking to the rest of the world. Few Americans have been fully exposed to the majority of the world, where countries and different religions are taught deep respect and honor for other human beings since birth. Children in these societies are expected to be fully trained by the time they are 10 to 13 years old in all aspects of showing honor and giving humble apologies in every situation. Bowing is used in many countries for a respectful greeting and for apologies. The duration and inclination of the bow is proportionate to age and the respect due. Think about it—what if every time you greeted someone, you were appropriately showing respect for that person before they even started talking to you? I cannot imagine what that would do to a world of anger out there!

Drawing attention to yourself as an individual is a huge faux pas in most societies outside of America. Personal space is also valued in other cultures; for example, even on super-crowded subways in China, no one would dare take your personal space or make eye contact. They do not stare at anyone, so everyone still feels like they have their own space—they are respected. Peace is kept in all circumstances. It would be very hard to find someone arguing. Respect is highly valued to maintain the society.

OUTDO ONE ANOTHER IN SHOWING HONOR

Be devoted to one another in brotherly love. Honor one another above yourselves. Never be lacking in zeal, but keep your spiritual fervor, serving the Lord. Be joyful in hope, patient in affliction, faithful in prayer. Share with God's people who are in need. Practice hospitality. Bless those who persecute you; bless and do not curse. Rejoice with those who rejoice; mourn with those who mourn. Live in harmony with one another. Do not be proud, but be willing to associate with people of low position. Do not be conceited. Do not repay anyone evil for evil. Be careful to do what is right in the eyes of everybody. If it is possible, as far as it depends on you, live at peace with everyone. Do not take revenge, my friends, but leave room for God's wrath, for it is written: "It is mine to avenge; I will repay," says the Lord. On the contrary: "If your enemy is hungry, feed him; if he is thirsty, give him something to drink. In doing this, you will heap burning coals on his head." Do not be overcome by evil, but overcome evil with good. Romans 12:10-21

At one time, Judaism set the standard for all respect, honor and politeness for the world—the Queen of Sheba even came to see King Solomon out of respect and honor.[1] People were awed at the behavior of Jerusalem and the respect that the Jews had for their leaders. Christians at one time were also known for having the highest standard of manners and etiquette. The early Christians not only greeted one another with a holy kiss, but they were told to outdo one another in showing honor. When in the presence of enemies, they turned the other cheek in full self-control and allowed graciously the confiscation of their homes.[2] They accepted being burned at the stake for the sake of Jesus Christ.

> THOSE WHO HAVE FOLLOWED CHRIST FOR LONGER ARE BRIGHT LIGHTS—THEY MAKE YOU SMILE, BECAUSE THEY ARE SO APPRECIATIVE OF THE SMALLEST THINGS. THEY ARE TRULY CHILDLIKE.

But you are a chosen people, a royal priesthood, a holy nation, a people belonging to God, that you may declare the praises of him who called you out of darkness into his wonderful light. Once you were not a people, but now you are the people of God; once you had not received mercy, but now you have received mercy. Dear friends, I urge you, as aliens and strangers in the world, to abstain from sinful desires, which war against your soul. Live such good lives among the pagans that, though they accuse you of doing wrong, they may see your good deeds and glorify God on the

---

1   *I Kings 10*

2   *You sympathized with those in prison and joyfully accepted the confiscation of your property, because you knew that you yourselves had better and lasting possessions. Hebrews 10:34*

day he visits us. Submit yourselves for the Lord's sake to every authority instituted among men: whether to the king, as the supreme authority, or to governors, who are sent by him to punish those who do wrong and to commend those who do right. For it is God's will that by doing good you should silence the ignorant talk of foolish men. Live as free men, but do not use your freedom as a cover-up for evil; live as servants of God. Show proper respect to everyone: Love the brotherhood of believers, fear God, honor the king. I Peter 2:9-17

Again, a "Christian," a "gentle-man," would be one highly educated in polite manners and etiquette. One who was careful of his words—saying nothing that was not completely gracious. As has been said, we have been called to be a Holy Priesthood. This standard of nobility and behavior is the same for all of us. Honor God first and foremost, honor Christ, honor the king, honor one another, and then give proper respect to outsiders.

HONORING THE AGED

It is safe to assume that the longer you have lived, the more you have suffered, but this is especially true the longer that you have been committed to God and His Church. In Leviticus 19:32, it says, *Rise in the presence of the aged. Show respect for the elderly and revere your God. I am the Lord.* We must truly revere what our more experienced Saints say, for they have lived longer. They are priceless jewels who have no anger toward anything but the unrighteousness in the world that hurts God. These people are rare, but those who have chosen the path of self-denial are happier and very encouraging to be around. They have the pleasing aroma of Christ. These Saints are sacrificial and are able to wash the feet of others. They are at peace.

Those who have followed Christ for longer are bright lights—they make you smile because they are so appreciative of the smallest things. They are truly child-like. When you have lived longer, you are more appreciative of God's grace. When you have lived thru many battles, you become more impressed with the sinless and perfectly sacrificial example of Christ. It is an appreciation that is the ingredient of happy, aged Saints, and they are full of energy as they ignore that the body is more challenged physically. It is all in their focus.

The world around them seems to disappear as the aged Saints become consumed with the House of the Lord, and they care for the place and the people more than their own life, their own home. King David said in Psalm 137:5, *If I forget you, O Jerusalem, may my right hand forget its skill.* The House of God is on the mind and in the heart of the aged Saints.

Honor those who have gone before. The aged are close to God, and anyone close to God has access to answered prayers and to the blessings that come with the approval from God. Their prayers and their righteous lives are the very glue that is needed to secure the presence and the favor of God. Do you not try to preserve the battery in your computers? Do you not try to fix the electricity the minute it goes out? Do you not try to protect the money in your bank? The answer, of course, is a resounding, "Yes!" We take care of the engines that drive our lives and especially those that drive the Kingdom and usher in the Presence of our God Almighty. These are the True Saints, those who have laid down their lives for the Kingdom of God. Now, though they might look less powerful as the Lord allows outward physical atrophy, they are those who are inwardly most powerful.

Honoring the Church Body

Having a reverent respect to God and to your authorities and living an upright and pure life transforms all those around you. It is amazing, and it all comes down to *love*, for without love, you cannot genuinely honor. Without love, you cannot even get under authority—you will despise the authority instead of loving it as unto God.

True honoring takes away fear. When there is true respect, there will be no fear in the home, but only beautiful peace. When we abide in the Vine, he lives in us, as Jesus said in John 15.[3] So this way of interacting thru honoring is reflecting the Spirit and charac-

teristics of Christ. Then take it a step further. In these interactions, you should be seeing the Spirit of Christ himself, as Christ is in you. We are clones of Christ—Christians, Christ followers, Disciples—so his humility and mercy and sacrificial love will fill the community of Believers. It is Christ interacting with you—unbelievable!

I Corinthians 12:27 says, *Now you are the body of Christ, and each one of you is a part of it.* But what is so amazing is that Jesus Christ

---

3   *Remain in me, and I will remain in you. No branch can bear fruit by itself; it must remain in the vine. Neither can you bear fruit unless you remain in me. John 15:4*

appears to us today thru the members of the Church—the called out, the Ecclesia—the Kingdom of God.

Imagine a community that shows great honor to God, Christ, and then to each other! It is a light to all the world, a peaceful, beau-

> THE REAL WAY TO HONOR CHRIST IS TO LIVE AN HONORABLE LIFE.

tiful community built on honor. It is a glimpse of the Kingdom of God, a society worth beholding and fighting for. Imagine giving and receiving honor, going from the youngest to the oldest, and then learning about honoring positions appointed by God. I pray that we all take the challenge to live as thoughtfully and respectfully as humanly possible to God first, and to Christ, and then to each other.

The Ten Commandments call us to honor our parents, and the way to do that is to live an honorable life. If you are dishonorable, it embarrasses your parents. In the same way, the real way to honor Christ is to live an honorable life. The way to honor God is to live an honorable, upright life and pass it on to others as your cup overflows.

You have found the secret—following and imitating Christ—and that honors all the Kingdom. It honors God, His Church and His Christ, and it brings about the righteous, royal life that you are dreaming of.

You must put your all into pleasing your authorities. Give them your undivided attention. Every day is a chance for you to submit to your authority. We get to do this as unto God and submit with respect as unto Christ. All of this is what sets us apart and makes us a Godly, holy people. Let us stop expecting and let us start giving respect, compliments, love and honor due to those above us every day. Page 359.

Showing Christlike Respect

CHAPTER 27

Children, obey your parents in the Lord, for this is right. "Honor your father and mother"—which is the first commandment with a promise— "that it may go well with you and that you may enjoy long life on the earth." Fathers, do not exasperate your children; instead, bring them up in the training and instruction of the Lord. Slaves, obey your earthly masters with respect and fear, and with sincerity of heart, just as you would obey Christ. Obey them not only to win their favor when their eye is on you, but like slaves of Christ, doing the will of God from your heart. Ephesians 6:1-6

Genuine honor and sincere respect speak volumes. True respect, honor and awe toward God and authority proves your morality, for no one would choose to obey an authority unless it was for God. The Remnant upholds the ancient, revered words of the Most High God of the Universe, and we know that honor and respect of God first and our authorities second is one of the principle foundations of our faith. We are called to serve those over us—to follow that line of authority and look for ways to obey our authorities.

The average person focuses only on their own personal situation under an authority: "I cannot believe this difficult job." "No one else has a supervisor like mine." "Surely God does not want me to submit to someone who is always in a foul mood." "My parents are always telling me what to do." "My spouse overspends." Such people feel like *they* are the ones who get no respect, that *they* have been treated poorly, and *they* are the victims. So what they give back to their authorities is what they feel like they are receiving from their authorities—if they get yelled at, they yell back. They nag their parents if they feel like their parents are nagging them. They punish their boss for their boss's behavior. They may smile to their supervisor's face, but they turn around and sabotage an assignment or neglect their duties and end up making the boss look bad. They talk behind his back, and they get the whole crowd to resist until the boss is not ruling at all. Then they threaten to sue if they are fired, so the business goes under. It is criminal to take a paycheck from a boss while talking behind his back and therefore destroying him and his business.

It does not matter if you think your boss is the least qualified person in the company or if you feel your husband is the least worthy of respect...you are missing the point! We have the *opportunity* to submit to our authorities—from the least to the greatest—so that every authority has full respect...every husband, every leader, every parent. It does not matter how much money your husband makes; it does not matter what your boss is like. *You* start by being the one to show respect, and you look for their positive qualities.

Genuine Respect

Give everyone what you owe him: If you owe taxes, pay taxes; if revenue, then revenue; if respect, then respect; if honor, then honor. Romans 13:7

Growing up in America today, it can be difficult to truly know how to treat an authority. What does genuine respect look like? For starters, we are to treat those over us with great fear and honor as if they were the top CEO in the company. Treat them like royalty, like a king. The big secret is that when you give respect to others—even though they have not given respect back, or in other words, when you give a compliment even though they have not given you a compliment—then *you* will be treated with respect.

Teach slaves to be subject to their masters in everything, to try to please them, not to talk back to them, and not to steal from them, but to show that they can be fully trusted, so that in every way they will make the teaching about God our Savior attractive. Titus 2:9-10

God works thru this authority line, and we should never take our authority at face value, but rather, see Christ thru our authority. We jump to serve them as we would for Jesus Christ. *You* anticipate; *you* figure out their wants and their needs so that they do not even have to tell you beforehand, and *you* show FULL respect for them, never taking anything personally. It is not about you! It is about God and His training of you. It is a test of the Saints, and it is a promotion of God and His Kingdom. This has a dual purpose. By watching us give honor where honor is due, it proves the existence of God.

> GIVE IT TIME. *YOU* GO FROM NAGGING TO NICE, FROM COMPLAINING TO COMPLIMENTING.

Not only does the Word of God promote this authority, but the entire animal kingdom is controlled by authority and is a good example for us to study. The animals all know their position in life. They do not try to take another type of animal's position, and they patiently wait their turn. It is instinctive; they know it, and it glorifies God. They could have devoured one another long ago, but they all know their place, and it is beautiful. Babies in the animal kingdom are tuned in to their parents. Their mother or their father will nudge them to get in line. God teaches all the offspring, and their attention to authority spares and extends their life. That is how they live—by following their authority and showing respect.

Give it time. *You* go from nagging to nice, from complaining to complimenting. A true compliment is an expression of esteem, of respect, affection or admiration. Give a compliment every day—not insincerely, but genuinely—formal and respectful recognition.

Do not correct your authority. *Respect* is better than accuracy.

We need to stop waiting for a compliment before we give one. We need to stop waiting for respect before we give it to our bosses, our husband, our parents. Stop expecting anything from anyone. Know and trust that God rewards those who earnestly seek Him and His Jesus Christ.[1] You can count on God.

---

1 And without faith it is impossible to please God, because anyone who comes to him must believe that he exists and that he rewards those who earnestly seek him. Hebrews 11:6

From this moment forward, do not look for or expect any compliments or any respect for yourself, but rather find opportunities to give compliments and respect. Ask questions; get advice from your authorities. Do not correct your authority. It is demeaning for the one under authority to say, "You are wrong," or "You do not understand." *Respect* is better than accuracy. Be very careful, as if you were serving unto God, and God will bless it.

The world owes you nothing, and besides, this world cannot give anything to you. But if you do what is right, then God comes back in and blesses you. It is a beautiful thing. You *will* be blessed if you just remain focused up and positive.

To those who are in positions of authority, I ask, would you want to work for yourself? Would you want to be under your own authority? And to those who are under authority, I ask the question, what does your authority really think of you? Does the one in authority over you want to keep you employed, or would they secretly be fine if you leave? Is your husband fine not coming home because he is coming home to constant nagging? Men would rather have a continual toothache than have a complaining wife who is always stirring something up. Would your spouse cry if you never came home again…or would they be delighted?

You must put your all into pleasing your authorities. Give them your undivided attention. Your work for your husband or your boss could be perfect, but if you do not show respect and honor, they will reject your work. Respectless dinners—your husband does not want them. Respectless tasks on the job—forget it. You cannot work your way into the heart of your authority without genuine respect in your heart. Respect is the glue. Respect is the foundation.

Every day is a chance for you to honor your authority. Every day is a chance for the children to be honoring to all of their teachers and to their parents. We get to honor the ruling government in America by obeying it, and we get to do all this as unto God and submit to our spiritual leaders in a beautiful way with respect as unto Christ. All of this is what sets us apart and makes us a Godly, holy people. Let us stop expecting and let us start *giving* respect, compliments, love and honor due to those above us every day.

The Purpose of Authority

If you are really under God, then you will accept the good and the bad that comes your way. Are you under God, or do you act like you are over God? The only way God is going to know the answer is by how you treat your earthly authorities and others. You are tested when you are at home; you are tested when you are driving down the road; you are tested when you are coming in; you are tested when you are going out. You are tested when you get up, when you go to bed and in the middle of the night. This is a spiritual war; and when you choose this path, you will not get out of the testing. There is no drinking alcohol to forget about it. There are no drugs that are going to erase it. There is nothing that will relieve the pain except to hear the words from your Father who is trying to prepare you and grow His Church up to be the place it is supposed to be.

This University has more exams than Harvard, and Saints do not really graduate from it—but they rise above. What is your goal? It must be to rise above the spiritual warfare. Conquer it! Master it so that it does not master you.[2] You are not overcome with the evil; you overcome evil with the good.[3] Then you are promoted in the ranks into being the generals of this spiritual war. Think about the men and the women, the Christian soldiers, who have marched

---

2   Genesis 4:7
3   *Do not be overcome by evil, but overcome evil with good. Romans 12:21*

into war day after day, year after year, and who have fought spiritual battles without complaining or giving up. They wake up expecting it, they go thru their day conquering it, and they go to bed being victorious—it is beautiful! They are the ones we should decorate with Purple Hearts, the ones we should look at and admire.[4]

ADVANCED SPIRITUAL TRAINING

I know this authority is the answer—the answer to salvation—the answer for life. It is the life of Christ that is the light to all mankind. This original word of authority that was there from the beginning is the answer for the purity of the Church. But sometimes, we really do have authorities who might appear harsh. How do you respect those authorities? You must learn quickly not to take anything personally. You need to see the authorities as being under the control of God, like a marionette. And you see that it is God who is allowing this situation for your training and that this training is invaluable. Men receive and put up with jealous negativity all the time in the workplace, and it is great training when you learn to rise above it. I do not encourage quickly trying to get out of a situation that appears harsh. If you do leave, you are likely to have the same situation in the next job, and the next, until you learn to overcome it and pass the test. It is not about you or your work. You should not go looking for a job so people can see how great YOU are! No, this is about your training. You have a

> LET US STOP EXPECTING AND LET US START GIVING RESPECT, COMPLIMENTS, LOVE AND HONOR DUE TO THOSE ABOVE US EVERY DAY.

---

4 *One example is the Apostle Paul in II Corinthians 11:23b-29*

short period of time in this life to learn to get under authority and to accept that God is over all authority on this Earth.

A Spiritual Training Ground

God knows exactly where you are and what you are going thru. Remember, *...the one who is in you is greater than the one who is in the world. I John 4:4b* Greater is God than satan and his demons. God has not left you alone in this trail of trials. God allows spirits to enter and leave, to come and go, and the person who He uses will have no memory of the event—they may even deny that they ever acted in such a way. If you do not understand this concept, you might feel like you are losing your mind. But if you do not take anything personally, then watch and see that you *can* pass this test.

> THIS IS A HIGH-PRICED UNIVERSITY OF THE NEW JERUSALEM, AND THIS CONCEPT WILL REVOLUTIONIZE YOUR LIFE, FOR IT WILL ENDEAR YOU TO GOD LIKE NOTHING ELSE.

The authority will often come back in a little while and act as if nothing negative has been said—they will be as nice as they can be!

This is also a test to make sure you do not hold a grudge and that you have learned to respond to the mood of the authority. Let the boss set the mood, the parents set the mood, the husband set the mood. You are not in control. This is a high-priced university of this New Jerusalem, and this concept will revolutionize your life, for it will endear you to God like nothing else. You will depend on Him for everything and pray about everything and be prepared for warfare for this life and the next. You will realize that part of being Spirit-led is to be sent to the front lines of combat. We are soldiers of Christ expanding a Kingdom of peace, proving that the Will of God is superior. If we can be on our guard and get ready for the daily examination, the adversity, or hardships and become alert to the spirits that war against God—these anti-authority spirits that war against being under authority—then we will be rewarded by God. Who knows whom you may impact by your actions? As Paul said in his first letter to the Corinthians, *How do you know, wife, whether you will save your husband? Or, how do you know, husband, whether you will save your wife? I Corinthians 7:16* How do you know? You may convert someone, or you may help an immature Saint.

You must go all the way. The half-hearted effort of being under authority will only backfire. As Saints we must not take negative behavior personally. We must not look at the evil—but rather the *potential*—of those caught up in sin. We must understand that there is a higher purpose or calling. If your motive is just for your own peace, your own self-control, your own household, then you are never going to rise above. But if your motive is for the expansion of the Kingdom, to teach this to your children, then you will fight harder and you will win more battles. Be the first to give, the first to change. Even a small change on your part can make a great change in others.

Seeing beyond the surface and removing yourself, loving the unlovely, is the powerful answer.[5] It is proof of a loving God who does that for you every single day. What is there to fear? A loss of pride? What if you just gave up your pride? What are you waiting for? What is so bad about finding out that you were wrong? What if you looked for the *good* in your spouse or in your authority, and you just gave a little more? What if giving in a little more made a drastic

---

5   *For more about loving the unlovely, please see Chapter 22 of* <u>The History of the Love of God</u>, *Volume II: A Love More Ancient than Time*

change in your authority? Who knows? Is returning good for evil too great a price to pay for the power to transform?

We must wake up and accept our positions as soldiers in a war, so we can be on our guard for these tests and baptize every word and every act into humility. Thereby we will hopefully and prayerfully be helping mankind and those around us to transform from arrogant, spoiled and bratty, to humble and appreciative. Oh, how needed is this heart change. So many have been given this mercy but are not extending it. It is a big breach. There is a void of respect and honor given to God and Christ and then earthly authorities as unto Christ. It is so tragic. It is heartbreaking.

> WE MUST WAKE UP AND ACCEPT OUR POSITIONS AS SOLDIERS IN A WAR, SO WE CAN BE ON OUR GUARD FOR THESE TESTS AND BAPTIZE EVERY WORD AND EVERY ACT INTO HUMILITY.

On the other hand, I want to give you a vision: Imagine this Kingdom, this Royal Remnant Revival, and this humility…if it were promoted more than ever before, promoted not half-heartedly but in full. Imagine if it grew and the world became *full* of pleased bosses, pleased husbands, pleased parents. Imagine all the authorities giving back generously because they are so pleased. What a concept! Heaven is going to blow us all away. It will be breathtaking, a true Paradise, like the Garden of Eden before the fall of man. Please, dear Saints, honor and respect others while taking nothing personally and giving love in return. Let us all do our part in promoting this honor and this respect to our authorities for the sake of the Kingdom of God. What if obedience to this goal glued this broken world back together? Join with me in doing our own small part.

Showing Christlike Respect

PRAYER

Father, we praise you for your words from the Prophets of old and for this incredible secret that everyone wants peace at home and everyone wants respect, but the secret is that respect is given when we give it away first. Then you come back in, and you make us into someone who is respected. O God, how beautiful is all of this! Please help us understand the incredible need to be respectful and honoring, for the children to honor their parents thru obedience, for the wives to understand that their husband is to be honored as they are the head of the household. God, may every person honor their bosses, and may every person honor their spiritual leaders. Father, we pray that we all grow up in this so that we love it, and then we are a pure body of people, shining like stars as Christ shines in the night like the morning star. May we shine in a dark world of hate. May this world see that obeying you by giving honor and respect is the most glorious thing in the world, the most freeing thing in the world, the most beautiful thing in the world and the happiest thing in the world. O God, you are wonderful. Thru Jesus Christ's name we pray all of this together, Amen.

Humble yourselves and seek correction and direction. Have you conquered humility? Consider the sermons as direction, take notes and accept conviction. Then go back and follow up; keep track; look back at it and tackle any areas that were convicting, because that is how you get close to God. Page 371.

Accepting Loving Redirection

Chapter 28

To be a part of this Royal Revival, we must all search out and seek for Truth. Followers of Christ should be different. The husbands are different, the wives are different, and the children are different. That is the light to the world, and we must have a relationship with God to endure.

This is the verdict: Light has come into the world, but men loved darkness instead of light because their deeds were evil. Everyone who does evil hates the light, and will not come into the light for fear that his deeds will be exposed. But whoever lives by the truth comes into the light, so that it may be seen plainly that what he has done has been done through God. John 3:19-21

This concept of light is essential, a light of revelation of what is inside our heart. You must be in the light to have a relationship with the Most High God. Correction and confession play a vital role, but they are so misunderstood in today's society. In fact, they are the most misunderstood concepts on the face of the Earth. People are so afraid of correction and confession, and they allow pride, projection, family protection and self-protection to block this life-giving information. Look at these Scriptures:

You will say, "How I hated discipline! How my heart spurned correction! I would not obey my teachers or listen to my instructors. I have come to the brink of utter ruin in the midst of the whole assembly." Proverbs 5:12-14

In vain I punished your people. They did not respond to correction. Your sword has devoured your prophets like a ravening lion. Jeremiah 2:30

Whoever loves discipline loves knowledge, but he who hates correction is stupid. Proverbs 12:1

He who ignores discipline comes to poverty and shame, but whoever heeds correction is honored. Proverbs 13:18

A fool spurns his father's discipline, but whoever heeds correction shows prudence. Proverbs 15:5

A mocker resents correction; he will not consult the wise. Proverbs 15:12

He who ignores discipline despises himself, but whoever heeds correction gains understanding. Proverbs 15:32

To be in the light means that we are in constant communication with God.

Not everyone who says to me, "Lord, Lord," will enter the kingdom of heaven, but only he who does the will of my Father who is in heaven. Many will say to me on that day, "Lord, Lord, did we not prophesy in your name, and in your name drive out demons and perform many miracles?" Then I will tell them plainly, "I never knew you. Away from me, you evildoers!" Matthew 7:21-23

Draw near. Get close. Be known by God. The whole relationship is wrapped up in this verse because there are many who will say that they have done great things, but they do not *know* God, and they do not know Christ. Part of knowing God is getting under the authority over you.[1] When you get a smile from your authority, then you know you are on the right path.

If you feel a distance with your employer, with your spouse, or with your parents, then there is something wrong with your relationship with God. The first step is to repent and look to God for direction. *They turned their backs to me and not their faces; though I taught them again and again, they would not listen or respond to discipline. Jeremiah 32:33* Many people have their backs to God, just like a child who is looking back over their shoulder at the parent instead of following in the parent's footsteps. Their actions and their whole lives are based on going their own way.

> CORRECTION IS LOVE, AND THERE IS NO WAY TO HAVE A RELATIONSHIP WITH AN AUTHORITY UNLESS YOU CHECK BACK IN ON A REGULAR BASIS LIKE A MOTHER TO A CHILD—CHECKING IN WITH YOUR HEAVENLY FATHER AND HIS HOLY SPIRIT.

You repent. You turn toward God to find what He wanted thru the existing authority that He has set up for you on Earth. To be corrected is simply to be given direction, and I liken it to a mama duck swimming down a stream. She is whispering back to her children saying, "Go this way, now go this way. This is where we will find food. This is where we are safe." This is a beautiful picture of kind and loving attention and a totally new mindset. Proverbs tells us *The Lord disciplines those he loves, as a father the son he delights in. Proverbs 3:12* The Apostle Paul confirms this in Hebrews:

---

1 Romans 13:1-7, I Peter 2:13-17

Endure hardship as discipline; God is treating you as sons. For what son is not disciplined by his father? If you are not disciplined (and everyone undergoes discipline), then you are illegitimate children and not true sons. Moreover, we have all had human fathers who disciplined us and we respected them for it. How much more should we submit to the Father of our spirits and live! Our fathers disciplined us for a little while as they thought best; but God disciplines us for our good, that we may share in his holiness. No discipline seems pleasant at the time, but painful. Later on, however, it produces a harvest of righteousness and peace for those who have been trained by it. Hebrews 12:7-11

A harvest of righteousness and peace...God is whispering to His children, to those He *loves*. Correction is love, and there is no way to have a relationship with an authority unless you check back in on a regular basis like a child checking in with the mother—checking in with your Heavenly Father and His Holy Spirit. If you do not want to be corrected by those in authority over you, then you will not have a relationship with them nor with God. You are missing this royal calling, this priceless opportunity. Later in Proverbs we find, *Buy the truth and do not sell it; get wisdom, discipline and understanding. Proverbs 23:23* We must long for this correction and direction. If you do not want to call it correction, write the word "direction" every time you see it. I *long* for direction. I continue to get up every night and cry out to God to be corrected and redirected.

> MOMENTS OF CONVICTION ARE WHISPERS OF LOVE AS GOD WHISPERS TO US IN THE PRIVACY OF THE NIGHT, AND THE HOLY SPIRIT MOVES YOU.

CLINGING TO CONVICTION

You know what the idol is that God has called you to lay down. Are you doing it? Or are you making your own list of what you are going to do and fulfilling your own requirements? *Since they did not know the righteousness that comes from God and sought to establish their own, they did not submit to God's righteousness. Romans 10:3* They made their own rules. If you make your own list and fulfill your own requirements, then when your authority asks you for something, you have no energy left. You are exhausted from trying to please yourself and doing things that are self-right. Your list, your focus, needs to be directed from up above. When you get up in the morning, it must be God's agenda you are seeking.

How are you going to accomplish this? A good way to begin is with a journal. You need to keep track of what God and your authorities are asking of you. You can use it to track your daily work schedule and your spiritual goals. Do not just ask others, "What do you see in me?" Instead, look to God for His conviction and consider what your authorities have already asked of you. Keep that list, and then check back in with those over you on how you are doing. Ask if there is anything else you need to change or improve. You will become self-disciplining. Paul says in II Timothy, *For God did not give us a spirit of timidity, but a spirit of power, of love and of self-discipline. II Timothy 1:7*

Humble yourselves and seek correction and direction. Have you conquered humility? Consider the sermons as direction, take notes and accept conviction. Then go back and follow up; keep track; look back at it and tackle any areas that were convicting, because that is how you get close to God. You should long for your employer to approach you so that you can show them your list and what you have done and ask for their feedback. This is vital because you do not have a relationship with God if you do not have a relationship with the authority over you.

Watch the animals—they are teaching their children. The baby animals stay near their parents, and they watch everything that the parent teaches. As the cardinal flies to one spot, the baby is close behind. They dare not venture away. Fear is our missing element. We must draw near. The mother whale cannot chase down the baby whale; the baby must stay near her side. The mother duckling cannot chase down all four ducklings going in different directions. The only safe place is in the middle of the Will of God, following His authority line.

Moments of conviction are whispers of love as God whispers to us in the privacy of the night, and the Holy Spirit moves you. Turn the television off, close the refrigerator door, and then you find God. Make your list, and look for that conviction.

Train yourself to listen to the gentle and sweet voice of God. If you can learn to listen to the gentle and the sweet, then you are training your mind to hear God. But if you are waiting for the loud, angry voice, you are training your mind to listen to a demon or yourself. God's voice is quiet. With Elijah, God was not in the thunder or the earthquake...He was not in the loud; He was in the quiet, gentle whisper.[2] Why would God keep Himself invisible if He did not prefer to guide you with gentle prompting instead of being a dictator? That is why parents have to learn to be that way, and the

---

2 *The Lord said, "Go out and stand on the mountain in the presence of the Lord, for the Lord is about to pass by." Then a great and powerful wind tore the mountains apart and shattered the rocks before the Lord, but the Lord was not in the wind. After the wind there was an earthquake, but the Lord was not in the earthquake. After the earthquake came a fire, but the Lord was not in the fire. And after the fire came a gentle whisper. I Kings 19:11-12*

Accepting Loving Redirection

Shepherds have to learn to be that way... to be like God. Or otherwise, we are altogether not like God.

It is about a habit of hearing correction and then repenting and changing. The journal is a barometer to measure change, but there is no legalism on this journaling. Your goal is to get to the root of the issue and make sure that it is about your heart changing. We move at such a fast pace in this life, and we seldom reflect like we should. Journaling or even writing it down in your phone is one way to keep track. It is an incredible gift to be able to go back and look at this journal between you and the Lord of your life.

It is your responsibility to take this conviction and record of changes and communicate your progress to the one over you. It is the job of the one under authority to report in. It is the child's job, the wife's job, the employee's job, the Church member's job to stay near their authority and follow up. It is not up to the teachers to track down the students to make sure that they are handing in their homework. It is not up to the bosses to track down all their employees to make sure they are doing their job. It is not up to the spiritual leaders to track down the members who are caught up in sin. You need to be the one to initiate checking in.

> IF YOU CAN LEARN TO LISTEN TO THE GENTLE AND THE SWEET, THEN YOU ARE TRAINING YOUR MIND TO HEAR GOD.

CRAVING DIRECTION

It is very important to *know* your authority: study what they want, know how they want you to report in and how they like you to communicate. Children need to keep their eyes on the parents; the employee needs to look for direction and the approval of the boss. Why is this difficult? Why would a man resent another man directing his life? Normally, it is because men look for praise from other men, and correction is the opposite of what they crave. It is like taking food away from the overeater or alcohol away from the alcoholic. If you cringe when you are corrected, it is because you eat the praise of man; and when you are redirected, you just missed a meal.

However, if you are in love with God alone, you see nothing but the face of God and look only for His approval. You must lose the desire for the praise of man if you are to ever win the approval of your authorities and of God. You cannot have it both ways. The irony is that the man who loves God first and foremost gets support from fellow brothers and sisters in Christ who are so grateful to be corrected and connected to the Mainframe Computer. They now have electricity for the life in their little terminals, and their little computer screen starts lighting up when a man directs them on how to plug into God. This correction and redirection is so exciting, so beautiful and so comforting. I look for the words of direction and redirection and correction from God daily. We must turn correction into redirection of our minds. If we are headed the wrong way and someone gently leads us back to the right direction, that is pure love!

Are you avoiding correction by trying to make yourself look better or only going to those who you know will remove conviction and guilt? Do you hate the correction? Do you seek your child's approval over your husband's? In a work situation, are you more concerned about the customer's approval than your boss's? Correction is one of the mysteries that connect people to the light. It is probably one of the most misunderstood concepts of all time, and yet it is essential and connected to the doors of eternity. We must learn to crave it. Look up every day. Look upward to your authorities. Take care of them. Stay close. Correction and redirection are love.

Join the revival of those who walk on a constant path of no expectations and who look for redirection from above. When we do that, we will become a beacon of light so bright that it will run evil far away and draw only the pure-hearted. How beautiful would every home and workplace be if each soul let the light of Jesus Christ be our plumbline—with a moment-by-moment mindset on the Heavenly Father and His goals. Happiness abounds as each Saint rises above and advances the glorious Kingdom of God.

PRAYER

Father, we praise you for correction and redirection. May we be the most respectful and loving people to authority, looking for their every move, every glance. May we know everything about our authorities as unto Christ, and may we translate that to knowing you and loving you with everything we have. O Father, we pray in the name of Jesus Christ that you will shower us with love, and we will love you back and love others while we have the chance to love, to get it right and to go the right direction. In Jesus' name we pray, Amen.

The Christian home is both physically cleaned up and spiritually cleaned up, and it is filled with Truth and prayer. In a Christian household, it should not be unusual to see the children praying, to see the father studying and praying, to see the parents having a devotional. Prayer would be something common. These homes are lights to the world because everything in the home is peaceful, and it is evident by the fruit of your lives. We are in love with God, and we want to share that love with others. Page 385.

What does a Christian Household Look Like?

Chapter 29

Here is a trustworthy saying: If anyone sets his heart on being an overseer, he desires a noble task. Now the overseer must be above reproach, the husband of but one wife, temperate, self-controlled, respectable, hospitable, able to teach, not given to drunkenness, not violent but gentle, not quarrelsome, not a lover of money. He must manage his own family well and see that his children obey him with proper respect. (If anyone does not know how to manage his own family, how can he take care of God's church?) He must not be a recent convert, or he may become conceited and fall under the same judgment as the devil. He must also have a good reputation with outsiders, so that he will not fall into disgrace and into the devil's trap. Deacons, likewise, are to be men worthy of respect, sincere, not indulging in much wine, and not pursuing dishonest gain. They must keep hold of the deep truths of the faith with a clear conscience. They must first be tested; and then if there is nothing against them, let them serve as deacons. In the same way, their wives are to be women worthy of respect, not malicious talkers but temperate and trustworthy in everything. A deacon must be the husband of but one wife and must manage his children and his household well. Those who have served well gain an excellent standing and great assurance in their faith in Christ Jesus. Although I hope to come to you soon, I am writing you these instructions so that, if I am delayed, you will know how people ought to conduct themselves in God's household, which is the church of the living God, the pillar and foundation of the truth. I Timothy 3:1-15

I Timothy 3 is a beautiful picture of what the Christian home should look like. It should be a small micro-unit or subunit of the Church, as we discussed previously. A Christian home should reflect Christ and his beautiful example of authority with the head of the household and the wife and children all under authority and everyone serving each other for the glory of God.

This chapter of Timothy begins by talking about "overseers," which is another word for Shepherds, or the King James Version calls them Bishops. Sometimes, they are called Elders. *"Now the overseer must be above reproach…"* *Above reproach* means there is no question that this is a Godly man. You would have no worry about what he might say if he were to speak in the Assembly. If you went to dinner with him, you would not dream of thinking that he would get angry and storm out or that he would say anything offensive at any time.

The husband of but one wife… They are faithful to their spouse. *Temperate…* Temperate means no anger—a person who is even and consistent. They do not have mood swings where they are up one day and down the next. They are constantly pleasant, approachable, happy, an even-tempered personality. You would never worry about finding them in a bad mood, angry, depressed or sullen.

Self-controlled… They are in full control of their actions and their words. They can stop eating when they are full. They can stop drinking when they have had enough and have not overindulged. They are not out of control in any of the Fruits of the Spirit: love, joy, patience, peace, kindness, goodness, faithfulness, gentleness.[1] A self-controlled person has God's spirit in him because God is self-controlled.

---

1   *Galatians 5:22-23*

What Does a Christian Household Look Like?

Respectable… These men and women are honorable and upright—it is recognized and acknowledged by others. They show it by their actions and words. Think about the impact on the children and family when mothers and fathers are not respectable… when there is arguing in the home or over-drinking or a disorganized household or overspending. That is not glorifying to God. A Christian household is honorable at all times.

> NOTICE IT MAKES YOU HAPPY INSIDE ONCE YOUR ROOM FEELS CLEAN. IT IS A LITTLE PIECE OF HEAVEN.

Hospitable… Hospitable means that someone is willing to open up their home and let others come over for dinner or to host other families. You are friendly and welcoming. Your home is open and used for the Kingdom of God.

Able to teach… These shepherds would be able to stand before others and be clear in their instruction. They can gently guide members and help those who are seeking.

Not given to drunkenness, not violent but gentle... They are in control with their drinking and with their emotions.[2] They are very gentle, patient and kind.

Not quarrelsome, not a lover of money... This is a person who is not argumentative and not worried about having to be "right." They also do not love money; they generously share what they have been given to further the Church and those in need. They are not interested in accumulating money just to spend it on themselves.

> THE REMNANT IS MADE UP OF HOUSEHOLDS OF MEN, WOMEN AND CHILDREN WHO HAVE CHOSEN TO TAKE ON THE PERSONAL RESPONSIBILITY AND LOVE THAT HAS BEEN GIVEN ACCORDING TO JESUS CHRIST.

He must manage his own family well and see that his children obey him with proper respect... Sometimes a father wants to hand that responsibility over to the mother, but a Godly father welcomes this responsibility, making sure the children are respectful and obedient. He pays attention to what his children are doing, what they are learning at school and how they are treating one another at home. Are they learning to be kind, patient, charitable and giving? A father can delegate some responsibilities, but he needs to be involved with his children and take care of some of the direct teaching.

If anyone does not know how to manage his own family, how can he take care of God's church? This means if someone is not doing something right, the overseer is able to kindly direct them to the right path. *You* manage it. You make sure the children are all learning. If you let

---

2 For more about over-drinking, see Weigh Down Works! Chapter 20, "Alcohol, Tobacco and Drug Abuse"

the children go their own way and you overlook it or ignore it, the next thing you know, children will realize that they can get away with that behavior, and the behavior will increase. Children need you to stop them from behaviors that are unsafe or not in God's will. You want to make sure that you are managing the house and managing the finances. You are making sure that the lion's share of your children's time is spent learning to be like Jesus Christ, and you are showing them this example in your own words and actions. That is your main goal.

He must not be a recent convert… This means that a leader is not someone who just recently joined the Church. A Church Overseer needs years of training, watching the examples of others and showing the fruit of their own changed lives. Keep in mind that once a person becomes an Elder he will naturally face heavy testing. This testing will be from the Father: *From everyone who has been given much, much will be demanded; and from the one who has been entrusted with much, much more will be asked. Luke 12:48b* You are often tested and then retested, with heavy testing at times for your own refining. When you have been given more responsibility, more is expected.

Or he may become conceited and fall under the same judgment as the devil. Some people turn a position of leadership into a prideful thing. You should never have pride in your role because those who are conceited will fall into the same trap into which satan fell. You must be accountable at all times, always mindful of your own heart, and willing to accept questioning and correction if given. You may even be asked to step down from the role of Leadership if needed. If you are not willing to step down, it shows you are greedy for the praise of man, and something is wrong with your heart.

He must also have a good reputation with outsiders, so that he will not fall into disgrace and into the devil's trap. Another way to fall into the devil's trap would be in disgrace with the public. There is a difference between disgrace (because you have not done what is right) versus persecution (where you are doing everything right but satan is slandering you). Jesus was mistreated in public, and they crucified him, but that was all from persecution. He did not bring disgrace upon himself. We are to avoid the disgrace that comes from doing what is wrong. You are making sure that you have never done anything questionable with your job or your personal life…never hiding things, avoiding taxes, speeding down the road or being flippant with your words. You should not be too lavish with your spending or too showy so that you can get the praise of others. The world will be a judge. Even the world does not like conceited people or prideful people. They do not mind being that way themselves, but they can certainly sense it in others and shun those qualities.

If anyone sets his heart on being an overseer, he desires a noble task. In other words, this is a good desire. If you do aspire to this role you need to let Church Leadership know that you would love to be in training for this. Start learning what would be expected of you and what is missing in your own household. We all have blind spots, and we all need each other, if for no other reason than to be a watchdog over one another's souls. Too often the way we see ourselves and the way others see us are two very different things. That is why we help each other out. Even the children help each other out—in fact, children are much more candid when things seem out of line. They have a very strong sense of right and wrong, and they will tell it like it is to the other children. Adults tend to be more politically correct, and therefore we do not share what we see with others as easily or we overlook it. Do not let this happen to you and your family; seek out guidance and accountability from others around you who are living out this Truth.

What Does a Christian Household Look Like?

THE CARE OF THE HOME

The care of the physical home is also a part of this Christian household. If family members are self-controlled, they are ready to invite people over and can pick up the house in a few minutes. All of nature does it—all the birds keep their nests clean, and all the little rabbits keep their burrows neat. All of them are so organized—ants are organized, and bees have a magnificently organized home. Organization is such an essential part of showing a reflection of respect to God, and it shows that He is present.

> YOU HAVE STEPPED OUT OF THE MUNDANE, BORING LIFE AND INTO A VERY EXCITING LIFE OF GETTING EVERYTHING RIGHT AND HAVING THE POWER TO DO IT!

It is hard on the family if the mother is doing all the cleaning and the father does not help out or on the other hand if the father is doing the cleaning and the mother does not play a role. It should be shared. We are not to be lazy. We do not just drop things on the floor or leave them someplace they do not belong. We all need to pick up and clean up after ourselves. Take care of your home and what you have.

If you feel like your situation could be improved, then make your home better. Open up the windows, bring in wildflowers, bring your smile, bring the aroma of Christ, make the home beautiful inside and out. Take what you have and take care of it with love, appreciation and delight!

Notice it makes you happy inside once your room feels clean. It is a little piece of Heaven. You can teach the children that if they are feeling sad and want to do something that makes them feel happy, then go and clean up their rooms or clean up a closet or bathroom.

Suddenly, happiness comes! I cannot tell you how that happens, but it happens! It is fun. Cleaning up your room brings joy to *you*. It is not from someone else cleaning it up for you, but you cleaning up the way you like it…that makes you happy.

We are also to be good neighbors and be respectful in how the outside of the house looks, representing the Royal Priesthood well. We need to be aware of what the people around us think and be thoughtful of others—make sure we have favor with our neighbors. *Make it your ambition to lead a quiet life, to mind your own business and to work with your hands, just as we told you, so that your daily life may win the respect of outsiders and so that you will not be dependent on anybody. I Thessalonians 4:11-12* We want to make sure that we are painting that picture described by Paul—a people who are seen as quiet. We are joyful, but joyful at the right time and appropriately. Joy is drawing, but then being quiet and respectful to others is alluring. That is what people would really notice.

> ONCE YOU CROSSED THE LINES OF COMING OUT OF THE WORLD, YOU CAME IN AS KNIGHTS IN SHINING ARMOR, GALLANT KNIGHTS OF THE ROUND TABLE.

Keeping the house and home cleaned up inside and out is not only a reflection of the heart but also a readiness to be hospitable. Once your own household is in order, you can help others. Then this loving example of Christ spreads as you help others get their homes cleaned up physically and spiritually.

In addition to being physically cleaned up, the home is spiritually cleaned up and filled with Truth and prayer. Instead of being surprised to see someone praying in your house it should be something you see all the time. It would not be unusual to see my granddaughter Grace leading the young ones in a prayer. I have watched all of my grandchildren stop to pray with others all throughout the day. In a Christian household, it should not be unusual to see the children praying, to see the father studying and praying, to see the parents having a devotional. Prayer would be something common. In addition, surrounding the household with Truth is essential. Playing All Access drives out lies and evil spirits.[3] In the home, you would see the Bible and other resources that point your family to God sitting out and being used frequently by family members as a way to tell others who you are. They would know by everything in your home being peaceful and by the fruit of your lives. We are in love with God, and we want to share that love with others.

PERSONAL RESPONSIBILITY

Carry each other's burdens, and in this way you will fulfill the law of Christ. If anyone thinks he is something when he is nothing, he deceives himself. Each one should test his own actions. Then he can take pride in himself, without comparing himself to somebody else, for we are each responsible for our own conduct. Anyone who receives instruction in the word must share all good things with his instructor. Do not be deceived: God cannot be mocked. A man reaps what he sows. The one who sows to please his flesh, from that flesh will reap destruction. The one who sows to please the Spirit, from the Spirit will reap eternal life. Let us not become weary in doing good, for at the proper time we will reap a harvest if we do not give up. Therefore, as we have opportunity, let us do good to all people, especially to those who belong to the family of believers. Galatians 6:2-10

The Remnant is made up of households of men, women and children who have chosen to take on the personal responsibility and love that has been given according to Jesus Christ. Personal responsibility

---

3   *For more about All Access, see the Appendix or visit www.WeighDown.com.*

is an essential explanation of Christianity, and this comes from within versus without. It is a want, an internal desire to love. You *want* to do more; you want to be more involved. It may take some time of experimenting with this "all," as you learn thru each opportunity that every time you give a little more, you receive much more in return. Alternatively, if you give less, things do not go as well for you. The longer I live and the more I am in the Word and understand God, the more I see that He has been trying to get thru to all of us about this line of authority. There is only one way for this line of authority to be accomplished, and that is for all of us to take on more personal responsibility. This is not frightening—the more time you give Him, the more He will give you back time. The more you give up your idea of "fun," the more He makes your fun time truly exciting. The more you give up of your money, the more He gives back. Experimentally, we have found that when you give more and then you implement more of God's Truth in your life and your family's life, everyone is better in your family—even your children are better and happier. You cannot outgive this God. In the past you may have experienced worldly churches that drained you like a battery pack and robbed you of all of your time and energy, but True Christianity is a well-kept, fantastic secret to actually having more and doing more.[4]

A New Job Description

Do you remember the first time you realized that you could deny yourself—that you could change and stop overeating or over-drinking? You could push away from the table, put the food down, set the drink down, and do without. You were elated! You were able to take on personal responsibility thru the power of the Holy Spirit, thru God and His son Jesus Christ. What an opportunity! In the

---

4   For more about this concept, see <u>History of the Love of God</u>, Volume II, Chapter 3, "Love… The Ancient Religion."

What Does a Christian Household Look Like?

past your life was computer games or shopping or indulgences, but now you know you are going to be accountable for every word and every deed on the Day of Judgment.[5] We all have work to do, and we need to step it up. You have been called into a *Holy Priesthood*. This is not just an everyday church. This is an *opportunity*. You have stepped out of the mundane, boring life and into a very exciting life of getting everything right and having the power to do it! This life is a joyous adventure. It is so fun to lose weight. It is thrilling to get everything right. It is so exciting to be awakened by the Holy Spirit in the night and realize thru God's gentle prompting that you should have done something differently. Then you can put it into practice the next day. It is such a delight to come into a Church where you have a job and a purpose. You may not be the most popular man at your work, but in this Pure Community of Love, you will be known, and you will be honored. God will know. Your deeds are written in the Books, and every job is important, every single one.[6]

This is all about the Kingdom of God. These jobs that you have in the world are gifts that you are using to be able to provide for your homes; then we have the time to spend serving the Church and building God's Kingdom. So God keeps us busy, but it keeps us out of trouble and it sets a beautiful example for the next person that we can say, "I am not living for this life. I am not living for just temporary pleasures. I am living for God!"

I have always told the children that if there is a lot of play and not enough work even the games that they play are not fun anymore. You may hear whining and complaining or arguments, but when

---

5   *For we must all appear before the judgment seat of Christ, that each one may receive what is due him for the things done while in the body, whether good or bad. II Corinthians 5:10*
6   *I tell you that men will have to give account on the day of judgment for every careless word they have spoken. Matthew 12:36*

you give them a job to do—chores or something to help with—the next time that they get to play, they are so excited about playing, and they are happy. If you have unhappy children, more than likely they are bored from not enough responsibility. Likewise, if you find yourself experiencing the feeling of boredom it is from not enough responsibility and work for God's Kingdom.

> YOU ARE HIRED, AND YOU ARE NEEDED. WE ALL HAVE A JOB TO DO IN THIS KINGDOM OF LOVE.

You are hired, and you are needed. We all have a job to do in this Kingdom of Love and have further to go. You know there is a need to have your home organized, to improve your marriage, to help your children—a need for confession and cleaning up the hearts of your family members. The Church is highly organized and full of responsibility, and that responsibility is the most ironic thing in the world. You may worry about taking on a new responsibility, but when you do it brings back happiness one hundredfold. We want to make sure that we carry one another's burdens so that the load is distributed. Every person is needed. You cannot compare yourself to someone else; you are looking at your own work. You *are* a part, and all of us are working together so that the workload is spread out.

How beautiful the growth of this would be if there was an equaling of the distribution of all of the needed help, working and balancing—helping the widows and those who are less fortunate, seeing to it that everyone's needs are being taken care of and that all sin is purged out of the Church. You have a role in this beautiful Kingdom, and you need to let your gifts and abilities be known so that you can use them to serve God's Church. When you do get that job and it is your responsibility, you are going to feel very different about your life. You will have a pep in your step; it is so fun. All these parts come together and all work in unity to build the Kingdom.[7] It is a beautiful, doable picture.

When you come into the Remnant, you are coming into a *Royal, Holy Priesthood*. This is no ordinary calling. You are a Holy Priesthood of men with royal wives who are Queens and children who are Princes and Princesses. Once you crossed the lines of coming out of the world, you came in as knights in shining armor, gallant knights of the round table. This is a much higher calling. You must keep this picture in mind of who you really are. Therefore, *every* home should look like the description in I Timothy 3 of overseers, deacons and deaconesses. These are aspirations that we all should have because you are a Royal and Holy Priesthood, and you are at the foundation of this *Royal Regal Revival*.

PRAYER

Father, I know you have such a beautiful picture of what the home looks like…reflecting Christ and the head of the household, the wife and the children, everyone under authority and everyone serving each other—it is all a beautiful thing. Father, we owe this back to you. I pray for the gift of organization. I pray for the gift of unity in the homes. I pray that more prayer will be seen and heard. I pray that love will be everywhere, that the older children are gently teaching the younger ones and that the younger ones are looking up and respecting the older ones. I pray the parents are lovingly hovering over their children. I pray that this beautiful picture of the home, with the children learning to clean and help and all the organization, that this is something that will build with each generation. I pray that you will teach us to help others after we have made our own household straight. I pray we pass this down to future generations to come. In Jesus' name we pray, Amen.

---

7 I Corinthians 12:12-31

I have given them the glory that you gave me, that they may be one as we are one: I in them and you in me. May they be brought to complete unity to let the world know that you sent me and have loved them even as you have loved me. John 17:22-23 Page 396.

A Picture of the Church

CHAPTER 30

Once, having been asked by the Pharisees when the kingdom of God would come, Jesus replied, "The kingdom of God does not come with your careful observation, nor will people say, 'Here it is,' or 'There it is,' because the kingdom of God is within you." Luke 17:20-21

Jesus did not build a single building during his time on Earth. The Church that he established was the Kingdom of God, an invisible Kingdom in the heart. Over the centuries there have been countless churches that have come and gone. What makes the difference? What is it that creates a True Church that will survive the coming centuries until Jesus Christ returns? The difference will be the foundation of laying down your entire life, your entire agenda, your old way of thinking, and your old way of doing things.

God has laid a firm foundation of hearts that know how to extend His light. We keep the light, the flame, going in the Churches that are not in buildings, but they are the soft, repentant hearts. These people are carrying around the Church. You do not **come** to church; you **are** the Church. You are not looking at a Holy Priesthood; you *are* the Holy Priesthood. The vision that Christ gave us was not "here or there"—but he laid a foundation that spans from sea to sea—a community of people who are in love with the Father, following in Christ's footsteps so that they can imitate him and then they can be the apple of God's eye, too, knowing that God loves them.[1] *Whoever has my commands and obeys them, he is the one who loves me. He who loves me will be loved by my Father, and I too will love him and show myself to him. John 14:21*

As we read before in Matthew 7, *Not everyone who says to me, 'Lord, Lord,' will enter the Kingdom of Heaven, but only he who does the will of my Father... Matthew 7:21a* This is a community of people who will bow low, not because we have to but because we *want* to. When I woke up this morning, I could not wait to bow down. My knees wanted to get down. My whole body felt the magnetism of getting low before God. "Oh God, I am awake! I cannot believe You! I cannot believe Your mercy, Your faithfulness, this relationship. I cannot believe that I can commune with You, that I have a piece of You. I owe You everything! I love You, God. I love the amount of sleep You gave. I love You waking me up. I love everything!"

Faith and Deeds

The Body of Christ is a grouping of pure Saints. Think about these units in each household coming together to worship. He has put us in these family units to practice, but again, I call upon the men, these mighty men of God. It is time for you to get in the driver's seat because everyone is looking to you. You need to be following Christ so much that people can see in you the behavior of Jesus Christ with all of his characteristics: no laziness, no rage, no anger; only the gentle nature of a gentle man, relying on Godly leadership and watching their lives, imitating them as they imitate Christ.[2]

---

1   *Keep me as the apple of your eye; hide me in the shadow of your wings. Psalm 17:8*
2   *Follow my example, as I follow the example of Christ. I Corinthians 11:1*

A Picture of the Church

*But someone will say, "You have faith; I have deeds." Show me your faith without deeds, and I will show you my faith by what I **do**. James 2:18* There is your faith—you measure your faith by your deeds. Your journals should be a list of your deeds—by the deeds, you will know. We have to understand that God has this light that He has given us. It is there not for us to snuff it out, but He has gone to that much trouble to extend Himself. He did not have to give us any piece of His magnificent Being, but He trusted us. He trusted *you* enough to give you a piece of His light, a piece of His love.

What a revelation to know that doing good deeds, living this life, and getting your family up to speed is what we need to be doing for the Kingdom of God—starting in the home and sticking with the home. Men, you need to understand that when you take a back seat or you are lazy or you want to let your mind wander from all your problems, and you think no one is seeing it that Jesus said, *For there is nothing hidden that will not be disclosed, and nothing concealed that will not be known or brought out into the open. Luke 8:17* In the past, many men have taken a back seat spiritually and have been

> THE VISION THAT CHRIST GAVE US WAS NOT "HERE OR THERE"—BUT HE LAID A FOUNDATION THAT SPANS FROM SEA TO SEA—A COMMUNITY OF PEOPLE WHO ARE IN LOVE WITH THE FATHER, FOLLOWING IN CHRIST'S FOOTSTEPS.

tempted to hide out. Though you might think you are hiding out, whatever is done in darkness will be brought to light. You cannot hide sin from God. Your life is an open book. It is as if your life is being filmed—every word you have said, everything that you have texted or read or looked at or done is stored and then shown on a big jumbotron screen for all to see. It is analyzed, and it is judged, and it is going to be known. God and all the Heavens know as well as the dark world and all the demons who are cheering you on to entertain self. Even if you can ignore your conscience and think no one is looking, take note that your choices are affecting God's reputation, and once again, you owe everything back to God.

Make a tree good and its fruit will be good, or make a tree bad and its fruit will be bad, for a tree is recognized by its fruit. You brood of vipers, how can you who are evil say anything good? For out of the overflow of the heart the mouth speaks. The good man brings good things out of the good stored up in him, and the evil man brings evil things out of the evil stored up in him. But I tell you that men will have to give account on the day of judgment for every careless word they have spoken. For by your words you will be acquitted, and by your words you will be condemned. Matthew 12:33-37

What if you are just neutral? In Matthew 12:30 Jesus says, *He who is not with me is against me, and he who does not gather with me scatters.* If you are not with God, you are not with Christ, and you are not building the Kingdom. Your neutral stance does not help you, your family or the Kingdom.

To the angel of the church in Sardis write: These are the words of him who holds the seven spirits of God and the seven stars. I know your deeds; you have a reputation of being alive, but you are dead. Wake up! Strengthen what remains and is about to die, for I have not found your deeds complete in the sight of my God. Remember, therefore, what you have received and heard; obey it, and repent. But if you do not wake up, I will come like a thief, and you will not know at what time I will come to you. Revelation 3:1-3

This is a wake-up call for all of us. Do you think you are alive, do you think you are doing "good," but you are really dead in your sins?

A Picture of the Church

God is calling a *Royal Priesthood*. We must take up the calling before it is too late and the thief comes in.[3]

Are you trying to get thru life by living as three people—one person in public, a different one at home, and a third person in the privacy of your own room? You must stop—you cannot have three lives and keep your sanity. It will eventually come to light—in fact, those around you probably already know more about it than you think. If you do not repent, eventually it will lead to instability, insecurity and unpredictability at home and at work. To the contrary, a God-fearing man will be even more righteous at home than he is in public and will be even more adored by the family. He will be the same person from his room, to the home, to the public setting of work or Church—one man. When you become that one man, then it is a sight to behold, inspiring to everyone. All those who have been defeated and confused—this whole hurting world—will be in awe. They are watching more than you think. You will be *extraordinary*, and you will become a light to others. No matter what your position at work—you could have the lowest position at the office, but you will have the highest respect of every man in the building because they will want to be like you. Even one righteous man in this dark world is an astounding phenomenon—it impacts the world, it changes the world.

> EVEN ONE RIGHTEOUS MAN IN THIS DARK WORLD IS AN ASTOUNDING PHENOMENON— IT IMPACTS THE WORLD…IT CHANGES THE WORLD.

---

3   *The thief comes only to steal and kill and destroy; I have come that they may have life, and have it to the full. John 10:10*

How do you avoid temptations when work, home and spiritual warfare are so challenging? It is a fact that the pain in life is great, and during testing, the pain is predominant. The Truth is that men are very sensitive. Sensitivity was purposed by God, and it is very valuable to be able to obtain the lead of God. The world tries to dilute sensitivity or drown the feeling of a bothered spirit or conscience with drugs or drink or other indulgences. If you feel all the pains of life *and* mix it with a cocktail, you might find yourself spewing pain onto your wife or children, those you value the most. You are too ashamed to ask for help. You wake up the next day, and you know you are not doing what is right, but you still do not know what to do with that pain. The day starts over, and you just repeat it and repeat it until you are locked into a prison of anger and rage. You are back to how you used to be, yet you still go to Church and say, "I am good. My family is good." Then you go home, and you are the different person. That pain was intended to cause you to go to God, to bring you down to your knees and on your face seeking Him. There is no way Jesus Christ came home and lost himself in a computer game, TV, sports or alcoholic drinks to ease the pain of all the pressures of life. He went only to the Father.

> THIS HEALING IS BETTER THAN ANY CLINIC, HOSPITAL, THERAPY SESSION OR TREATMENT THAT ANYONE HAS EVER DESIGNED!

A Unified and Humble Community

Jesus created a unified community, and in John 21 he told his disciples that if they loved him, they would feed his sheep. His last prayer in John 17 was for unity:

I have given them the glory that you gave me, that they may be one as we are one: I in them and you in me. May they be brought to complete unity to let the world know that you sent me and have loved them even as you have loved me. John 17:22-23

Unity...keep them together. May they be unified. May this Church—this Body—love each other, help each other, feed each other and take care of each other. Without the Body of Christ, you cannot lay sin down. If the burdens or satanic lies are high, bring it to Godly Leaders who have the fruit and characteristics of Christ in their lives, and you will get advice on exactly how to handle these demands. God may lead you to answers that were right there all along, but you could not see them—not because there is anything wrong with you or your intelligence but simply because we *need* each other. One person may have a gift that you need, and it leads you to go to them, but then you have a gift that they need, and it draws them to you. Blessed be the tie that binds. He is sewing us together. Unity is the sign of God, the sign of Christ, the sign that God loves us. The true journey of Christianity is that we lean on God and not our own understanding, but we also need the Church.[4] We do not try to take control of our lives, but we use the Body of Christ to get wisdom and sound advice from the Heavens, thru the Church, thru Jesus Christ as the head. Then the next thing you know, your pressures will be lifted. You will then get more respect from your wife and more praise from your in-laws, more admiration from the children, and then acceptance from the Heavens, which all go to completely restore your sanity and peace. No more anger, no more self-induced pain. Each day more burdens are lifted off of your shoulders.

What stops you from fully putting this into practice is what you learned in a counterfeit message of false grace: "I am good. We are doing fine." Oh, the proud words: "I am a man. I can handle this. It

---

4   *Trust in the Lord with all your heart and lean not on your own understanding. Proverbs 3:5*

is my family. I can take care of the problem. I do not want to bother the Church. I can handle it on my own." Pride. To not need the Body of Christ would be like a foot that is infected, but it does not want to tell the brain; it does not want to bother the heart or the circulatory system or any of the antibodies that could heal it. Then the whole body hurts until finally you have to amputate the leg because gangrene has set in.

> WHEN YOU PLUG INTO GOD AND THE TRUE CHURCH, THEN YOUR LIFE IS HEALED, AND IT PASSES TO THE NEXT FAMILY THAT IS HEALED, AND THE NEXT, AND IT CONTINUES TO BUILD.

We like to think we have everything together. Making the outside cleaned up, polishing it for appearances, but the inside are dead men's bones.[5] Not only is it wrong not to function as you should with the whole body working together to ease the burdens, but it is even worse because many men take this pain out on the spouse. Pride will never go to Heaven. I think about all the pain, all the marriage trouble, all the children who are hurting, and the problems that could have been avoided by functioning as Christ taught in the Church thru the community of love. Then in addition to the guidance and help, add on top all the prayers from the righteous Saints. This healing is better than any clinic, hospital, therapy session or treatment that anyone has ever designed!

We have witnessed that here at the Remnant—healing in the homes with happy husbands, delighted wives and joyful, obedient children. We all started at the bottom, and we have all been lifted up. We have humbled ourselves, and grace has brought us thru. Now

---

5   *Woe to you, teachers of the law and Pharisees, you hypocrites! You are like whitewashed tombs, which look beautiful on the outside but on the inside are full of dead men's bones and everything unclean. Matthew 23:27*

we are no longer babes in Christ; we are going further and learning more. So you do not have to come in and feel overwhelmed or embarrassed. That feeling comes from pride. The Church helps you on this journey. It has helped us all and continues to help us keep growing to reach this full vision of God's beautiful Kingdom of Love in the heart. This group is moving mountains. This is the Kingdom of Love—relationships must be a priority—the home must be a beautiful reflection of Christ. When you plug into God and the True Church, then your life is healed, and it passes to the next family that is healed, and the next, and it continues to build.

Separating Good from Evil

If anyone does not provide for his relatives, and especially for his immediate family, he has denied the faith and is worse than an unbeliever. No widow may be put on the list of widows unless she is over sixty, has been faithful to her husband, and is well known for her good deeds, such as bringing up children, showing hospitality, washing the feet of the saints, helping those in trouble and devoting herself to all kinds of good deeds. I Timothy 5:8-10

This passage is referring to having a relative in the Church who is a Saint and is known by their good deeds. It was not referring to antagonists. In fact, Paul says in II Timothy…

But mark this: There will be terrible times in the last days. People will be lovers of themselves, lovers of money, boastful, proud, abusive, disobedient to their parents, ungrateful, unholy, without love, unforgiving, slanderous, without self-control, brutal, not lovers of the good, treacherous, rash, conceited, lovers of pleasure rather than lovers of God—having a form of godliness but denying its power. **Have nothing to do with them.** *II Timothy 3:1-5*

God is separating evil from good as He is building His Kingdom. He called for us to live out this separation in many Scriptures.[6] But how do you know the difference between those who are mockers and those who just do not understand? There *is* a difference. Those who have potential to understand will have a conscience. Someone who has a conscience may have gone against you in the past, but when they are shown the Truth, they can see, and they can change. The people who are true mockers have no conscience. They literally do not want Truth. They will jump subjects; they will draw you back in just to tear you up again—like a cat playing with a mouse. Worldly advice tells us to go to the extremes with people who are mockers—either turn the other cheek and always spend all the time you have on those people, or cut those family members off completely and never see them again. However, God's Word tells us that we are to avoid extremes.[7]

To Be Worthy of this Calling

Do not suppose that I have come to bring peace to the earth. I did not come to bring peace, but a sword. For I have come to turn 'a man against his father, a daughter against her mother, a daughter-in-law against her mother-in-law—a man's enemies will be the members of his own household.' Anyone who loves his father or mother more than me is not worthy of me; anyone who loves his son or daughter more than me is not worthy of me; and anyone who does not take his cross and follow me is not worthy of me. Whoever finds his life will lose it, and whoever loses his life for my sake will find it. Matthew 10:34-39

---

6   See also: Ephesians 5:5-7, I Corinthians 5:1-13, II Corinthians 6:14-7:1, Revelation 18:1-5, Psalm 1, Acts 2:40, and Revelation 21:23-27

7   *The man who fears God will avoid all extremes. Ecclesiastes 7:18b*

A Picture of the Church

This passage is alive and well today, and the reason why these separating situations happen is for God to see if you are going to obey Him, or are you going to obey man? Do you love your family more than you love God? Do you want peace with your family members and peace here on Earth more than you want peace with God? Then you are not worthy of this calling, and many people fall to the wayside. Just pass the test. Keep telling God that you love Him more, and then prove it by your deeds. When it comes to most day-

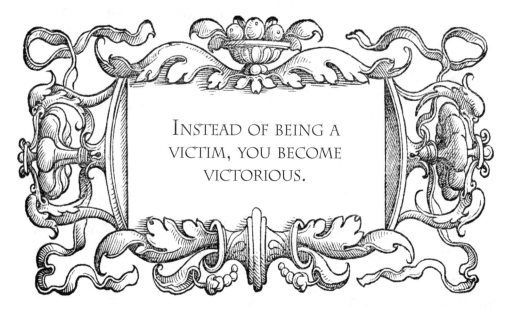

INSTEAD OF BEING A VICTIM, YOU BECOME VICTORIOUS.

to-day situations, just submit to your family authorities. But when it comes to doing the Will of God, *you obey God*.[8]

Separation within the household will bring times of suffering, but you know that God is the God of peace. He does not want complete turmoil. He is separating good from evil, but there is peace in doing His Will. There are times for separation, but we need to understand

---

8   But Peter and John replied, *"Judge for yourselves whether it is right in God's sight to obey you rather than God."* Acts 4:19

that all this suffering and this demonic warfare is all screened by God. When you understand that, you can live this life out like you were intended to live it—as a bright light, stable, not blown and tossed by the winds.[9] You will be a constant light every day with love every day, getting back up no matter what is said to you. You are returning evil with good, and you are loving the unlovely, responding with a gentle answer to something that is harsh.[10] The gentle answer turns away wrath—so wrath is leaving, and you are overcoming the evil.[11] You are remaining where you have been placed, but your mind and heart are for the Saints.[12] You are plugged into the Church and into Leadership. You are confessing to the Saints so that everything is surfaced. You will have a constant, contrite heart looking for what else needs to be changed. You will consistently join in with the Saints—in person or taking advantage of God's technology to stay close and stay connected. You will come to visit when you can and get to stay with Saints in their homes, seeing their beautiful changed lives.

> THIS BEAUTIFUL CHURCH OF A ROYAL REMNANT REVIVAL, A TRUE HOLY PRIESTHOOD, IS A VISION OF A UNITED ARMY MARCHING IN STEP TOGETHER. IT IS A DREAM OF FAMILIES, ALL AT PEACE AND IN UNISON, UNDER THE AUTHORITY OF THE FATHER.

---

9   But when he asks, he must believe and not doubt, because he who doubts is like a wave of the sea, blown and tossed by the wind. James 1:6
10 For more on this subject, please read *The History of the Love of God, Volume II*, Chapter 22, "Loving the Unlovely." See Appendix for more information on this book and other resources.
11 A gentle answer turns away wrath, but a harsh word stirs up anger. Proverbs 15:1
12 Each one should remain in the situation which he was in when God called him. I Corinthians 7:20

Instead of being a victim, you become victorious, and you realize that wherever you are, you can feed God's Sheep. Do you love Him? Then live it. Love your household; keep being a light and a constant. Keep reaching out to encourage others—use social media or write letters, make a phone call. You can do what is right in your own life, which is a light to the world, and then feed the Sheep.

> ALL THESE FASCINATING, REFRESHING, JOYFUL LIVES ARE ONE BECAUSE WE SERVE ONE GOD THRU JESUS CHRIST, HIS SON, AND BECAUSE OF THAT, THIS CHURCH CAN *BUILD*.

Do you love? God will know it by your deeds. You have picked up your cross, yet you have been positive, and you have been a light. Your children can see it, and your grandchildren and great-grandchildren will see it, and you will have answered a noble, royal calling to a very worthy life.

A Beautiful Vision

God's Church is growing, and these hearts are being purified more each year—purified of sin and pride—and they are filling that void with humility, meekness, love, purity and holy service on God's Holy Hill. This is a beautiful place because it is filled with faith, commitment and self-sacrifice. This beautiful Church of a Royal Remnant Revival, a true Holy Priesthood, is a vision of a united army marching in step together. It is a dream of families, all at peace and in unison, under the authority of the Father. It is a picture of all men in full respect, taking care of their families, having concern for each other and the Church and in step with the direction of God. This vision of distributed responsibility and concern for the spirituality of those around us is a breathtaking vision. It is clearly changing the landscape from this point forward with a Remnant of purity that has a fellowship connected by the authority line, thru leaders all the way up to Christ and God.

You are that Royal Priesthood, and you are a part of this beautiful group of changed lives that grows every year. All these fascinating, refreshing, joyful lives are one because we serve one God thru Jesus Christ, His Son, and because of that, this Church can *build*. God's decision to build on the right foundation is electrifying, for the Glory returns, and we are now marching forth with God as our guide and God as our rear guard! God will be in the midst of this Remnant—the Mighty One who will save us and take away the shame and replace it with honor and praise. Our God and our Christ will rejoice over this Church, and Christ *will* return one day and take her Home forever. No more half-hearted men or women filled with death and decay, but only wholehearted, joyful, fully-focused Saints, boldly advancing the Kingdom of God!

A Picture of the Church

When Solomon built the Temple, he prayed a prayer of dedication to the Lord and said, "May the Lord our God be with us as he was with our fathers; may he never leave us nor forsake us. May he turn our hearts to him, to walk in all his ways and to keep the commands, decrees and regulations he gave our fathers. And may these words of mine, which I have prayed before the Lord, be near to the Lord our God day and night, that he may uphold the cause of his servant and the cause of his people Israel according to each day's need, so that all the peoples of the earth may know that the Lord is God and that there is no other. But your hearts must be fully committed to the Lord our God, to live by his decrees and obey his commands, as at this time." I Kings 8:57-61

Taking Care of God's House

Chapter 31

"A son honors his father, and a servant his master. If I am a father, where is the honor due me? If I am a master, where is the respect due me?" says the Lord Almighty. "It is you, O priests, who show contempt for my name. But you ask, 'How have we shown contempt for your name?' You place defiled food on my altar." Malachi 1:6-7a

This is what the Lord Almighty says: "These people say, 'The time has not yet come for the Lord's house to be built.'" Then the word of the Lord came through the prophet Haggai: "Is it a time for you yourselves to be living in your paneled houses, while this house remains a ruin?" Now this is what the Lord Almighty says: "Give careful thought to your ways. You have planted much, but have harvested little. You eat, but never have enough. You drink, but never have your fill. You put on clothes, but are not warm. You earn wages, only to put them in a purse with holes in it." This is what the Lord Almighty says: "Give careful thought to your ways. Go up into the mountains and bring down timber and build the house, so that I may take pleasure in it and be honored," says the Lord. "You expected much, but see, it turned out to be little. What you brought home, I blew away. Why?" declares the Lord Almighty. "Because of my house, which remains a ruin, while each of you is busy with his own house. Therefore, because of you the heavens have withheld their dew and the earth its crops. I called for a drought on the fields and the mountains, on the grain, the new wine, the oil and whatever the ground produces, on men and cattle, and on the labor of your hands." Haggai 1:2-11

"Will a man rob God? Yet you rob me. But you ask, 'How do we rob you?' In tithes and offerings. You are under a curse—the whole nation of you—because you are robbing me. Bring the whole tithe into the storehouse, that there may be food in my house. Test me in this," says the Lord Almighty, "and see if I will not throw open the floodgates of heaven and pour out so much blessing that you will not have room enough for it. I will prevent pests from devouring your crops, and the vines in your fields will not cast their fruit," says the Lord Almighty. "Then all the nations will call you blessed, for yours will be a delightful land," says the Lord Almighty. Malachi 3:8-12

The books of Haggai and Malachi are the all-time most heartbreaking books ever recorded in history. These Prophets felt God's pain from being the Creator…yet being reduced to last choice. The description is being everyone's last one to please—the feeling of being rejected. These two Prophets penned the greatest insights into the human crimes against the Eternal Vessel of Love. Imagine God as the largest conglomerate and collection of love, and He emotionally risks creating man in hopes of acceptance, yet His beloved children use and abuse Him. These children of God neglected, ignored, robbed, cheated, disregarded and used God—and if perchance they gave anything back, it was leftovers simply to appease their Creator. No

> TO HAVE THE TRUE CHURCH, PLEASING GOD IS THE FOUNDATION AND LAYING DOWN ALL SIN AGAINST GOD AND ELIMINATING ALL LEGALISM, WHICH IS RULES MADE BY MAN AND NOT GOD, IS THE ANSWER.

doubt God has allowed all of us to feel those same pain-filled emotions so that we can possibly grasp His enormous pain.

Hurting God's feelings is the most serious delinquency, but second would be neglecting His house while taking care of your own. God does not ask for too much—only for your love and for you to take care of His House. At every level, we have our own homes, and even children have their own rooms, and we have all felt the anxiousness of neglect and worry about our houses, the feeling of wanting to clean our rooms up. When we act on this driving feeling, we love it. How sad to rob God of this joy.

God's Church is not just a building—it is dynamic and alive, so how do you clean God's House? The answer is shared responsibility. First of all, you clean up your own heart—His primary Home. Take the log out of your own eye first.[1] The concentration should be on bearing your own fruit.

Matthew 18 ... Love for God's House

Those who are called out to serve God each have personal responsibility to take care of His House, starting with your own sacred temple (your heart), then your household (your family), and then the Church Body. It is shared, calling us all to the attention of our gift of teaching and counseling, instruction and reproofing. You train up your family, continue to encourage those walking in the light, lift up the downcast and discouraged, and finally, the hardest part—confront the stubborn.

Brothers, if someone is caught in a sin, you who are spiritual should restore him gently. But watch yourself, or you also may be tempted. Galatians 6:1

---

1   *You hypocrite, first take the plank out of your own eye, and then you will see clearly to remove the speck from your brother's eye. Matthew 7:5*

From the words of Christ, *If your brother sins against you, go and show him his fault, just between the two of you. If he listens to you, you have won your brother over. But if he will not listen, take one or two others along, so that "every matter may be established by the testimony of two or three witnesses." If he refuses to listen to them, tell it to the church; and if he refuses to listen even to the church, treat him as you would a pagan or a tax collector. Matthew 18:15-17*

Pray with those who are caught up in a sin—asking God for the perfect, correcting, loving words with great forgiveness, longsuffering and loving redirection—while Saints with the gift of encouragement surround the seeker to keep the spirits uplifted. Everyone takes their own personal responsibility and cleans up their own households; then all can share healing gifts and work together for the struggling Saint caught up in sin, because otherwise it would be a heavy burden.

> A YEAST-FREE, CLEANED-UP, PURE CHURCH IS ESSENTIAL SO THAT THE ECCLESIA—THE CALLED OUT, THE CHURCH—CAN ACTUALLY GROW... THEY CAN SPRING FORTH!

The True Church would obey this Scripture and have pure leaders who could boldly say that laying down your idol is not hard, because they had done it themselves. If the leaders were also caught up in sin, they would relax the commands for the members. If the pews are full of sinners and only a few righteous people, then the Church is already dead and there is no hope. The lifeless will drain and suck the remaining sap from the vine. Paul had great alarm for sin left in the congregation.

It is actually reported that there is sexual immorality among you... And you are proud! Shouldn't you rather have been filled with grief and have put out of your fellowship the man who did this? Even though I am not physically present, I am with you in spirit. And I have already passed judgment on the one who did this, just as if I were present. When you are assembled in the name of our Lord Jesus and I am with you in spirit, and the power of our Lord Jesus is present, hand this man over to Satan, so that the sinful nature may be destroyed and his spirit saved on the day of the Lord. Your boasting is not good. Don't you know that a little yeast works through the whole batch of dough? Get rid of the old yeast that you may be a new batch without yeast—as you really are. For Christ, our Passover lamb, has been sacrificed. Therefore let us keep the Festival, not with the old yeast, the yeast of malice and wickedness, but with bread without yeast, the bread of sincerity and truth. I have written you in my letter not to associate with sexually immoral people—not at all meaning the people of this world who are immoral, or the greedy and swindlers, or idolaters. In that case you would have to leave this world. But now I am writing you that you must not associate with anyone who calls himself a brother but is sexually immoral or greedy, an idolater or a slanderer, a drunkard or a swindler. With such a man do not even eat. What business is it of mine to judge those outside the church? Are you not to judge those inside? God will judge those outside. "Expel the wicked man from among you." I Corinthians 5:1-13

Jesus had left the synagogues and started over to get the percentages right. He knew that leaving even one person in sin would corrupt the Church. At the time that Jesus started his ministry, the synagogue had already allowed sin in, and the ruling preachers of the day were firmly established and were not leaving—in fact, they kicked out those who followed Christ's strong religious teaching of symbolically cutting off your hand if it caused you to sin.[2] So Christ left and started over. Likewise, in the late 1990s, the church was long past where they could expel *one* immoral brother. God called me to exit these churches, and it was evident that these churches wanted the righteous to believe that you *cannot* stop sinning.

Why is the road so narrow? Why are there so few churches that teach this? There is a world of persecution if you want to believe it, much more if you decide to teach it, and even more if you truly confront sin as in Matthew 18. In the end, the true Saints will love you. You imagine it to be hard, but because it is so surrounded in gentle, compassionate love, it is a beautiful experience.

THE THEFT OF GOD'S AUTHORITY

The early Christians confessed and repented of sins and met together daily and shared all their possessions together.[3] They knew each other and were very close to each other because of the external persecutions. They thrived because they laid down their sins and purged the Church of the immoral. Three hundred years later the Roman Emperor Constantine combined the church and the Roman government, which transferred the policing or discipline of the church to the government. This practice has been maintained without question as it is today. Note the government policies of selective man-made rules along with a few commands from the Bible: speeding, drinking while driving, stealing, murder, child abuse, tax evasion, lust crimes. The church counts on the government to be the heavyweight. Secular governments legislating abortion and making decisions on divorce and child support leave so much in the hands

---

2   *And if your right hand causes you to sin, cut it off and throw it away. It is better for you to lose one part of your body than for your whole body to go into hell. Matthew 5:30*
3   Acts 2:42-47

of the godless. This worldly judicial court neutralizes the church and steals its authority. Again, what business is it of ours to judge those outside the church? Are we not to judge and confront those inside? God will judge those outside.

From 325 to 2017 A.D., the religious government churches copied the church and institutionalized what should have belonged solely to the Church for the glory of God alone. This includes care for

IF YOU STUMBLE, GET BACK UP AND RUN FOR THE CROWN.

the sick. The hospitals were all originally built and run by the Saints, and many hospitals still bear the names of Saints. Counsel was taken from the Church Shepherds and given to psychologists. The judge and jury had been in Jerusalem and the Church, but now it was run by the government. Prisons themselves are a form of excommunication. This shift was not the fault of the governments but was the fault of the fear of man by the religious leaders. All of this belongs to the Church, but the weak churches were happy to give the responsibility away. Governments trying to play the role of legislating morality is wrong on so many levels. While a few of the Ten Commandments were legislated, most of God's rules were ignored. No one has ever seen anyone come to the door and handcuff someone for having pride, coveting, having private lust, overindulging in too much television or computer games, talking back to parents or having the sins of the disposition such as rage. Have you ever seen the gavel go down in a courtroom when the greatest crime of all has been committed—the neglect of the First Commandment? "Guilty—you are sentenced to imprisonment for failing to love God with **ALL** of your heart!" God allows the government to legislate some morality because the church has neglected it, for God will not be mocked, but how shameful for the government to hold a higher standard than the church.[4]

> WITH TRUE REPENTANCE, ACCESS TO GOD'S SPIRIT AND THE HELP AND SURROUND OF THE CHURCH, YOU WILL BE VICTORIOUS AGAIN.

To have the True Church, pleasing God is the foundation and laying down all sin against God and eliminating all legalism (which means following rules made by man and not God) is the answer. This cannot be done on your own but necessitates continual sermons of Truth, righteous Shepherds laying their lives down for each family and member, and truthful brothers and sisters who give loving honest evaluation using Christ's Matthew 18. Even the greatest of sermons are ineffective without all of this in place.

Do you see the shared burden, the shared responsibilities, the picture of all the men's shoulders working together to carry the load? How beautiful. If you have a parent who reads the rules of the house but never enforces them, the children will never obey and will grow up to hate the parents while becoming increasingly

---

4 *Do not be deceived: God cannot be mocked. A man reaps what he sows. Galatians 6:7*

disrespectful. Police departments that never enforce laws against theft or the speed limit leave society to be taken over by criminals. While the world has been full of harsh and unloving discipline, that does not mean we abandon this command of Christ. Correct discipline brings about a love for God.

Ninety percent of this building of the Church is the teaching that you *must* and *can* lay down sin. Jesus said, *Be perfect, therefore, as your heavenly Father is perfect. Matthew 5:48* Simply put, love God first and man second. Can you be perfect in loving God and then loving man? The answer is absolutely yes! Most know the history of this Remnant restoration movement. I traveled the country and spoke in all denominations to the largest crowds. These churches were full of sin and hurting people. They lined up to hear this teaching because they were hungry for the green grass. This green grass was the hope that comes from taking personal responsibility for your own sin—and thru obedience you would receive God's Spirit that would help you and give you a whole new, beautiful personality.

Jesus made the procedure for God's beloved Church very clear. In Matthew 18, this loving protocol is placed between the need to personally lay down your own sin—cut off your hand if it causes you to sin[5]—and then seeking out the lost...

What do you think? If a man owns a hundred sheep, and one of them wanders away, will he not leave the ninety-nine on the hills and go to look for the one that wandered off? And if he finds it, I tell you the truth, he is happier about that one sheep than about the ninety-nine that did not wander off. In the same way your Father in heaven is not willing that any of these little ones should be lost. Matthew 18:12-14

---

5   *Matthew 18:8-9*

Ninety-nine righteous and one sinner. Leave the righteous sheep on the hill and go seek the lost. Again look at the percentage of righteousness needed to be able to help the sinner: ninety-nine percent. This is why a church full of sin is sick and on its deathbed with a terminal prognosis. This chapter in context provides clearly a very loving atmosphere for the protocol of correction given by Christ. Matthew 18 is flanked by the strongest admonition—forgiving your brother who sins against you and then understanding how God detests double standards in the Parable of the Unmerciful Servant who was forgiven his debt and then condemned others.[6] No secular court could ever duplicate the love surrounding this precious, loving redirection of the sinner. First, clean up your own life, then the righteous majority can seek the wanderer—not just waiting for them to come in, but privately and gently reaching out, encouraging and forgiving with all your heart and with your own sins in mind, and finally bringing to the Church. It is gently done. It is a process bathed in love.

The Shepherds at Remnant Fellowship Churches are unified on long-suffering love and learning to walk a mile in the sinner's shoes of financial stress or hardships, and they are also unified in going the extra mile to help and encourage. God has taught me to hope all things and think the best first, but to look for the pattern of sin and then teach true repentance. Envision each struggler in the future as possibly restored as the prodigal son, and run to meet them when they are walking back with no shameful embarrassing hurdles to jump over to repent and come back...but with perfect, long-suffering love extended.

---

6   Matthew 18:21-35

Taking Care of God's House

How long has God put up with your shortcomings? Those without sin were told they could cast the first stone at the woman caught in adultery.[7] Jesus was sinless and never picked up a stone. That is our example. Notice the immediate instruction he gave—go and sin no more.[8] Put to death therefore whatever belongs to your earthly nature, rid yourself, repent, turn.[9] It must be sincere repentance, and therefore, with your actions; you prove your repentance by your good deeds, good behavior, your rapid weight loss, and more.[10] When the tax collector made retributions to those he had wronged, his transformation was instant.[11]

PRUNING THE VINE

I am the true vine, and my Father is the gardener. He cuts off every branch in me that bears no fruit, while every branch that does bear fruit he prunes so that it will be even more fruitful. You are already clean because of the word I have spoken to you. Remain in me, and I will remain in you. No branch can bear fruit by itself; it must remain in the vine. Neither can you bear fruit unless you remain in me. I am the vine; you are the branches. If a man remains in me and I in him, he will bear much fruit; apart from me you can do nothing. If anyone does not remain in me, he is like a branch that is thrown away and withers; such branches are picked up, thrown into the fire and burned. If you remain in me and my words

---

7   When they kept on questioning him, he straightened up and said to them, "If any one of you is without sin, let him be the first to throw a stone at her." John 8:7
8   Jesus declared. "Go now and leave your life of sin." John 8:11b
9   Put to death, therefore, whatever belongs to your earthly nature: sexual immorality, impurity, lust, evil desires and greed, which is idolatry. Colossians 3:5
10   First to those in Damascus, then to those in Jerusalem and in all Judea, and to the Gentiles also, I preached that they should repent and turn to God and prove their repentance by their deeds. Acts 26:20
11   Luke 19:1-10

remain in you, ask whatever you wish, and it will be given you. This is to my Father's glory, that you bear much fruit, showing yourselves to be my disciples. John 15:1-8

Why do you need to prune the dead branches? Dead branches block growth. Pruning—getting rid of the dead branches during winter dormancy—helps the tree produce a vigorous burst of new growth in the spring.

A yeast-free, cleaned-up, pure Church is essential so that the Ecclesia—the Called Out, the Church—can actually grow. They can spring forth! But most of all, it is because one bad apple spoils the whole barrel of good apples, and this destruction can happen overnight. Keeping watch over the Church is a full time job.

Here is the point: if you stumble, get back up and run for the crown.[12] Indeed, do not give up. Do not quit. The only thing you can do wrong is quit. The Bible does not teach that you excommunicate yourself, but if you tarry too long in defiance, you confuse yourself and others and can lead others to sin. With true repentance, access to God's Spirit and the help in being surrounded by the Church, you will be victorious again. Look at the fruit of those in the middle of the pack. There is so much hope with the True Church functioning as Christ commanded.

It is the responsibility of all members, from the oldest to the youngest, all of the Ecclesia, to judge yourself first and your home, but then to be able to discern if there is sin left in the Church. This takes the whole Church, and the burden is spread out among the strong. What a precious occupation of the Church, and these corrections are like a kiss to the righteous. Correction is the opposite

---

12 *Everyone who competes in the games goes into strict training. They do it to get a crown that will not last; but we do it to get a crown that will last forever. I Corinthians 9:25*

of what you think—it says, "I love you," and it is among the most precious moments on Earth when a brother or sister listens. It *builds* relationships—not destroys them. The Remnant of the Kingdom of Love was reestablished from the Early Church upon these foundational teachings, and the result has been a healthy Church.

Surely the day is coming; it will burn like a furnace. All the arrogant and every evildoer will be stubble, and that day that is coming will set them on fire," says the Lord Almighty. "Not a root or a branch will be left to them. But for you who revere my name, the sun of righteousness will rise with healing in its wings. And you will go out and leap like calves released from the stall. Malachi 4:1-2

Let us continue with this good foundation and remove the sin so that His Vine, the New Jerusalem, will take root and the fruit will fill the nations.

The building of the True Church and care for this Kingdom on Earth results in a Community that is phenomenal. It is the picture of Acts 2 and the early Christians. The immediate love and connection members feel with other Saints is amazing—they are no longer alone, but instead have instant fellowship and friends for adults and children, no matter where they live. Page 427.

The Super Community of Love

Chapter 32

For Zion's sake I will not keep silent, for Jerusalem's sake I will not remain quiet, till her righteousness shines out like the dawn, her salvation like a blazing torch. The nations will see your righteousness, and all kings your glory; you will be called by a new name that the mouth of the Lord will bestow. You will be a crown of splendor in the Lord's hand, a royal diadem in the hand of your God. Isaiah 62:1-3

As you know, the world is troubled and lost, and their solutions do not include repentance and turning to God to lead the world. In addition, satan is mounting his troops against the Saints. There will be difficult, challenging times ahead and ultimately, in the end, God has declared destruction of this Earth. Without God's Presence we cannot survive. Without the True Church—the Kingdom of God on Earth as it is in Heaven—we have no shelter or protection.

There was a time in Israel's history when The Glory departed because of sin.[1] God eventually allowed the Philistines to steal the Ark of the Covenant containing the stone tablets of the Ten Commandments. Due to overwhelming idolatry and sin, we are in those days again. It is going to take everyone choosing to go ALL IN and getting rid of every offensive vice so that God can reside in the

---

1   I Samuel 4, Ezekiel 10

heart on Earth as He does in Heaven—so that a light can be left for our children and our children's children.

What do we need to do? This generation needs to wake up, and we need to live and teach the pure, unadulterated reform of repentance taught by Christ. We then prove our repentance by our deeds.[2] We need to surrender everything, throw off the pressures of the secular and allow God to reside in our hearts, and the Church needs to fight to uphold this high standard. Numbers do not matter. Even if it is only a few totally pure people left carrying the Spirit of the Almighty God in their soul, that is more powerful than the seven billion people that are on the planet. It is more powerful than all the armies in the world put together. I want God on Earth! His Kingdom come, His Will be done. We must concentrate on this one goal, and we must fight for God's Kingdom; and then we must teach this around the world, for the Church is universal—there is no race, creed, color, continent—it is those who are in love with God.

How do we start? It begins in our *own* heart. We repent of our sins, and then we love God with abandon, with all we have—heart, soul, mind and strength.[3] Have you fully repented of greed and a selfish agenda? What are you waiting on? Those who have laid down sin, those who are focused on God above, are the ones who can love. What is distracting you? Have you taken time to seek your Heavenly Father and love Him? Then the love of God will spill over for the family of Saints.

We must follow God's lead of tenderness each day, starting with those closest to us. Have you been purposefully kindhearted today

---

2   First to those in Damascus, then to those in Jerusalem and in all Judea, and to the Gentiles also, I preached that they should repent and turn to God and prove their repentance by their deeds. Acts 26:20
3   Mark 12:29-31

with your children? Have you been completely patient with your spouse? Have you given a thought to someone in need, much less been charitable? Have you encouraged even one hurting Saint? If someone were to ask me what was the one thing you could do to enhance your love by 100 percent instantly, it would be to slow down, to pause, and even stop what you are doing, pray for God's lead, think on other's needs and love! The Ten Commandments creates the Super Community. Now that is something worth living for.

> IF SOMEONE IS CONSISTENTLY CHOOSING VIRTUE AND LAYING DOWN ALL SIN IN EVERY AREA, THEY ARE GOING TO CHANGE THEIR LIFE, CHANGE THE WORLD, AND THEY WILL LIVE FOREVER.

Love gives more than anything on Earth. Someone who responds to hate with love, with the virtues of gentleness and quietness, is the prodigy. If someone is consistently choosing virtue and laying down all sin in every area, they are going to change their life, change the world, and they will live forever; they have chosen wisely, and they are the brilliant spiritual-billionaires who will live forever—the best investment of all. The narrow-sighted will entertain anger, greed for money or food, television, computers, shopping, alcohol, food, or lust every evening and weekend with an increasing desire for more.[4] Yet, the Saint will be rewarded with a crown, for God is gathering together on this Earth the Saints who love, which eases the burdens of all those involved, and later take them back to His Castle of Love because that is what He is building. Do you believe?

---

4   *Having lost all sensitivity, they have given themselves over to sensuality so as to indulge in every kind of impurity, with a continual lust for more. Ephesians 4:19*

The New Jerusalem

The following is Isaiah's vision of the Kingdom of Love on Earth:

"Behold, I will create new heavens and a new earth. The former things will not be remembered, nor will they come to mind. But be glad and rejoice forever in what I will create, for I will create Jerusalem to be a delight and its people a joy. I will rejoice over Jerusalem and take delight in my people; the sound of weeping and of crying will be heard in it no more. Never again will there be in it an infant who lives but a few days, or an old man who does not live out his years; he who dies at a hundred will be thought a mere youth; he who fails to reach a hundred will be considered accursed. They will build houses and dwell in them; they will plant vineyards and eat their fruit. No longer will they build houses and others live in them, or plant and others eat. For as the days of a tree, so will be the days of my people; my chosen ones will long enjoy the works of their hands. They will not toil in vain or bear children doomed to misfortune; for they will be a people blessed by the LORD, they and their descendants with them. Before they call I will answer; while they are still speaking I will hear. The wolf and the lamb will feed together, and the lion will eat straw like the ox, but dust will be the serpent's food. They will neither harm nor destroy on all my holy mountain," says the LORD. Isaiah 65:17-25

This picture of a Royal Priesthood is being lived out in this community, people who have been transformed and who are lights—wherever God has placed them, no matter their job, they light up the world. It is a delight to have the opportunity to walk around people who are constantly telling the Truth, full of joy, full of positive attitudes instead of being chronic liars or always in a bad mood or sarcastic and depressed.

The most amazing fruit, both physically and spiritually, are the children. They are beautiful in their pursuit of God, their respect for their parents, their maturity and their spiritual, academic and physical gifts. We are witnesses here at the Remnant of children who want to go to Church rather than go see a 21st century rock star. The subject of Christ and God is interesting to them; in fact, it is their everything…a community that lives, sings, dances, reads and follows Christ's virtues and his love.

WE MUST FOLLOW GOD'S LEAD OF TENDERNESS EACH DAY, STARTING WITH THOSE CLOSEST TO US.

Real love for God is what Christ had. When you have that same genuine love for God, it brings out a totally new, born again person. It births something phenomenal—it is called a sacrificial, loving life. This can happen all the way from the youngest to the oldest—it is never too late to start—and everyone gets along, helping one another.

The Kingdom of Love could be best described as people who give and give again and then give again; and when they think they cannot give any more, they GIVE, to both God and to man. This creates the Super Community founded on Christ. God is gathering a Kingdom of pure adoration, a Kingdom of Saints, and a Holy Royal Priesthood of childlike hearts who have focused on Christ so much that they are altogether different, born again with sacrificial love. You have a Community of childlike hearts, so there is singing and dancing, and no one is afraid that they will be judged. There is no back-biting, snide remarks or competition, as everyone wants the best for each other and considers others better than themselves. In the absence of self-focus, a miracle happens—liberty abounds. It is the definition of popular; everyone wants their company and a community like that because it is a constant encouragement. Instead of leaving downcast, you leave filled up.

THE BUILDING OF THE TRUE CHURCH AND CARE FOR THIS KINGDOM ON EARTH RESULTS IN A COMMUNITY THAT IS PHENOMENAL.

They devoted themselves to the apostles' teaching and to the fellowship, to the breaking of bread and to prayer. Everyone was filled with awe, and many wonders and miraculous signs were done by the apostles. All the believers were together and had everything in common. Selling their possessions and goods, they gave to anyone as he had need. Every day they continued to meet together in the temple courts. They broke bread in their homes and ate together with glad and sincere hearts, praising God and enjoying the favor of all the people. And the Lord added to their number daily those who were being saved. Acts 2:42-47

The building of the True Church and care for this Kingdom on Earth results in a Community that is phenomenal. It is the picture of Acts 2 and the early Christians. The immediate love and connection members feel with other Saints is amazing—they are no longer alone, but instead have instant fellowship and friends for both adults and children, no matter where they live. Every conversation we have and everything we do has a purpose. We are not aimlessly getting together just to hang out or have dinner; the fellowship and the food that we are seeking is to do the Will of the Father.[5]

Immediate answers and assistance are available for financial, parenting and marriage issues. Members also have help with any area of need from other Saints who are willing to lay down their lives and use their gifts for others—from basic needs like clothing and food, to moving (including packing, loading, unpacking and people willing to drive cross-country to help), career and resume advice, medical advice, people willing to freely share their automobiles, give rides and help with decorating and construction advice and services. They go from having no help in a world by themselves, lonely and depressed, to walking in and suddenly being surrounded by thousands who have wisdom, generosity and love. In Zion, it is the description of Isaiah 65, and there is an endless supply of energy to serve and untold numbers of volunteers who almost compete for the opportunity to serve. The vitality is beyond belief.

---

5   "My food," said Jesus, "is to do the will of him who sent me and to finish his work." John 4:34

Though it may not happen overnight, each member is financially uprighted. Think of a Community that helps each other, saving thousands over each generation. It begins with a young married couple starting off in the Remnant and how much they may save thru the Church and Ministries including: moves, medical, handyman services, daycare, day camp, tutoring, weddings, and lessons in music, ballet, academics and athletics. The costs avoided include: marriage counseling, credit card interest, and excess prescription drugs—not to mention avoiding excess doctor bills as a result of improved health. There is more—the money saved every day from eating less, jobs assistance (resume writing and job placement help, plus people are making more because they are learning how to get under the authority of their bosses), sharing clothing, food distribution, and so much more. Members are helped to move up in their business, and so income is higher. The women assist the men and their household; their hands are not idle, so their work is profitable. This place is not just drug free but practically debt free with the exception of homes. We are now teaching and watching a generation learn to obtain college scholarships with higher ACT scores and testing out of many college courses so that they are graduating early with zero debt.

The savings continue as each generation is taught not to be greedy, so they do not waste money on things that depreciate like new cars, and they are not piling up consumer debt. Each member is personally and gently helped to get out of debt and learn how to invest and save, which gives even more revenue. What God is giving to pass down is unbelievable. The Jewish people skipped generations to distribute the inheritance, considering that investments in real estate and stock took more than one generation to grow. When you live God's way to start with, the family and the Church helps each person to be financially stable. It grows in each family, and with selflessness at the helm, it is passed down to the next generation and the next, as each parent makes one selfless decision after another. It is beautiful; it is peaceful. In a world that is "each to his own," everyone here is helping each other instead. It builds little by little, but it is a solid foundation because the parents are passing down their wisdom at a very early age so that their children do not have to go thru the pain that they did. So many now own their own business and are not just getting established, but are bypassing their competition.

A Transformed Family

This is God's Church, led by His unspoiled son, and Christ is calling repentant people who are not going to mourn over having to give up extra morsels of food. They are not going to complain about the job or position in life that God has given them. Instead, they are going to *praise* God for every single gift and opportunity He has given!

Each man should take responsibility to honor Leadership and to love God with all of their hearts. Then they should teach constantly, daily taking responsibility to lovingly guide each family member in adoring God with all of their hearts, all of their souls, all of their minds and all of their strength. These will be responsible men, answering to their designated leaders. Godly men who live by the Truth are anxious to come into the light.[6] They are anxious for accountability and guidance so that they and their families can find their way home.

---

6 *Everyone who does evil hates the light, and will not come into the light for fear that his deeds will be exposed. But whoever lives by the truth comes into the light, so that it may be seen plainly that what he has done has been done through God. John 3:20-21*

As a leader of your family, you now have renewed hope with this vision of distributed responsibility. It *will* work for you and your family! This will give all the men a newfound joy and a pep in their step as they fulfill this powerful and blessed responsibility with even more friendships and more fellowship with each other in this shared leadership. Pride will be eradicated and replaced by purity and humility that walks daily with full respect to authority, and especially to Godly leaders at every level. There will immediately be a heightened level of accountability to the Spirit of God thru leadership with no defensiveness, but rather with a love for the Light and the Truth—no more hiding in the darkness. This will automatically birth more prayer, more preparation, more organization, more focus, more concentration and more effort with ever-increasing strategizing against the enemy.

> ULTIMATELY, THE SPIRIT-FILLED MEN AND WOMEN AND CHILDREN WILL ACHIEVE FEATS BEYOND THE LIMITS OF WHAT WAS ONCE BELIEVED...THROWING MOUNTAINS OF HATE INTO THE SEAS OF LOVE.

A GOAL FOR EVERY HOUSEHOLD

How will this vision of the Kingdom of God be accomplished when we are surrounded by anti-authority and discord in today's world? With a tighter fellowship and more purity, each man will be more active in the Kingdom and will take more responsibility—*full* responsibility—and they will learn how to counsel within their family. If you are responsible and accountable and are counseling your own loved ones, you will hang on to every word from sermons and the Bible. If you have never taken notes during lessons and sermons, you will want to start because you will want to take these words back to your family and redirect more than just yourself. You become the sacrificial life and the daily encourager and the counselor…each and every man guiding his children as they grow up. Then the children marry, and you are now helping these new young couples to be counselors for their own marriage and then for their own children—all for the Kingdom of God, making skillful warriors out of *every* family member. Each and every member gains wisdom and knowledge and is challenged to go forward, the bar raised, knowing more scriptures, knowing more than they have ever known about the spiritual warfare. You cannot enter the Kingdom of Heaven unless you have been born of this Spirit, this Spirit of being under authority, and then teaching about this authority line and guiding those under you to desire and follow their authorities. Each person needs to look for God's lead and seek out the authority over them, ready for the task, longing for direction and taking responsibility for their own family. This is going to change your life! Responsibility makes you grow up. It changes everything—fewer hobbies, more accountability, more dependability, more conscientiousness, more reliability and more trustworthiness.

The Church is built of holy households—not just a few selected households, but the whole group being holy. Waiting any longer to lay down your sin will be devastating for God and His Church. This foundation has been laid, and the question is—do you want to be a part of it? Humility is the key ingredient to pour into the heart, and humility implies joyfully submitting to the authorities God has put over you.

This is a rich heritage for us and our families. I praise God for Jesus and Paul and all the Godly men who have walked before us. We have been called to be a people who are totally in love with God, which turns men and women into a Royal Nobility because they are so secure in their relationship with God that they have the ability to show kindness and love to all, especially to their families.

BUILT ON A SOLID FOUNDATION OF LOVE

It is all about who you love, and with the Spirit of God in our hearts, it is a Community of stress-free peace. In a world of unpredictable people, manic depressives, hidden hate and backstabbing, violence and lawsuits…in a world of uncertainty, there is a place of certainty—the focus on God, like a child, brings life and love…a place called the New Jerusalem, the City of Peace. Beyond a doubt, this is an absolute possibility for your life and your family's lives—a deep healing is available for each and every person and liberation from unwanted habits, dependencies, lifestyle choices and behaviors that have been destroying our lives and relationships. You would have to come and see the dependable power of the True Church. It is a Church built on the Rock of Jesus Christ who said, *"the world must know that I love the Father and I do exactly as he commands me."*[7] It is an abundant life of hope, of beautiful relationships, of financial freedom, of health, and most important of all, of a relationship with God that is beyond anything we have ever experienced before.

God has given us this focus, not because He is self-centered, needy or demanding—but because miraculously this focus of love gives *us* a life of love that is wondrously blessed. God is gathering Love into a Spiritual City on Earth with a final destination of the Celestial City—a concept that brings a smile to my face.

This planting of pure love has just begun. God is taking a piece of Himself—His Spirit—and building a Super Community consisting of charity as we have tasted, but know that what the future holds

---

7   John 14:31a

will be far beyond our imaginings and more formidable than any nation known to man because it is the most prevailing substance to found an institution on, the most powerful substance on Earth.

God is alluring and gathering the beautiful, positive, warm, endearing and delightful emotions that feel best, and severing them from the worst, hateful emotions in the world. It is the Church, the Ecclesia, the Called Out, a Fellowship to commune with one another on Earth…answering the prayer of Christ—His Kingdom is coming, His Will is being done on Earth as it is in Heaven. It is a Heavenly City on Earth located in the hearts of mankind, that is not just in one location but also connected around the world.

> WHEN THE CHURCH IS TAUGHT THE TRUTH, IT PRODUCES THE GENTLEMEN OF OLD, THE KNIGHTS IN SHINING ARMOR…AND THE ROYALTY OF KINGS AND QUEENS, PRINCES AND PRINCESSES WILL COME FORTH LIKE THE SUN RISING IN THE EAST TO LIGHT THE WORLD.

For those who do not believe there can be such a place and since there is not enough time to describe all elements of pure worship to God, you will have to come and see for yourself—a place of no lies, no rudeness, envy, or lust, just layers upon layers of goodness, kindness and charity. This substance flows from the Spirit of God when we put Him first and adore Him like He says, and then it overflows to man, a spring of love to give to others as we are simply empty conduits, vessels or pipelines for the redistribution of the sea of love from the Heavens. We have found *true love*.

For those who know it is real, you know that there has been a Remnant of a Royal Priesthood all along, a root of God's Kingdom waiting to grow where the branches fill the Earth.[8] There are thousands of things that could distract us; however, we have been called to re-establish God's Holy Priesthood, His Royal Revival, starting with your own heart and family and then beyond. Think on these spectacular, awe-inspiring things. Think generations out, for our God is limitless! What we have experienced so far on Earth is amazing and convincing enough. Look at the results in less than twenty years. There is no telling where this is going.

A Dream of God's Kingdom

Pray and dream for the Remnant of Believers and its future—God's Kingdom, His dreams. No doubt you do not want to miss what this brilliant Star of Life is building, because it is advanced and there is more to see. It is The Plan of the Ages, God's strategy from antiquity, that of forming a Super Community out of Love, derived from the dissection of evil from good.

Pray against the counterfeit of love movements, since the true City of Peace, the Kingdom of God on Earth, has active antagonists and impostors.[9] The counterfeit of Christianity is convincing to most, but it has a bitter end. Those who see the difference between the True and the fake are part of this profound and impactful movement and will want to unite. No matter what your location, you are going to want to unite in heart, goals and purpose, and promote and protect this life-changing, profound movement. We have heard that love will never fail.[10] Paul pointed out that even if you give away all

---

8 *In days to come Jacob will take root, Israel will bud and blossom and fill all the world with fruit. Isaiah 27:6*

9 *For false Christs and false prophets will appear and perform great signs and miracles to deceive even the elect—if that were possible. Matthew 24:24* and *For such men are false apostles, deceitful workmen, masquerading as apostles of Christ. II Corinthians 11:13*

10 *Love never fails… I Corinthians 13:8a*

you own and then give your body to be burned, if you do not have love, you are "nothing."[11]

When you finally find this obedience that leads to the Spirit of the Most High God in you, you will not be able to brag or boast or take credit for anything that you thought you accomplished. Before your life is over, you will come to realize that when connected to God, you have extraordinary skill and self-control, but when disconnected from God, you are nothing and you have nothing. God is Love, and without God (Love) inside of you, you gain nothing and you are nothing. In the end, you will see that God (Love) inside of you is everything. Only then can you comprehend man's value to God's plan for His Kingdom of Love. His brilliant purpose for every man, woman and child is their capacity to house a piece of His power and Spirit, which in turn endows these hearts with a small piece of His superpowers with which they can do or perform things that they never thought or imagined. Each person should be respected as a cherished creation made in God's image with supernatural potential—beyond Marvel Comic fantasies. It will take time and practice for each born again human, but ultimately, the Spirit-filled men and women and children will achieve feats beyond the limits of what was once believed, throwing mountains of hate into the seas of love. "Love will never fail" is simply another way to say God inside you will never fail. There is Victory in God's Church.

When the Remnant began years ago, the noble men and women of God arose out of the ashes and launched God's ethical Priesthood, with each generation growing stronger than the one before it. The people who were rough around the edges became polished and

---

11 *If I have the gift of prophecy and can fathom all mysteries and all knowledge, and if I have a faith that can move mountains, but have not love, I am nothing. I Corinthians 13:2*

gracious. Each person had their own journey, but all were helped by the camaraderie. From rags to riches, from unpresentable to presentable. From ignoble to noble purposes. You will know them when you see them. They are calm in all contexts, with an inner peace, never overreacting in any circumstance. Embracing this calling produces mighty men and women who are gracious in life and accepting when facing death, ready for the call to return home.

When the Church is taught the Truth, it produces the gentlemen of old, the Knights in shining armor and regal women, Queens with a noble calling. The royalty of Kings and Queens, Princes and Princesses will come forth like the sun rising in the east to light the world, taught to declare the praises of God who called us out of darkness into his wonderful light.[12] It is time for God to have His Holy Priesthood. Who would not want to be a part of this rising Royal Remnant Nation—a nation inside a nation? May the men listen to this calling and join Noah, Daniel, and Job. May the women join with Sarah and Esther and choose to live up to this regal Kingdom-calling for the purpose of giving God all the glory. In the end it brings back the delight of God—the noble, Royal Priesthood of the New Jerusalem.

---

12   *But you are a chosen people, a royal priesthood, a holy nation, a people belonging to God, that you may declare the praises of him who called you out of darkness into his wonderful light. I Peter 2:9*

The Super Community of Love

Appendix

Our Family Lineage

But you are a chosen people, a royal priesthood, a holy nation, a people belonging to God, that you may declare the praises of him who called you out of darkness into his wonderful light. I Peter 2:9

Father _____ Mother _____

United in Marriage on _____(date)

Children:

Name: _____ Date of Birth: _____

Name: _____ Date of Birth: _____

Name: _____ Date of Birth: _____

Name: _____ Date of Birth: _____

Name: _____ Date of Birth: _____

Dedication Record

Name: _____ Date: _____

Notes: _____

_____

_____

_____

Name: _____ Date: _____

Notes: _____

_____

_____

_____

Name: _____ Date: _____

Notes: _____

_____

_____

_____

Name: _____ Date: _____

Notes: _____

_____

_____

_____

Name: _____ Date: _____

Notes: _____

_____

_____

_____

Baptismal Record

Name: _____ Date: _____
Notes: _____
_____
_____
_____

Name: _____ Date: _____
Notes: _____
_____
_____
_____

Name: _____ Date: _____
Notes: _____
_____
_____
_____

Name: _____ Date: _____
Notes: _____
_____
_____
_____

Name: _____ Date: _____
Notes: _____
_____
_____

Confirmation Record

Name: _____ Date: _____
Notes: _____
_____
_____
_____

Name: _____ Date: _____
Notes: _____
_____
_____
_____

Name: _____ Date: _____
Notes: _____
_____
_____
_____

Name: _____ Date: _____
Notes: _____
_____
_____
_____

Name: _____ Date: _____
Notes: _____
_____
_____
_____

Our Family Story

As for me and my household, we will serve the Lord. Joshua 24:15b

Father's Personal Exodus Story

_____
_____
_____
_____
_____
_____
_____
_____
_____

Mother's Personal Exodus Story

_____
_____
_____
_____
_____
_____
_____
_____
_____
_____
_____
_____

Parent's Goals for Family Direction for the Sake of God and His Kingdom

Extended Family Members in the Church

Grandparents

Aunts, Uncles and Cousins

Spiritual Mothers and Fathers, and Brothers and Sisters in Christ

(Close, adopted, dear Saints who are special to the family)

For whoever does the will of my Father in heaven is my brother and sister and mother. Matthew 12:50

_____
_____
_____
_____
_____
_____
_____
_____
_____
_____
_____
_____
_____
_____
_____
_____
_____
_____
_____

Records of Marriages and New Extended Family

Name of Child: _____
Spouse: _____ Date: _____
New Extended Family (Spouse's parents and siblings, etc.):
_____
_____
_____
_____
_____

Name of Child: _____
Spouse: _____ Date: _____
New Extended Family (Spouse's parents and siblings, etc.):
_____
_____
_____
_____
_____

Name of Child: _____
Spouse: _____ Date: _____
New Extended Family (Spouse's parents and siblings, etc.):
_____
_____
_____
_____
_____

Records of Marriages and New Extended Family

Name of Child: _____
Spouse: _____ Date: _____
New Extended Family (Spouse's parents and siblings, etc.):
_____
_____
_____
_____
_____

Name of Child: _____
Spouse: _____ Date: _____
New Extended Family (Spouse's parents and siblings, etc.):
_____
_____
_____
_____
_____

Name of Child: _____
Spouse: _____ Date: _____
New Extended Family (Spouse's parents and siblings, etc.):
_____
_____
_____
_____
_____

Wedding Memories

Wedding Memories

Records of Grandchildren and Great Grandchildren:

Name: _____ Date of Birth: _____
Parents: _____

Name: _____ Date of Birth: _____
Parents: _____

Name: _____ Date of Birth: _____
Parents: _____

Name: _____ Date of Birth: _____
Parents: _____

Name: _____ Date of Birth: _____
Parents: _____

Name: _____ Date of Birth: _____
Parents: _____

Name: _____ Date of Birth: _____
Parents: _____

Name: _____ Date of Birth: _____
Parents: _____

Name: _____ Date of Birth: _____
Parents: _____

Name: _____ Date of Birth: _____
Parents: _____

Name: _____ Date of Birth: _____
Parents: _____

Name: _____ Date of Birth: _____
Parents: _____

Name: _____ Date of Birth: _____
Parents: _____

Name: _____ Date of Birth: _____
Parents: _____

Name: _____ Date of Birth: _____
Parents: _____

Name: _____ Date of Birth: _____
Parents: _____

Name: _____ Date of Birth: _____
Parents: _____

Journal Pages

(Special notes, memories, events, answered prayers and records for a lasting legacy for the family)

Journal Pages

(Special notes, memories, events, answered prayers and records for a lasting legacy for the family)

Note About Artwork

Artists include Gustave Doré and Julius Schnorr von Carolsfeld. Some of these images were altered digitally for various purposes and modesty. Digital editing done by Ryan McCauley and directed by Gwen Shamblin Lara and Erin (Elle) Shamblin—the graphic arts team.

Note About Writing Style

You may notice a difference in the capitalization of certain terms. It has been decided to honor (via capitalization of the first letter) all terms that are referencing God, the Kingdom, His Holy Servants, and True Love. Likewise, you will see a trend toward de-emphasizing (via using lowercase of the first letter) religions not founded by God. Notice "SATAN" and all his diabolical titles will often be recognized by an eerie font. I have noticed in modern writings that references to "pharisees," are capitalized, but there is no capitalization of God's Priests or Holy Priesthood. Now what is with that?! There are no capitalizations in the Hebrew language. It is an absolute crime that all references to common denominations have ensured capitalization of their organization but there is no capitalization when referencing God's Church or The Kingdom of God. Bear with me as I am trying to right this wrong in this prayerful work. These changes are intentional. May other literature follow suit.

In addition, for simplicity and clarity, some grammatical terms and traditions have been adopted for ease of reading. An example of this is the spelling of word "thru." The use of the spelling of this word dates back to the mid-1800s and was proposed by many spelling reform boards and dictionaries, including the Council of the Spelling Reform Association, the American Philological Society and the American Philological Association.

NOTE FROM THE AUTHOR

My life is very, very full, and everything is so fun! God has given me family and extended family who all live nearby. We have many good times together, especially since all of them have such a great sense of humor! We travel together, work together and play together. God has given me a beautiful relationship with my husband, Joe Lara. My children and the 8 little ones are together all the time!

My highest joy is God's Kingdom, and I am amazed as He unfolds the New Jerusalem—The Kingdom of God in the heart. Every day is an adventure and Heaven becomes more inviting with every year.

God-Fearing Families

Appendix

For more pictures, visit GwenShamblinLara.com.

GOD-FEARING FAMILY RESOURCES

Weigh Down Ministries is the non-profit publishing house sponsored by Remnant Fellowship Churches. It has been producing resources for over 35 years that have proven to help participants stop overeating, alcoholism, gambling, drugs, sexual sins, materialism, and any other stronghold or dependency. Please visit WeighDown.com to find out more about these materials or call us at 1-800-844-5208!

MORE ABOUT THE AUTHOR
www.GwenShamblinLara.com
For a complete list of finished works: www.GwenShamblinBooks.com

ADDITIONAL VOLUMES IN THIS SERIES
History Of The One True God Volume I: The Origin Of Good And Evil
History Of The Love of God Volume II: A Love More Ancient Than Time

WEIGH DOWN MONTHLY SUBSCRIPTION PROGRAM
If you have been moved by reading the pages in this book, and want to learn more about putting God first in your family, we encourage you to try out our monthly online subscriber program where you have access to hundreds of life-changing audios and videos. For more information and to sign up, visit WeighDown.com

CHILDREN, YOUTH & FAMILY
- Children's Books: Inspirational and educational children's books depicting powerful spiritual lessons: *A to Zion, In the Beginning* and *The Garden of Eden*
- Child's Dedication & Memory Book: Record your most precious moments for your children and document their spiritual journey as they grow from birth to age 13.
- Zion Youth Series: Video lessons and a comprehensive workbook—excellent resources for parents and children to watch and work thru together, pointing the entire family up to God.
- Zion Kids: 30-minute videos that are a fun and exciting combination of music, dance, and Bible lessons to help children learn the basics in a way that is just as much fun for the parents as it is for the child.
- Feeding Children Physically and Spiritually: video and audio lessons for parents.
- Zion Kids: Lessons for the Parents
- The Last Exodus: A video series for teens and young adults.

GWEN SHAMBLIN LARA LIBRARY
- Weigh Down Works! Practical advice to help you on the path from physical hunger to spiritual fulfillment.
- Rise Above: A follow-up book to *Weigh Down Works*
- The Legend To The Treasure: This book contains powerful spiritual lessons on how to lay down the last bit of self and praise of man, coupled with practical, true statistics of what life is like without God.
- For a complete list of titles, see www.GwenShamblinBooks.com

Spiritual Warfare Resources
- The Power to Overcome Set
- You Are Not a Victim Series
- Focus Up Set
- Weigh Down at Home
- Strongholds at Home

Godly Music
Fill your home with Godly uplifting music to help you thru any spiritual testing.

Weekly LIVE Teaching
- Watch Gwen's weekly *You Can Overcome* TV Show on Wednesdays at 6:00 pm central on www.WeighDown.com/weigh-down-tv/
- Hear sermons at Remnant Fellowship Church on Saturdays at 9:00 am central on www.RemnantFellowship.org.
- Check WeighDown.com to see if Gwen is coming to your area on a Weigh Down Tour.

Bible Studies
Overcome whatever is causing you pain in your life thru online and local Bible studies. Visit WeighDown.com to watch orientation videos: *Weigh Down Basics, Exodus Out Of Egypt, Exodus From Strongholds, The Last Exodus, History Of The One True God, Breakthrough, The Legend To The Treasure, Weigh Down Advanced, Feeding Children Physically and Spiritually* and the *Zion Kids Series*.

Social Media
- Follow WeighDown, Gwen Shamblin Lara & Remnant Fellowship on Twitter.
- Find WeighDown, Gwen Shamblin Lara, Remnant Fellowship & Remnant Fellowhip Youth on Facebook.
- Watch WeighDown, Gwen Shamblin Lara & Remnant Fellowship on Youtube.
- Find WeighDown & Remnant Fellowship on Instagram.

Free Resources
The WeighDown App: Available for Apple and Android devices
WeighDownatHome.com: Free online weight loss videos and audios
GwenShamblinLara.com daily devotionals. Weight loss and encouragement tips sent to your email every morning

Remnant Fellowship Publishing
Remnant Fellowship Church sponsors this author and her works. The Church was established in 1999 and has over 175 locations around the world. Please visit www.RemnantFellowship.org

WeighDown.com 1-800-844-5208

CPSIA information can be obtained
at www.ICGtesting.com
Printed in the USA
LVHW021149140319
610644LV00001B/1/P